Appraisal and Acquisition

Innovative Practices for Archives and Special Collections Series Editor: Kate Theimer

This dynamic series is aimed at those working in archives and special collections as well as other cultural heritage organizations. It also provides students and faculty in archives, library, and public history graduate programs a resource for understanding the issues driving change in the field today.

Each book in the series tackles a different area in the field of archives and special collections librarianship and demonstrates the kinds of strategies archivists are using to meet these new challenges.

These innovative practices reflect approaches and ideas that will be new to many readers. The case studies featured in each book have been selected to keep in mind a broad spectrum of readers and enable the series, as a whole, to benefit a diverse audience.

Each book features case studies from both large and small organizations. Thus, some of the creative ideas presented are being implemented with costly tools and robust infrastructures, and others are being done on a shoestring. A hallmark of the series is that every case study incorporates ideas that are transferrable, even if the specific implementation might not be.

About the Series Editor
Kate Theimer is the author of the popular blog *ArchivesNext* and a frequent writer, speaker, and commentator on issues related to the future of archives. She is the author of *Web 2.0 Tools and Strategies for Archives and Local History Collections* and the editor of *A Different Kind of Web: New Connections between Archives and Our Users*, as well as having contributed chapters to *Many Happy Returns: Advocacy for Archives and Archivists, The Future of Archives and Recordkeeping* and the forthcoming *Encyclopedia of Archival Concepts, Principles, and Practices.* She has published articles in *The American Archivist* and the *Journal of Digital Humanities.*

Kate served on the Council of the Society of American Archivists from 2010 to 2013. Before starting her career as an independent writer and editor, she worked in the policy division of the National Archives and Records Administration in College Park, Maryland.

Titles in the Series

Description: Innovative Practices for Archives and Special Collections
Outreach: Innovative Practices for Archives and Special Collections
Reference and Access: Innovative Practices for Archives and Special Collections
Management: Innovative Practices for Archives and Special Collections
Appraisal and Acquisition: Innovative Practices for Archives and Special Collections
Educational Programs: Innovative Practices for Archives and Special Collections

Appraisal and Acquisition

Innovative Practices for Archives and Special Collections

Kate Theimer

ROWMAN & LITTLEFIELD
Lanham • Boulder • New York • Toronto • Plymouth, UK

Published by Rowman & Littlefield
4501 Forbes Boulevard, Suite 200, Lanham, Maryland 20706
www.rowman.com

10 Thornbury Road, Plymouth PL6 7PP, United Kingdom

British Library Cataloguing in Publication Information Available

Library of Congress Cataloging-in-Publication Data

Appraisal and acquisition : innovative practices for archives and special collections / edited by Kate Theimer.
pages cm. -- (Innovative practices for archives and special collections) Includes bibliographical references and index.
ISBN 978-1-4422-4953-0 (hardcover : alk. paper) -- ISBN 978-1-4422-3854-1 (pbk. : alk. paper) -- ISBN 978-1-4422-3855-8 (ebook)
1. Appraisal of archival materials. 2. Archives--Acquisitions. 3. Libraries--Special collections. I. Theimer, Kate, 1966- editor.
CD973.A77A67 2015
025.2'814--dc23
2014048167

∞™ The paper used in this publication meets the minimum requirements of American National Standard for Information Sciences Permanence of Paper for Printed Library Materials, ANSI/NISO Z39.48-1992.

Printed in the United States of America

Contents

Introduction

Appraisal is, arguably, the most important thing archivists do. After all, determining what materials are preserved dictates the future of the archives. However, in practice, archival appraisal is often just as, if not even more, affected by the concerns of the present rather than the possible needs of the future. The literature of the archival profession is rich in theoretical discussions of appraisal, but the decisions archivists make in their work are influenced by a host of concrete issues. This is not to say that archivists do not take future needs into account in making their decisions but rather that what is often presented as a theoretical exercise is actually a very practical one. The question "What should we collect?" turns into a series of more pragmatic questions, such as "How can we collect these materials?," "How can we provide access to them?," "How would these materials be used?," "How can we preserve them?," and "Where will we store them?"

When appraisal develops into acquisition, materials that were accepted as an aggregate can reveal a host of individual and unique problems. All too often what an archivist thinks he or she has agreed to accept is not quite the same as the materials that arrive on the loading dock. And when resources of all kinds are limited for most repositories, ensuring that transferred materials are worth investing in has become a priority. Therefore making wise decisions at a high level about what to collect has become even more important, and making prudent decisions at lower levels has become a necessity.

Appraisal and Acquisition: Innovative Practices for Archives and Special Collections explores how archivists and special collections librarians in organizations of different sizes and types have approached these kinds of challenges, as well as exploring opportunities to acquire new kinds of materials and conduct thoughtful reappraisal. These case studies show a range of strategies and processes, but all were selected because they demonstrate ideas that could be transferred into many other settings. They can serve as models, sources of inspiration, or starting points for new discussions. This volume will be useful to those working in archives and special collections, as well as other cultural heritage organizations, and provides ideas ranging from those that require long-term planning and coordination to ones that could be more quickly implemented. The chapters also provide students and educators in archives, library, and public history graduate programs a resource for understanding the varieties of issues related to appraisal and acquisition and how they can be addressed.

ABOUT THE INNOVATIVE PRACTICES SERIES

I debated with myself for some time over the title of this series, *Innovative Practices for Archives and Special Collections.* After all, what is innovative and new to one person is often standard procedure to another. Another option was to call them "best practices" and follow the model of a series of similar books from the same publisher featuring case studies from libraries. But this seemed equally problematic. In a field that seems to embrace the phrase "it depends" as a mantra, putting forward the experience of any one archives as best practice seemed ill advised.

It is the very diversity of our field, though, that caused me to stick with my "innovative" label rather than shying away from it. There are new ideas in these books or at least ideas that will be new to many readers. My philosophy in selecting case studies for the books in this series has been to keep in mind a broad spectrum of readers and to position the series so that it will be as valuable as possible for a diverse audience. In each book, you will find case studies from both big organizations and small ones. Some of the creative ideas presented are being implemented with costly tools and robust infrastructures, and others are being done on a shoestring. In determining what to include, I wanted to ensure that every case study incorporates ideas that are transferrable, even if the specific implementation might not be.

This commitment to making the series broadly valuable and practical has meant striving for a balance that favors more approachable innovations over implementations that are aggressively on the "cutting edge." The ideas presented here are within the reach of most archives and special collections—if not right away, then in the near future. They represent the creativity and commitment to serving and expanding our audiences that I think are the defining characteristics of the archival profession in the early twenty-first century.

Because archival functions and processes are interrelated and don't always fit neatly into compartments, and because most archivists perform several of those functions and processes in the course of their daily work, the contents of each of the volumes in this series has both its own clear focus and overlapping relationships with the others. Case studies in reference and access touch inevitably on description and outreach. The overarching purpose of description is to facilitate use, so issues relating to reference, access, and outreach are components of the case studies in that volume. The case studies on educational programs in this volume have a clear relationship to outreach and touch on the areas of management, reference, and access. These interrelationships are inevitable given the nature of archival work, and most practitioners and students will find all of the volumes useful.

Just as the activities archivists undertake depend on each other, so too have I depended on the assistance of my friends and colleagues who generously agreed to review the case studies. My thanks to Rodney Carter and Amy Cooper Cary for the time and careful consideration they have given to improving the latest two books in this series.

ABOUT THE APPRAISAL AND ACQUISITION CASE STUDIES

When considering how innovation is displayed in the case studies in this collection, perhaps the largest single theme that emerges is the ways in which the archivists seek to ensure their repositories' resources are being invested to provide the best possible value—in every sense—for both the intuitions and their users. Archivists must act as responsible stewards, considering as carefully as possible both the needs of the present and the future.

This kind of consideration is demonstrated in Maurita Baldock's discussion of the New-York Historical Society's decision to accept the records of the Children's Aid Society, a large part of which would remain closed to public access. She describes in her case study the analysis that resulted in the society's decision, as well as her perspective on the results and impact of that decision for staff and users. In their case study, Will Hansen and Matthew Farrell similarly outline the questions Duke University's Rubenstein Rare Book & Manuscript Library posed in deciding whether or not to accept the donation of vintage computer equipment with a unique provenance.

While often archivists rely on their own knowledge and judgment in making such decisions, Shelley Sweeney has enlisted a group of "spider advocates" to assist her in both seeking out appropriate donations for the University of Manitoba Archives & Special Collections and in providing professional advice about possible acquisitions. These advocates draw on their own networks and expertise in advising and help determine how the archives should invest its limited resources. Similarly, when faced with a mandate to document and provide records management support for the range of activities of the University of Wyoming with only a quarter-time archivist, Laura Uglean Jackson assembled a team to decide which offices she should prioritize for support and acquisition of records.

As responsible stewards, the case study authors also describe how the future use of the materials under consideration factored into their decision making. Baldock examines the value of the nonrestricted Children's Aid Society records for education and outreach, as well as research, and also how the acquisition of the collection affected the use of other collections and the donation of similar materials. Hansen and Farrell also discuss how the potential use of the vintage computer equipment by researchers and for exhibits factored into their final decision.

In some case studies, outreach and advocacy are more directly related to acquisition activities. In the case of the Georgia LGBTQ Archives Project, as described by Morna Gerrard, a central aspect of the project is to encourage and promote the donation of private collections, publications, ephemera, and oral histories to a suitable repository and to educate potential donors about how to care for their materials. In a sense, outreach is the fundamental purpose of the project, along with advocacy for the importance of LGBTQ collections. Outreach is also at the heart of Tiah Edmunson-Morton's work to create the Oregon Hops and Brewing Archives. In starting a new collecting initiative for Oregon State University's Special Collections and Archives Research Center, a primary focus of her work is identifying potential donors and partners and talking with them about the new collection, as well as promoting the new archives to the public. Shelley Sweeny's "spider advocates," as the name suggests, help promote and advocate for the archives as they work to identify and facilitate the donation of appropriate collections.

Brad Houston found himself with a different kind of outreach challenge in implementing an active electronic records acquisition program at the University of Wisconsin–Milwaukee. In addition to addressing the difficulties presented in processing electronic records transfers, and so selecting that which needed to be kept from non-record material, he had to first convince creating offices that their digital materials were indeed records and needed to be transferred to the archives. The authors from the Library of Virginia, working with the email created by the administration of Governor Tim Kaine, did not face that particular challenge, as the status of email as a record was well established. But their intent to make the records available to the public online meant that they needed to develop processes to review the millions of messages and determine which among them were actually records and in addition which ones needed to be restricted. In this case, the library's plan for providing access dictated their appraisal strategy.

Working with the digital records of the Ford Foundation International Fellowships Program presented yet a different kind of challenge to Jane Gorjevsky and Dina Sokolova and the staff at Columbia University. They needed to define and implement processes for acquiring records from offices all over the world, from a variety of systems, some of which were created in languages that used non-Roman character sets. They needed to coordinate with staff who were already also in the process of shutting down their operations, many of whom had little time to devote to sorting and segregating records before transfer. Like the archivists at the Library of Virginia, they also had to address problems of privacy and restricted information in records while considering how they planned to provide access to the collection.

Each of these case studies—the University of Wisconsin–Milwaukee, the Kaine email collection, and the records of the Ford Foundation International Fellowships Program—also demonstrates the need to work effectively with records creators to acquire significant records and also to assist in more efficient processing and selection, particularly with digital materials. Working with donors to address the challenges of providing access to restricted materials is also a key challenge the New-York Historical Society faces in helping the public use the Children's Aid Society records and in particular the files regarding children from the orphan trains. In all of these examples, it was essential during appraisal and acquisition to develop a good working relationship with the donors to help the archives do its job more effectively and efficiently.

Establishing good relationships with donors is also critical to the work of Shelley Sweeney with her "spider advocates," as well as to the success of the fledgling Oregon Hops and Brewing Archives and the Georgia LGBTQ Archives Project. All of these archivists are in a sense working with the donors, as well as the larger community of which they are a part, to build a collection that reflects that community. The approach taken by the University of Maryland's Special Collections in Performing Arts to appraise and acquire the records of Washington, DC's Studio Theatre shows the value of taking a more formal approach to this collaboration. With their limited resources in mind, the archivists negotiated with the theatre to provide both financial and logistical support for an intern to appraise and select materials for transfer to the special collections. This arrangement allowed the intern to gain understanding of the operations of the company, as well as earn the trust of the staff, both of which were essential to ensuring that the most valuable records were entrusted to the archives.

The responsible stewardship demonstrated by all the case study authors as they weighed the challenges of acquiring collections, worked with donors to build trust, and considered how they would provide effective access does not end after materials are acquired. Increasingly, archives and special collections are creating programs to actively review materials in their holdings and consider how well they serve users' needs. Creating robust reappraisal programs is the subject of two very different case studies: one from a national archives, Library and Archives Canada, and one from the archives of a small liberal arts institution, Dickinson College. While the scale and processes are very different, for both organizations, making effective use of resources was the driving factor for reappraisal, and in both cases, the primary consideration in appraising collections is how well they meet the organization's mission and audience. The two case studies illustrate that reappraisal, while a daunting prospect for some, can be integrated into the effective management of archives, strengthening the organization and contributing to a more productive future.

While each case study in this collection describes a specific response to a challenge or opportunity, I think each also reflects a philosophy of experimentation that is perhaps the most critical ingredient necessary for any organization interested in developing its own "innovative" practices. In this regard, I hope this book and the others in the series encourage all readers to consider how their own work could benefit from the exploration of new ideas and tools. Although this series of books can, by definition, include only a small sample of the kinds of approaches being developed by archives and special collections around the world to meet the challenges of staying relevant and adaptable in today's complex environment, I am sure these case studies will give readers many useful ideas to consider, as well as the inspiration to come up with tomorrow's innovations.

ONE

"No Fame Required"

Collaboration, Community, and the Georgia LGBTQ Archives Project

Morna Gerrard, Georgia State University

Preserving the history of the LGBTQ community is particularly challenging. The AIDS epidemic decimated a generation of gay men, and many of their personal histories were lost and continue to be lost when relatives dispose of their materials either through ignorance or discrimination. Members of the LGBTQ community have traditionally been marginalized, and only relatively recently have their experiences been deemed important enough to document with intent. The Georgia LGBTQ Archives Project, a collaborative endeavor bringing together local archivists and activists, has been attempting to actively and purposefully engage and work with the LGBTQ community to educate its members about the importance of their history and to encourage them to embrace and take ownership of that history by working with archivists who seek to document it.

In the years leading up to the establishment of the Georgia LGBTQ Archives Project, archivists around the state had been quietly and slowly collecting the records of its LGBTQ community. The Kenan Research Center at the Atlanta History Center began collecting LGBTQ materials in the late 1980s, with its Atlanta Lesbian and Gay History Thing. Reflecting Emory University's strong partnership with the Centers for Disease Control (CDC), its Manuscripts, Archives and Rare Book Library (MARBL) had a solid reputation for collecting AIDS-related materials. At Georgia State University (GSU), the Special Collections and Archives had well-established Women's Collections. In early 2011, they were renamed the Women and Gender Collections, to reflect the fact that that LGBTQ materials were being collected. This coincided with a move to also rename GSU's Women's Studies Institute, which is now the Institute for Women's Gender and Sexuality Studies. The Auburn Avenue Research Library for African American History and Culture, a specialized branch of the Atlanta–Fulton Public Library System (AFPLS), had begun collecting the records of African American gay activists under the enthusiastic watch of gay archivist Wesley Chenault.

Collaborating across institutions was not new to me: in my role as GSU's Women and Gender Collections archivist, I had previously worked with archivists at Emory's MARBL and our state archives to transfer collections that were a better fit at GSU, and I had been collaborating with Wesley Chenault for quite some time. We each recognized that we were not and should not be collecting the same materials, and from time to time, we would direct donors or collections to one another. Wesley also made important introductions for me to members of Atlanta's gay community.

PLANNING

In 2011, Ann Edmonds, a librarian with oversight of the circulating collection of LGBTQ materials at AFPLS's Ponce de Leon Branch Library, began discussing the importance of preserving local lesbian and gay history with Atlanta activists Hillery Rink and Ann's predecessor at the Fulton County Public Library, Cal Gough. They had been attending SAGE (Services and Advocacy for Gay, Lesbian, Bisexual and Transgender Elders) meetings and regularly heard members talk about downsizing their homes and the fact that they didn't know what to do with their "things." Ann, Cal, and Hillery were concerned that if SAGE members were not sure what would happen to their own papers, it would be even less likely that their families would know what to do with them in the event of their deaths. And if SAGE members were uncertain about the future of their materials, surely this was a concern among members of the broader LGBTQ community. In response, in December that year, Ann invited local activists and archivists to join what would become the Georgia LGBTQ Archives Project.

I attended the first meeting, along with my department head, Stephen Zietz. Also in attendance were Ann, Hillery, Cal, Dave Hayward, who created and manages Touching Up Our Roots, a lesbian and gay oral history project, Kelly Caldwell, an archivist working at the Special Collections Department of the AFPLS's Central Library, Kerrie Cotten Williams from the Auburn Avenue Research Library, and Randy Gue, archivist at Emory's MARBL. Ann explained her vision, and it was wholeheartedly supported by those around the table. I personally remember a sense of collegiality, camaraderie, excitement, and determination. Here we were, archivists and activists, happy to put personal or institutional ego aside to ensure that a community's history was saved and celebrated. We were also thankful that we would have an established way to communicate with one another about our LGBTQ collecting and LGBTQ-focused activities. For the first two to three months, our discussions focused on creating our name, mission, and goals, as well as discussing possible additions to our membership and ways to let the community know about us and our activities. By March 2012, we were very clear that we wanted to: raise awareness about the importance of saving personal history, celebrate the role of LGBTQ citizens in Georgia, link donors and collecting institutions, and promote the appreciation of LGBTQ history. It was hoped that the project could not only inform the LGBTQ community that such archives existed and that they were actively seeking materials but also foster camaraderie among the archivists.

IMPLEMENTATION

Since the first gathering in December 2011, project members have continued to meet on the first Friday of every month, and from time to time, additional local activists have attended, looking for opportunities to volunteer, provide information, or seek advice. At the meetings, archivists share information about new and pending acquisitions and newly opened collections, and the whole group discusses project business and planned or possible future programming activities.

Soon after the project was established, Ann created a list of project member emails, comprised of individuals who attend meetings. This is not as sophisticated as a listserv, but it is useful for members who want to contact the group or individuals within the group. A Facebook page was established (www.facebook.com/pages/Georgia-LGBTQ-Archives-Project/257162497710554), and since we have no budget for website development or maintenance, this acts as our official web presence. Our group had discussed the possibility of creating a Twitter account but decided that managing it would be too time-consuming, and the kind of content that we wanted to present and publicize was better served using Facebook. Hillery Rink manages the general content of the Facebook page, and project members are given administrative rights to post as much and as often as they wish.

The Facebook page serves us well in a number of ways. First, it provides information about the member institutions: an archivist from each institution was tasked with creating a bookmark that could be handed out at public events. The bookmarks provide an overview of each institution's collecting focus and list some of the collections already available at each institution. Those bookmarks are digitized and available on the Facebook page for anyone who wishes to see them. The Facebook page also serves as a conduit for anyone interested in donating papers or doing oral histories: when community members contact the page, rather than directing individuals to particular institutions, Hillery forwards queries to all the institutions on our email list, and interested archivists follow up. The page allows project members to announce upcoming events and new acquisitions, and it allows archivists to ask community members if they have specific items or information that might help fill historical gaps. For example, the location of Georgia's ACT UP records was revealed through an August 2012 post that simply asked "Anyone out there know where the ACT-UP Atlanta files/archives are? A few people have heard they are stored in someone's closet. We'd love to help preserve this important part of Georgia LGBTQ history for future generations. Please get in touch with us if you have any information. Thanks! " Within hours, Jeff Graham, a local Georgia Equality activist, responded, "I've got a full collection of paper files and videos." To date, while Jeff has not yet decided where he will place his papers, he has been interviewed for GSU's Gender and Sexuality Oral History Project and is scheduled for a follow-up interview in the fall of 2014.

From time to time, we also use the Facebook page to post "archival tips" about saving, storing, or reformatting personal materials. These tips can be as simple as suggesting that people store archival materials in a dark, temperature- and humidity-stable environment, such as under a bed, to providing links to webpages such as the Library of Congress's "Personal Digital Archiving / Digital Preservation," or Lifehacker's "How to Back Up Your Computer to an External Drive." The page also provides a history of the community through its "This Week in History" postings. A number of years ago, project member Cal Gough created an LGBTQ-focused exhibit for the Central Library of the AFPLS. The exhibit included a timeline marking landmark dates in the history of the struggle for LGBTQ rights. Entries from that timeline and images from GSU's *Atlanta Journal Constitution* photographic collection are brought together by Stephen Zietz, and every few days, one or more LGBTQ-related photographs is posted along with a brief description of an event or activity.

An important goal for the project was to reach out to the community via public or group-focused events. In May 2012, the project organized an Out of Our Closets and Into Our History event at the Rush Center, a well-known LGBTQ meeting place in Atlanta. Our expectations for attendance were low, given that this was our first attempt at such an activity. However, on the day of the event, project members were astonished that the room was filled to capacity with attendees who clearly wanted to learn about who we were and what we could do to help them. Archivists from the Atlanta History Center, the Auburn Avenue Research Library, Emory

University, and Georgia State University talked about the process of donating papers and conducting oral histories, as well as discussing the importance of documenting the activities of the LGBTQ community. Archivists from each institution provided information about their existing collections and what they hoped to collect. Further, an academic, Daniel Rivers, discussed the importance of making LGBTQ history available for research, and a donor, Franklin Abbott, described his practical and emotional experiences as he made a number of donations to GSU. When their presentations were over, the archivists answered questions from the audience and then made themselves available for individuals to talk privately.

In March 2014, members of the project presented to the Atlanta Prime Timers, an organization for older gay men, at one of their regularly scheduled monthly meetings. At the heavily attended event, select members of the project came prepared with a more condensed and focused version of our talk that included a PowerPoint presentation that provided an overview of the project. Archivists from KSU and GSU explained the process of donating papers and conducting oral histories; a doctoral student, Andy Reisinger, talked about the research value of archival materials; and a donor, Jesse Peel, talked about his experiences with Emory University. The archivists then addressed questions from the audience.

In May 2014, upon a request from one of its members, Hillery Rink and I attended a meeting of the St. Jack's group of gay men at St. John's Episcopal Church in College Park. In front of a group of approximately twenty men, Hillery described the project, and then I talked about donating papers and doing oral histories. My remarks were not GSU-focused. Rather, they provided information that was applicable to any archival institution. This kind of presentation, focused on donating generally rather than to individual institutions, and "staffed" by only two members of the project, can be particularly effective, as the burden of promoting the project and archival institutions can be spread among members.

Not all community events are expected to result in immediate or imminent donations. In October 2012, Stephen Zietz and I attended a SAGE event to discuss the importance of estate planning. The main objective was to educate attendees about the importance of documenting end-of-life decisions regarding their personal papers so that they will not be discarded by friends or relatives. We had expected to talk for approximately half an hour, but interest was so intense that we stayed for more than two hours.

Most people who are being introduced to the world of archives are under the impression that one must be famous or "important" to be a donor. Therefore, whenever archivists talk to groups, we reinforce the "no fame required" mantra and the importance of the voices of the many in documenting a movement or a community. We explain that we want to show how the actions of the "important" people positively or negatively affected the lives of everyone within their community. We also try to talk more about what donating means to the donor rather than how important our own collections are. We hope to emphasize the community aspect of our work, highlighting collaboration and downplaying competitiveness. We always recommend that donors visit all the archives that interest them, ask archivists important questions about storage, access, outreach, and philosophy, and then make a decision about their preferred repository after they feel adequately educated. Each of our member institutions is different, and each has a unique focus. There is a place for everything and no need for us to be overly competitive. GSU is very grassroots, "bottom-up" in its collecting, Emory University focuses on AIDS and more prominent figures, Auburn Avenue Research Library documents the African American experience, the Atlanta History Center is more interested in political activities, and Kennesaw State University (which became involved in early 2013) is only interested in documenting local, northern Georgia activities.

In August of 2012, a local graphic designer, Carl Mattison, created a logo for the project, free of charge, and in December 2012, the group decided to apply for 501(c)(3) status. Members of the Stonewall Bar Association of Georgia Inc. (whose records are held at GSU) have been providing on-going pro bono legal advice and assistance.

RESULTS

The project's Facebook page has been cost effective in terms of time and resources. Not long after it was created, a local gay activist, Eric Watts, who had just discovered the page, contacted GSU to tell us about the papers of a friend of his, Thomas H. Crim Jr., who was deceased. Within weeks, Watts and Crim's niece, Mari Banks, donated a collection of his letters to various newspaper editors, most of which dealt with gay issues in the Augusta, Georgia, area. These letters are now all digitized and available on GSU's digital collections webpage. Our "This Week in History" posts have been particularly successful for creating online discussions as well as prodding potential donors to contact project members. On January 13, 2014, a photograph was posted showing a January 9, 1990, "die-in" protest that was held in front of the CDC by members of ACT UP (see figure 1.1). That same day, a local activist, Andrew Wood, commented, "I still have the sign I carried on that day, would the archives like to have it for their collection?" On March 17, Andrew brought his poster and other personal materials relating to ACT UP to Special Collections at GSU (see figure 1.2). That day, he signed a deed of gift and promised to give us more of his papers, particularly those relating to his activities with the Sisters of Perpetual Indulgence. He has completed two oral histories, and he has become a vocal and enthusiastic advocate for the archival endeavor and for Georgia State University.

The project's public events have been productive and instructional. At each event, we pay close attention to the questions from audience members, as they tell us what concerns potential donors may have. Two issues that are clearly at the forefront are end-of-life planning and privacy. When I am a presenter, I always discuss privacy issues as they relate to personal papers and organizational records. I explain that we try not to restrict or redact information, but that it is an option when the need arises, and I explain the scenarios in which it is appropriate. When documenting the LGBTQ experience, that need tends to arise more often than when documenting straight communities in which there is no fear of being "outed." I also let audience members know that if they want to do an oral history but are uncomfortable about being publically identified, there are options such as restriction, redaction, or using a pseudonym. Community members' stories are too important not to be told, and archivists can be very flexible in their efforts to ensure that the stories are captured and preserved. I make a point of watching the faces of our audience members when this is being discussed. Many visibly relax as they realize that not only can privacy be protected when necessary but

Figure 1.1. Police stand in front of the Centers for Disease Control as gay activists from ACT UP stage a "die-in" to protest the CDC's handling of the AIDS crisis, Atlanta, Georgia, January 9, 1990. ***AJCP178-017h, Atlanta Journal-Constitution Photographic Archives. Special Collections and Archives, Georgia State University Library.***

Figure 1.2. Morna Gerrard, Andrew Wood and Stephen Zietz at Georgia State University's Special Collections and Archives, March 17, 2014.

also that the professionals who want to document their stories are aware and sympathetic and are actively seeking ways to enable history to be told while respecting the very specific needs of the members of their community. This reinforces the notion that our collecting is donor focused rather than archivist or institution focused.

The majority of people we have reached through our presentations are over fifty years old, and many of them have lived through and survived the AIDS crisis, when so many of their friends and community members died without estate plans or instructions about what to do with their personal effects. Based on post-presentation questions, there are a number of members of the LGBTQ community who are not ready to donate their papers but would like to do so at some point in the future, and in the meantime, there is a clear desire for guidance about estate planning. To this end, archivists at GSU and Emory are currently working with their institutions' legal counsels to create a short, simple legal document that can be kept alongside future donors' estate files. When it becomes available, this document will be posted on our Facebook page, and copies will be made available with other handouts at any future presentations.

There have been some very clear, tangible results from our presentations. At the end of the Out of Our Closets and Into Our History event, community members had the opportunity to speak to the archivists. A local lesbian activist, Lorraine Fontana, approached me and thanked me and our project members for giving her the opportunity to so easily learn about each institution. A grassroots organizer, Lorraine felt that GSU was the best fit for her papers, and within a very short time, she not only donated them but also was processing them as a volunteer. Lorraine is an outstanding advocate for the work that we do at GSU. Likewise, AIDS activist Dr. Jesse Peel donated his papers to Emory very shortly after the Out of Our Closets event, and he continues to advocate for the project and his chosen institution. Within thirty-six hours of the March 2014 Prime Timers event, archivists at GSU had been contacted by four new donors, and an existing donor requested that project members present at another group's meeting. At the St. Jack's group event, one existing donor brought two additional boxes of papers, and a new donor brought a donation, completely unsolicited. In all, as of September 2014, GSU has acquired approximately 120 cubic feet of manuscript records and 12 oral histories that are directly related to project activities. Further, a great many periodicals have been donated as part of those manuscript collections, and they have been brought together to create a new Gender and Sexuality Periodical Collection that contains more than 400 titles and almost 5,000 items.

Beyond the tangible results of the project's Facebook activities and group presentations, our work has expanded LGBTQ-history activity beyond our metro Atlanta sphere into Cobb County, Georgia. In early 2013, as a direct result of hearing about the project, Jessica Duvall, who was the newly appointed program coordinator for GLBTIQ Student Retention Services at Kennesaw State University (KSU), heard about the project and asked Ann Edmonds if she could attend our monthly meetings. Not long after, she began working closely with KSU archivists, Heather Oswald and Anne Graham, to help focus their energies on documenting LGBTQ activities on campus and within the local community. Heather and Anne have been very active project members since spring of 2013. Throughout 2013, project members were available to support and provide advice to Jessica as she curated her first exhibit, Opening Doors, Outing LGBTQ History, which took the form of decorated doors that were placed at various locations across KSU's campus.

After one of the project's meetings, in the fall of 2013, activist project member Richard Rhodes approached Anne in the parking lot to ask if she knew of KSU alumnus David Neubecker. David had been a founding member of the university's student organization Gays and Lesbians United for Equality (GLUE), as well as the Pride of Peachtree Lesbian and Gay Marching Band. In 2004, David and his partner, Lee, were the first gay couple from Illinois to be married in San Francisco by Mayor Gavin Newsome, and the couple's daughter, Braiden, wrote an essay in defense of gay marriage that became part of an amicus brief for the U.S. Supreme

Court case *Perry v. Hollingsworth,* which questioned the constitutionality of California's Proposition 8. Since Anne did not know David, Richard made introductions, and within a few weeks, David traveled from Chicago to deliver his papers and to talk to the school's GLBTIQ student group about his experiences at KSU. This visit, which was attended by project members, was an important step toward healing for David, as his time at what used to be a very conservative university in a historically conservative part of Georgia had been difficult. Since donating his papers, David has also agreed to be interviewed, and his ex-partner, Jon Greaves, was interviewed in June 2014. Jon has been providing contact information for other local gay activists, and Anne and Heather plan take advantage of those contacts.

With remarkably little effort on our part, the project's activities quickly came to the attention of enthusiastic local news outlets and in particular LGBTQ newspapers, who have regularly supported the project by writing about its activities and providing information about its member institutions. In May of 2012, the *GA Voice* publicized the project and our upcoming Out of Our Closets event in the article, "GA LGBTQ Archives Project to Preserve Personal Histories."[1] In December 2013, the article "Atlanta Institutions Build Archives of LGBTQ Culture, Politics, History" appeared on the website ArtsATL,[2] and in January 2014, the *GA Voice* published another article, "GA LGBTQ Archives Project Working to Preserve Community's History."[3] Further, a local, gay-focused production company, Meak Pro Media, broadcast the Out of Our Closets event live over the radio.

Low-cost and low-key means of communicating within and about our project have been surprisingly successful. Using nothing more complicated than a Facebook page, our internal email list, and in-person meetings, archivists in Georgia are collaborating regularly and doing so meaningfully. We are not simply cheerleading for one another; we are also assisting each other. For example, KSU has been given permission to digitize a full run of the LGBTQ newspaper *Southern Voice.* They have most issues but are missing some. Member institutions are checking their own holdings for those that are missing, and we are all willing to loan them to KSU so that the run can be completed. Further, immediately after the project was established, Kelly Caldwell, the archivist (and acting manager) of the AFPLS's Central Library sought the help of Stephen Zietz and myself. The library was in possession of a number of LGBTQ collections, including the papers of gay film critic, Steve Warren, Atlanta's first Mr. Hotlanta, Jimmy Gray, and also the records of a local, gay competitive clogging group, the Buffalo Chips. Those collections had been acquired by a librarian who had recently retired, and the library was not equipped to manage or maintain them. Over a number of months, we worked with Kelly to transfer ownership of all but one of those collections to GSU, where they have been processed and made available for research. The one collection that did not come to GSU went to Emory, as it was AIDS related.

LESSONS LEARNED

One of the most important lessons learned in creating and developing the project has been the fact that it would not be possible to make this project work without the LGBTQ activists who work alongside the archivists. Making friends with a community that one is not a part of can be challenging. I am GSU's Women and Gender Collections archivist, and I have had a long and fruitful relationship with the feminist community in Georgia because I am part of that community. My constituents know me and trust me. While archivists have established relationships with gay and lesbian donors outside the orbit of the LGBTQ Archives Project, many new donors have been introduced to them via project activities. Being a member of the project has provided local archivists, most of whom are allies rather than members of the LGBTQ community, with a means to interact with those constituents. The local activists who belong to the project have been instrumental in building bridges to their communities and reinforcing the message that the work that the archivists do is essential and that the archivists can be trusted.

The importance of this symbiosis was at the forefront of our minds when the project decided that it was time to grow into a nonprofit organization, and the lawyers who were guiding us asked me to provide a list of officers. We had been managing ourselves quite comfortably as a leaderless organization up to that point but could not complete our paperwork without listing the names of our president, vice president, secretary, and treasurer. It was no accident that Hillery Rink was chosen to represent us as president, as he is a well-known and well-respected gay activist. Cal Gough, another gay activist was named treasurer, and Ann Edmonds and myself—both allies—were named secretary and vice president respectively. We have an unwritten rule that, if members of our group are invited to speak to a group, one of the presenters has to be gay/lesbian. It is also important that members of the LGBTQ community see the archivists at their own community events, and so some of us try to attend as many of those as possible, as well as attending LGBTQ-focused events at one another's home institutions. This is doubly useful, as not only do community members know that we are truly interested and invested in their activities, but also we become more educated about issues in the community that we as archivists are documenting.

Another surprising and satisfying lesson is that an organization such as the Archives Project can grow and thrive without any kind of budget. All members are volunteers, and any professional work that has been done for us, such as our logo design and 501(c)(3) legal services, has been done pro bono by friends or by donors who want to support our endeavors. The day that members of the Georgia Stonewall Bar Association visited me to drop off their first box of records, they asked, "What can we do for you?" Months later, when I asked for their assistance, an article about the project was placed in their professional newsletter, along with my contact information. I received a number of offers of assistance. Further, the lawyers that we chose to work with (at Atlanta's Bryan Cave LLP) have offered to pay any fees associated with our 501(c)(3) application and future filings and renewals. Each institution prints its own bookmarks, and any shared handouts, such as project flyers or guides to making donations, are printed by any member who feels that his/her institution can do it at that moment. In January of 2013, a national LGBTQ "Creating Change" conference took place in Atlanta. Our members wanted to host an exhibit to be shown at a pre-conference reception, and instead of trying to create one from scratch, Cal Gough suggested that we update a series of local LGBTQ history panels that he had created for an exhibit at AFPLS's Central Library. Our members brought together supplies from our garages and workshops, and together we made an old exhibit look somewhat new. It was reported that many of the young attendees at the reception admitted that they became educated about their own history for the first time when they saw the exhibit.

Similarly, over the past two and a half years, we have not paid for any of our meeting spaces. From December 2011 until early 2014, our monthly meetings took place at the Ponce Branch of the public library, before the building was open for the day. Once Ann Edmonds retired, we did not have access to the library. However, the Rush Center allowed us to use a small conference room on their premises free of charge. The Rush Center does charge for use of its large meeting space, and we have also used that, but thus far, we have not had to pay for its use, as we attended as presenters on the program at various LGBTQ groups' monthly events. Any further event costs, including those for refreshments, are also incurred by the hosting organization. Once we officially have nonprofit status, we do plan to raise money, but raising money will certainly not be a primary goal. At this point, we simply want to be able to accept and use any money that is offered to us. We would like to purchase a table runner and banner with our logo on them so that people can find our project members at public events. We would also like to purchase supplies when necessary, and we would dearly love to be able to pay for a booth at the annual Atlanta Pride celebrations.

One challenge with the project that will probably never completely resolve itself is the fact that while all members benefit from the work it does, not everyone plays an active role. Two of the member institutions have had difficulty providing representatives at our meetings, participating at events, or engaging on our Facebook page. The main reason for this is that they have experienced significant budget and staffing cuts or are undergoing major renovations. Those of us who are active do not ignore them however. Their membership in the project is made clear in our presentations, and they receive minutes and updates from the project's secretary. There has been some discussion about membership being tied to a certain level of activity, but thus far, we have agreed to take a relaxed approach. Every institution goes through trying periods, and it is hoped that when their issues are resolved, those who have been missing will become more actively engaged. Further, anyone who has participated on a committee or board knows that every organization has its active and less-active members. I strongly believe that the project is so important that those who are the doers simply have to put our egos aside and accept that we will be doing the bulk of the work. At the end of the day, what is more important is the fact that the history of our LGBTQ community is preserved and that community members feel a sense of ownership of their history and understand the importance of the archival endeavor.

CONCLUSION

Before the creation of the Georgia LGBTQ Archives Project, a few gay activists knew about the archival process through their personal interaction with local institutions, as they had donated their personal papers or organizational records. However, most members of the community were unaware that such institutions existed and that those same institutions would have any interest in their papers. This has certainly changed since 2011 and will continue to change: as we continue our outreach activities in Atlanta, we also plan to extend them to other parts of the state, particularly to populations in areas that have not enjoyed the same levels of acceptance and tolerance as communities within the state's capital. It is also hoped that membership in the project will grow and diversify, for example, the trans community needs to be represented, and we would like to see more faces and hear more voices of color at the table.

In Atlanta, the LGBTQ community members have welcomed their allies and embraced the notion that their common experiences should be documented for generations to come. They clearly see themselves as playing a very important "community service" role by donating their materials and acting as enthusiastic advocates. Thus, the community feels a greater sense of validation, its history is preserved, and archival institutions not only grow their collections but also are able to educate new constituents about the importance of the archival endeavor in the broadest terms.

Georgia, and in particular Atlanta, is a hub for gay activism in the South. As such, there are many lives and many activities to document, and no single institution has the capability or the donor appeal to do it alone. By taking a good look at the strengths of our various archives, we can see that we are well placed to cover all aspects of our state's LGBTQ history. Collaborating in this way moves us away from thinking only about ourselves as repositories, proud of what we have and sad about what we might not, toward a donor- and community-focused model: how can we best save all of our history, given our areas of focus? Why should GSU collect heavily in AIDS-related materials when Emory has been competently doing so for quite some time? Researchers are better served if like collections stay with like. This does not mean that I should turn away donors who actively choose GSU as a home for their papers or records if they are better suited elsewhere, just that we don't have to waste energy, time, and reputation by aggressively competing.

Educating our donors and potential donors about all of the options open to them, and then letting them make an educated decision about the repository that most suits them, not only empowers the community but also creates more buy-in, ownership, and long-term support. Academic and archival institutions are intimidating to most people who do not work within them. Demystifying the work that we do as archivists and showing donors that they and their histories have power and a place within those institutions can bring about nothing but good: good will, good collections, and good relationships. Showing donors that we as archivists are working together for the common good of the LGBTQ community engenders further collaboration between the community and the archivists and an ever-expanding pool of potential advocates for our institutions, and archives, in general.

Collaborative collecting may not be appropriate for every institution; however, in the case of clearly defined communities that include a wide variety of social, intellectual, and political groups, this kind of acquisition can be especially useful. For communities that have not been particularly well documented in the past, collaborating will ensure that no one institution has to take up the burden of acquiring, processing, housing, and making available the records of that whole community, and it enables individuals to be educated and empowered to choose the repository that most speaks to them. In the case of the Georgia LGBTQ Archives Project, the experience has been more successful than any of the project's members had anticipated: collections have found homes, donors are happy, and the community is empowered. At the end of the most recent presentation, one audience member stated simply, "Thank you for wanting to document our history, and thank you for respecting us."

Morna Gerrard *is the Women and Gender Collections archivist, special collections and archives, Georgia State University Library.*

NOTES

1. "Out of Our Closets," *GA Voice*, May 11, 2012, http://thegavoice.com/ga-lgbtq-archives-project-to-preserve-personal-histories-2/.

2. Anjali Enjeti, "Atlanta Institutions Build Archives of LGBTQ Culture, Politics, History," ArtsATL, December 24, 2013, http://www.artsatl.com/2013/12/atlanta-institutions-build-archives-lgbtq-culture-politics-history/.

3. Patrick Saunders, "Georgia LGBTQ Archives Project Working to Preserve Community's History," *GA Voice*, January 27, 2014, http://thegavoice.com/georgia-lgbtq-archives-project-working-preserve-communitys-history-2/.

TWO

Placed Out

Providing a Home for the Records of the Children's Aid Society and the Orphan Trains

Maurita Baldock, New-York Historical Society

From 1853 to 1929, the New York–based Children's Aid Society (CAS) sponsored an emigration program known as the "orphan trains." This program relocated thousands of children from New York City to new homes in the Midwest and West, many of them taken in as laborers on farms. While the program was idealistic in its goal to remove orphaned or vagrant children from conditions that might lead them to lives of crime, many of the children suffered from harsh working conditions and unsympathetic treatment. Today the program is a subject of great interest to scholars as well as to the families and descendants of the relocated children. The Children's Aid Society is still in operation and had kept many records relating to both the program and individual children. However, in seeking a repository to accept the donation of these records, the organization imposed conditions that would keep the vast majority of the donation inaccessible to most researchers indefinitely.

This chapter is a case study on the decision by the New-York Historical Society (N-YHS)[1] to acquire the records of the Children's Aid Society, despite the legal issues and specific restrictions. The appraisal decision this collection presented to N-YHS was a complicated one that required balancing the potential research value of the collection against the problems the restrictions would create for staff and the challenges presented by the collection's size of almost 700 square feet. The collection is now processed, and the N-YHS staff has experienced the benefits as well as the negative effects that custody of the collection has brought with it. While initially skeptical about the acquisition, I have come to believe that the organization made the correct decision to acquire the collection, restrictions and all.

PLANNING

The N-YHS began discussions with the CAS about its historical records in 2005. The CAS is one of the largest New York–based charitable organizations to assist children in need. Founded in 1853 by Protestant minister Charles Loring Brace, it is often recognized for its historic efforts to improve urban children's lives. In the mid-nineteenth century, orphaned or vagrant children were generally sent to almshouses or juvenile asylums. However, Brace believed these children would be better off with good homes, vocational training, and jobs. The CAS established lodging houses and industrial schools but perhaps is best known for its initiative to send orphaned and destitute children from the city streets of New York City out west to find homes. This program eventually became known as the "orphan trains" and placed out approximately 250,000 children to areas all over the country from 1853 to 1929[2] (see figure 2.1). Brace enthusiastically promoted his emigration idea as successful, and the system was soon imitated by other children's organizations. However, the CAS placed more children out on the trains than any other organization and did so for the longest amount of time, and so the CAS is the organization most strongly identified with the orphan train program.[3]

The records offered to N-YHS included material on the organizational history of CAS and its work with lodging houses, industrial schools, convalescent homes, health centers, farm schools, and, importantly, the individual case files of almost all of the children CAS sent west on the orphan trains. The CAS did attempt to stay in contact with the children as best they could, considering the limited communication available at the time. Thus many case files contain letters from the children and their new families that often truthfully describe their fate. The case files contain many tales of children from the orphan trains that were provided with good homes and saw success in their lifetimes. Two of the most notable examples are governors John Brady of Alaska and Andrew Burke of North Dakota. However, the case files also tell the stories of many children who had unhappy homes or could not escape their troubled past and became runaways or criminals. The case files also demonstrate that many children continued to write to the CAS as adults to let them know how they were doing or to inquire about their own past. Although there are a few later files, all of the records that the CAS offered (records and case files) extend only to the mid-1940s. This was a natural dividing line because that was when the programming at CAS began to change and

Figure 2.1. Children on a train to Texas, 1904. *The Records of the Children's Aid Society, The New-York Historical Society.*

shift more toward focusing on foster care for children closer to their homes.

There were many reasons for N-YHS to accept this material. The CAS records clearly fit into N-YHS's existing collections and its mission to collect materials that document the history of New York and the nation. The library at N-YHS already had the records of institutions created to assist children such as the Association for the Benefit of Colored Orphans and the Leake and Watts Children's Home. The CAS records contained one-of-a-kind documentation of the lives of children and the poor in New York City in the nineteenth and twentieth century. The lodging houses and industrial schools for children that Brace and the CAS created were a significant part of the city during this time and demonstrate the hardships often faced by immigrant families. Similarly, Brace's emigration program was based on the idea that children are better cared for in homes, rather than institutions, a concept that has become the foundation of the modern system of foster care. The emigration program also remains somewhat controversial. While it has been praised as a groundbreaking way to find new homes for children, it has also been harshly criticized as a mostly Protestant program that often put children in conditions close to indentured servitude if not slavery.

The potential research value of the collection was considerable, and the topic of children on the orphan trains was known to be popular. The stories of orphans and the orphan train program are of great interest to historians, survivors and family members, genealogists, and the general public. Many orphan train societies exist in various states and involve descendants of orphan train riders or those connected or interested in the orphan trains. Similarly, orphan train reunions are still held for the few remaining survivors all over the country. In 1995, the PBS program *American Experience* showed an episode on the orphan trains with survivors telling their stories that was well received.

However, there were two significant concerns about the potential acquisition. First, the CAS collection was very large, around 700 square feet, and would require N-YHS to reconfigure existing shelving to create a large-enough space for the materials in the stack area. Additional staff would also be needed to process a collection of that size in a timely manner. Thankfully, the CAS generously offered to donate funds for a processing archivist and for the preservation work needed for the materials. Thus, the second factor was the more serious long-term consideration: when discussing the donation, the CAS was upfront about the restrictions they wanted for the collection. While the records of the CAS organization and the files of the lodging and school efforts would be made available to general researchers, the case files on children sent out on the orphan trains would remain restricted indefinitely.

The CAS wanted restrictions on the collection for several reasons. The records of the children sent out west did present a legal conundrum, as it was not always apparent which records could be made available. Adoption laws vary by state, and the children were sent to various states and territories, and not all of them were actually adopted by their foster families, so it would be complicated to assess what laws applied to each case. Rather than doing research on all the records and their legal status, the CAS wished to restrict them all. However, there was another intangible factor involved. While the CAS has a history that dates back more than 150 years, it is also still currently active. Although the orphan train program was touted in its time as being successful, it later came under criticism as ideas changed about the best ways for assisting orphan children. It appeared that the CAS felt that it had to define clear limits on access, as it did not want these records to bring up past criticisms of its organization that might affect its current status as a highly successful nonprofit charity.

Legal research done by N-YHS showed that New York State did not have involvement in adoption proceedings until 1873, but any records from 1873 to 1924 related to New York state adoptions are publically available. So, the research concluded that documents relating to adoption in New York State predating 1924 were considered open to the public. Despite this, N-YHS's legal counsel was wary of allowing general access to the case files, as they did not want the N-YHS to be held responsible for breaking any laws. It was also not feasible to try to have N-YHS's reference staff try to determine, on a case-by-case basis, whether a particular case file could be made available based on the circumstances of the people involved and in what state the events took place—even if it was only to determine whether or not an adoption had taken place in New York. Thus it was decided that, if the records came to the N-YHS, the records of the agency would be open while the case files would be closed, except to those who had received special permission from CAS.

At the time of these discussions, the CAS was providing some information on orphan train children to the public, particularly to family members. Victor Remer, a social worker and a past executive director of the CAS, was caring for the archival files during his retirement.[4] He had worked on organizing the historical collection for many years and had spent much time providing genealogical and historical information to researchers from New York City and all over the country. He would not allow family members to view any orphan train case files records themselves but instead would research their requests and provide the information he felt it was appropriate to share. When he would correspond with researchers, he would not give them specific information, such as names of parents, but would rather provide "non-identifying" information from the files that they might find interesting or useful. For instance, he would tell a person that her mother was a small woman with brown hair and good health or that his grandfather had died of typhoid.

Since he was the only one responding to inquiries, how much detail he included was completely at his discretion. It appeared he was providing this information based upon what he felt was appropriate, rather than only giving specific information at the advice of any lawyers. He would occasionally provide general access to the case files to journalists or historians who were researching the emigration program as long as they promised to not publish any names. However, these requests were also handled on a case-by-case basis at his discretion alone.

Although Victor enjoyed his work and obviously felt attached to the materials, he was aging and realized the space for the material at the CAS was not appropriate. Victor and the current management at the CAS wanted the files to be placed in an appropriate repository for posterity. However, the CAS wanted to continue a similar type of reference procedure. In essence, it wanted the orphan train files to be restricted to the public but someone from the CAS would continue to provide information to selected individuals.

After an appraisal visit to the CAS building where the records were kept, it was apparent that about 80 percent of the approximately 700-square-foot collection would consist of these restricted case files. Was it serving the mission of N-YHS to accept material that would be mostly restricted? And was it practical to have N-YHS house the files while the

CAS determined who could use them? I heard through the grapevine from other archivists that a large New York City repository, as well as a large university in the region, had been offered the CAS records and had refused them based upon the size and restrictions. Like many of the children represented in the records, the material was having trouble finding a home.

IMPLEMENTATION

I had been working as an archivist at the N-YHS for six years but was promoted to the vacant position of curator of manuscripts soon after discussions began regarding the donation of the CAS material. As an archivist working on other projects, I had been aware of our talks with CAS but did not yet understand the complexity of the potential donation. Once I was made aware of the constraints CAS wanted to put on the collection, I became concerned that most of the material would be inaccessible to researchers for an indefinite period of time. I understood that the files of the children from the orphan trains might have legal complications. However, most of the children had been sent out so long ago that it was not clear how many of the people involved might still need to be protected. I wanted to negotiate on the restrictions. The N-YHS had the records of the orphanage of the Association for the Benefit of Colored Orphans, and its records relating to specific children were closed until after seventy-five years of creation. Since the association had mainly been active from the 1860s to the 1920s, most of the collection was now available. Perhaps this could be a model for access for the CAS files?

However it became clear that the emigration case files of the CAS were different from the records of the other orphanages. While the records of the Association for the Benefit of Colored Orphans generally include minimal information on the parents of children, the case files of the CAS emigration program include much more information on names of parents, both biological and adopted, as well as more details of a child's outcome. Another significant difference is that the Association for the Benefit of Colored Orphans is no longer in existence, while the CAS is still active as a foster care organization. The CAS views its orphan train placements as the beginning of its foster care system, with which it is still involved. Thus, its desire for restrictions was based on its understanding of laws that apply to its current practices. Even though it recognized that many who were involved with the emigration program are no longer alive, it viewed its historic records with the same approach as its current records. In this case, it wasn't historians or archivists who were making the decision, but foster care social workers trained to follow contemporary laws. Although not directly related, it may not have helped that a researcher who had been allowed to examine the case files extensively had written a book that was critical of the CAS's role in caring for children placed out on the orphan trains.[5] Thus, the CAS had grounds for being concerned about the risk to its current reputation based on access that was previously granted to its historic files.

Viewing the restrictions as a risk-mitigation strategy for both parties, the management of the N-YHS made the decision to accept the complete donation of CAS's historical files, along with funding for processing and preservation. The potential research value of the collection was deemed to be worth the challenges posed by the legal issues and restrictions. After going through various drafts, a deed of gift was signed in 2007 that outlined the materials that were restricted and those that were open to the public, citing specific New York state laws regarding confidentiality. The deed of gift also outlined reference procedures for accessing the archive at N-YHS. Now that Victor would not be around to provide his best judgment on who could access the materials, the deed of gift had to set up specific set of procedures. This included the appointment of a "specialist" by CAS who would determine which researchers would be allowed to view the restricted files and what they would be allowed to see.

While the deed of gift was being negotiated, we went to work to prepare for the acquisition of this large and complicated material. A project archivist, Cherie Acierno, was hired to process the collection, and she worked to build a relationship with our contacts at the CAS, including Victor, to learn the CAS material and oversee the transfer of the material to the N-YHS. She helped organize a series of transports of the material across Manhattan to the N-YHS by art shipping companies. Similarly, a part-time preservation assistant, Alegria Barclay, was hired for the conservation of the material. The stacks manager, conservator, and other staff members worked hard to condense existing collections and redo shelving to create a large-enough space for the materials in a stable environment.

RESULTS

The accession of the CAS materials was well received at the top level of N-YHS's administration as it cemented a relationship with a well-known and respected New York organization. The popular topic of the history of children in New York as well as the history of the orphan trains had enormous potential to generate publicity in the immediate and foreseeable future. Although I was initially skeptical about accepting the records with their restrictions, I soon became excited about the material. The attention this collection was generating could bring more interest to some of our other material relating to the history of children, which were smaller collections that I sometimes felt were overlooked. Although a large amount of linear feet was restricted, I began to see the materials that were open to the public still allowed for many views into children's lives in New York City and in the emigration program. For example, the open material included photographs and volumes describing children's facilities in New York City, pictures of companies of children being sent off on the orphan trains, diaries of agents encountering poor children in New York City and of chaperones sent out with children on the trains, and broadsides and ephemera from the program (see figure 2.2). The records also included architectural drawings by renowned architect Calvert Vaux, who designed some of the CAS buildings.

With the funds provided by the CAS, the processing and conservation of the 674 linear feet of material was successfully completed in about three years, and a finding aid encoded in EAD was posted online. Despite the large amount of organizing and rehousing needed, the files were generally in pretty good order when they arrived and even included a card index system of children names and their case file numbers. The finding aid clearly identifies which materials are open to the public and which are restricted. The N-YHS had recently implemented the Archivists' Toolkit, and the CAS finding aid was one of the first finding aids to be completed in the program. Cherie, the project archivist, won a finding aid award for it at the Mid-Atlantic Regional Archives Conference (MA-

Figure 2.2. Boys at the gym at the Newsboys Lodging House, circa 1910. ***The Records of the Children's Aid Society, The New-York Historical Society.***

RAC) in 2009. With a small amount of time left in the project, Cherie and Alegria, the preservation assistant, worked quickly to digitize a selection of photographs and key documents that had no restrictions. Because our digitization program was still in its infancy and also because of the limited time frame, we determined the easiest way to make the images available was to put them online through Flickr with a link to the page in the online finding aid.[6] We negotiated with the CAS that we could put images on Flickr if the images included a CAS watermark. The Flickr account was not set up to accept comments, as crowdsourcing was still a new idea and its value had not yet been determined. However, it was now easy to locate the finding aid with a link to digitized highlights of the collections (which could also be found by searching on Flickr). Many of these images have been requested by researchers and used by N-YHS staff for exhibits or promotional purposes.

However, one of the downsides of the new collection was that initially the restrictions and convoluted reference procedures for the collection left the manuscript reference librarians, and sometimes me, confounded. As it is N-YHS policy to provide access to unprocessed collections, researchers began requesting the files before the finding aid was available online to clarify the restrictions. Many people who had heard about the material at the N-YHS started calling, emailing, or simply arriving in the reading room thinking that they could instantly do research on their family. This left us continually explaining to researchers that even though the materials were there, we could not make them immediately available because they had to contact the CAS for permission or to have the CAS specialist provide them with the information they wanted. As more and more requests began to come in for information located in the restricted files, the CAS soon set up a system of approved volunteers to come into the reading room to assist the CAS specialist in dealing with all of the reference requests. This meant that Cherie and the manuscript reference librarians were now spending much of their time locating and pulling material for these CAS volunteers and the specialist.

LESSONS LEARNED

It now is apparent to N-YHS that the CAS collection was worth acquiring, despite its restrictions. The materials in the CAS collection are now regarded as some of the N-YHS's most treasured materials. The collection is one of the most requested collections in the reading room, especially by the CAS volunteers and specialist to research the restricted files for others. The materials are also used internally by the museum for various purposes. Many of the historic photographs and ephemera from the emigration programs and the lodging houses and industrial schools are commonly utilized for class or general presentations and exhibits. Cherie worked with the N-YHS education department to design a successful curriculum for high school students based on the collection. Museum curators also worked with Cherie to gather photographs and information on the orphan trains for the recently built DiMenna Children's History Museum located within N-YHS. The museum and website includes real and fictional historic characters, including an orphan train rider and a New York "newsie" based on composite information from the CAS collection. The Great Hall, which is a main attraction to a newly remodeled N-YHS, includes pictures and objects from the CAS.

It is also beneficial for the N-YHS library to have the original files on a topic that remains relevant to the public and popular culture. The orphan train emigration program most recently received attention with the 2013 book *Orphan Train: A Novel* by Christina Baker Kline. Her fictional story includes an older survivor of the orphan train who tells her story to young a girl who is currently in foster care. The book quickly became a number-one *New York Times* bestseller soon after it was published. Kline states that the idea for her novel began with a story that her husband's grandfather was possibly an orphan train rider, and she realized that it was a great idea for historical fiction.[7] Perhaps other works of art or fiction could be inspired by the stories of these children.

The publicity of the accession and our relationship with the Children's Aid Society eventually led to N-YHS acquiring similar collections on the history of children. As many leaders and board members of the CAS knew leaders from other children's organizations, we were soon contacted by other agencies wanting advice on what to do with their own historical records. The New York Foundling Hospital reached out to us to know if the N-YHS would be interested in its records caring for Catholic children. This organization also participated in placing out children in an emigration program and ran orphanages in New York. After some discussion, the New York Foundling Hospital did donate its records to us (79 linear feet) but decided to keep the case files from its placing-out program. Although permission is needed from the Foundling Hospital to view records that include personal information on children, not having specific case files makes the collection generally easier for researchers to access. Graham Windham, an organization created by a merger of two historical childcare organizations, also donated its records to N-YHS (81 linear feet).[8] It did not participate in any emigration programs, but its admission, discharge, and school records are closed for one hundred years from the date of creation. But, all records of the agency more than one hundred years old are open to the public. Following the CAS model, both of these organizations also provided financial assistance to process the materials. Luckily, since these two collections were much smaller than CAS and did not contain as many personal files on children, they were easier to appraise and process.

Despite the long-term success of the CAS acquisition, there were some arrangements that caused concern. One problem was the relationship of the N-YHS to the CAS specialist. The first person appointed to this position by CAS did not fully participate as planned, and this left us with limited ways to assist researchers who wanted access to the restricted material. Since the CAS appoints the specialist, N-YHS had little control over the situation. Although the CAS did appoint another specialist who carried out the responsibilities more successfully, this model of access does not seem sustainable for the long term. The person at CAS who is the designated specialist has changed several times since the collection was accepted. While some of the specialists appointed by CAS have been successful partners in the process of making materials available, others have been trained social workers who were simply given this duty on top of their other work, and so not all of them had the knowledge or the time needed to help researchers. It would be better in the future if N-YHS is able to work with CAS in determining who is appointed to the position. Ideally someone with archival training could be hired since this person is supposed to work closely with the reference staff on determining who can see restricted material.

CONCLUSION

When an archival collection is offered with any type of legal or donor-specified restrictions, an institution should cautiously consider its mission and how crucial it is to accept the material. Would the material be better in another repository? Will history suffer if the material is not kept? Will the institution benefit from having the materials, even with the restrictions? Even if the research value of the material is enough to compensate for any long-term restrictions, the institution needs to decide if it is willing to support the storage of a collection that few researchers may be able to access. Likewise, any conditions attached in a deed of gift should be feasible in the immediate as well as the long-term future.

In our case, the acquisition of the CAS materials was worthwhile, despite the difficulties. However, I hope that a few next steps might occur to make access to the collection easier. One step would include a reexamination of the complex reference procedures set up in the deed of gift when it was signed in 2007. There is a clause in the deed stating that the two parties agree to confer "on the two year anniversary of the signing of this Agreement and on a date every two years thereafter to a.) review the administration of / costs associated with maintenance of the Collection and b.) consider making mutually agreeable changes to this Agreement." That has not happened yet, but it certainly should in the future. The leadership of CAS has changed since the materials were donated, and the new leaders might be willing to reexamine its requirements for responding to requests from researchers. It is also not clear for how long the leaders at CAS might want to remain so involved with the agency's historic records. Ideally the N-YHS will be able to transition away from the need for a CAS representative mediating all reference on the case files, perhaps toward a model in which N-YHS reference staff have clear criteria to work from in adjudicating requests.

I also hope (and expect) that there will eventually be a reexamination of the indefinite restrictions on the children's case files. With the passing of time and changes in leadership, the CAS now appears to be more interested in the needs and successes of their current programs rather than concerns of how some children were treated in their emigration program. For instance, the CAS website has a section on the historical importance of Charles Loring Brace and the orphan train movement, which states: "Of course, much has changed since his time, including the concepts of children's rights and parental responsibility, but Brace's imprint remains an enduring one."[9] The CAS seems to be proud of the innovative and overall successful legacy of the orphan trains and less shamed by previous critiques in the program. Perhaps, N-YHS could reexamine its previous legal research and provide criteria for the reference staff to use, depending on what happened to the child, in what year, and in which state. While in 2007, and apparently still, CAS was clear that did not want these records open, as some of the files become almost 150 years old and almost all of the people referenced in them are deceased, perhaps CAS will be willing to begin declaring at least some of them open.

While there is ethical and practical guidance in archival literature on restrictions and privacy issues related to medical records and students' records, there is not much guidance on records of orphaned children. One exception is a 1997 article in *Archival Issues* by R. Jackson Armstrong-Ingram; in his article, Armstrong-Ingram observes that restrictions on adoption records that were intended to protect involved parties often now close information to those who were involved, such as the children and their descendants. He wonders if keeping adoption records closed for so long is serving the needs of the parents, the children, or the agencies. He argues that some biological and adoptive parents and children would actually prefer more open records.[10] I also believe that keeping the records of the orphan trains inaccessible for the long term is not the best use of the historical record. As the archival profession generally advocates that records and information be available to the public, these records should be made available to family members and the public in a legal and ethical manner.

Public opinion is also changing on the availability of adoption records. While adoptions were once closed to protect families from the shame of adoption, the recent popularity of more "open" adoptions are helping to break that stereotype. Indeed, many adoptees in New York have been asking lawmakers to change laws that prevent access to their birth certificates and to allow biological parents the option of being contacted by their children.[11] Perhaps these changing factors will encourage N-YHS to take a more active role in persuading the CAS to make its records more available.

Overall the appraisal of these records raised many unusual issues, but the N-YHS recognized the value in a rare collection and decided to accept it, despite the drawbacks. This acquisition would not have suited other institutions—as demonstrated by the rumors that others had passed on the opportunity. But perhaps because of its own long history, N-YHS was willing to take a longer-term view of the challenges. The N-YHS has been in existence since 1804, and many of the materials it accessioned many years ago with restrictions are now available to the public. Although never stated outright, it can also be assumed that N-YHS accepted the restrictions on the material believing that eventually they could be lifted. But even with the restrictions, the CAS records are one of the largest collections at N-YHS and receive substantial internal and external attention. These files remain as records of what happened to more than 250,000 children and their families in almost every American state and territory. While some practical issues still exist, the CAS materials were an accession that has come to represent one of the strengths of the library at N-YHS.

Maurita Baldock *is the assistant librarian and archivist at the University of Arizona Special Collections. Until July 2013, she was curator of manuscripts at the New-York Historical Society.*

NOTES

1. The New-York Historical Society was founded in 1804 when New York was still spelled with a hyphen. Thus the New-York Historical Society still officially includes the hyphen in its name.
2. Although the term "orphan train" is commonly used today to describe this emigration of children, none of the agencies that used this method ever used the term contemporary to the program. The exact number of children sent out west is still unclear, but it has been estimated to be about 250,000. Stephen O'Connor, *Orphan Trains: The Story of Charles Loring Brace and the Children He Saved and Failed* (New York: Houghton Mifflin, 2001), xvii–xix.
3. O'Connor, *Orphan Trains,* xvii.
4. The Children's Aid Society collection at the New-York Historical Society is officially titled the "Victor Remer Historical Archives of the Children's Aid Society" at the request of the CAS.
5. The author Stephen O'Connor was granted access to a large number of CAS files by Victor Remer. His 2001 book *Orphan Trains: The Story of Charles Loring Brace and the Children He Saved and Failed* discusses the history of CAS and is critical of CAS's management of its emigration program.

6. "Children's Aid Society Records," Flickr, accessed September 6, 2014, https://www.flickr.com/photos/n-yhs/collections/72157623964464144/.

7. "Orphan Train Historical Background," on Christina Baker Kline's website, accessed August 4, 2014, http://christinabakerkline.com/blog/my-next-novel/.

8. Graham Windham was created from a 1977 merger of the Graham Home for Children (founded in 1806 as the Orphan Asylum Society) and Windham Child Care (founded in 1835 as the Society for the Relief of Half Orphans and Destitute Children). "Guide to the Records of Graham Windham," New-York Historical Society Museum and Library, accessed August 4, 2014, http://dlib.nyu.edu/findingaids/html/nyhs/grahamwindham/bioghist.html.

9. "The Orphan Trains," Children's Aid Society, accessed August 4, 2014, http://www.childrensaidsociety.org/about/history/orphan-trains.

10. R. Jackson Armstrong-Ingram, "The Givenness of Kin: Legal and Ethical Issues in Accessing Adoption Records," *Archival Issues* 22, no. 1 (1997): 21–35.

11. Emily Brennan, "New York Adoptees Fight for Access to Birth Certificates," *New York Times*, June 15, 2014, accessed September 6, 2014, http://www.nytimes.com/2014/06/16/nyregion/adopted-children-fight-for-access-to-birth-certificates.html.

THREE

"I Really Can't Wait to Archive This Exchange"

Exploring Processing as Appraisal in the Tim Kaine Email Project

Benjamin S. Bromley, Roger Christman, and Susan Gray Eakin Page, Library of Virginia

In January 2010, the Library of Virginia accessioned approximately 1.3 million email messages from the administration of Governor Timothy M. Kaine (2006–2010). By law, the library must make processed gubernatorial records accessible to the public. But how does one process 167 gigabytes of email records received as Outlook Data Files (PSTs)?[1] And how does an institution serve them up to the public? This case study will describe how the Library of Virginia's decision to provide online public access to the Kaine email necessitated a "processing as appraisal" approach in order to balance our open access mission with the laws that restricted access to certain types of records. An additional challenge was presented by the presence of email related to the April 16, 2007, mass shooting at Virginia Tech and its aftermath, which required additional appraisal and access procedures. Documenting our item-by-item appraisal criteria was crucial in ensuring that it was applied consistently by the library's processing archivists and to prevent the accidental release of privacy-protected material. Consistent and careful processing was, in turn, crucial in building and maintaining a good relationship and level of trust with the record creators—representatives of the former governor—

and for the library's on-going relationship with the Office of the Governor.

The Library of Virginia has a long and impressive history of preserving and providing public access to the records of state and local government, dating back to the nineteenth century, and since 1950, governors have been required to transfer their records to the library upon leaving office. In January 2006, we accessioned our first transfer of born-electronic gubernatorial records from the administration of Mark R. Warner (2002–2006). The shift from purely paper-based to increasingly electronic records creation has posed challenges not only to the Library of Virginia but also to archives across the United States and around the world. Since our accession of the Warner records, we have developed policies in support of the creation, transfer, and management of this kind of content. We understand and take seriously our responsibility to ensure secure and stable management of this material, as well as to provide open and free public access to the archival records of our government regardless of format.

Budget challenges, staff vacancies, and the absence of definitive professional best practices hindered our ability to move forward as quickly as we would have preferred in making the Kaine emails accessible to the public. However, Kaine's April 2011 announcement of his candidacy for the United States Senate and the potential inquiries regarding his administration's records gave us an increased level of urgency to reassess and reconsider our priorities around these records, especially the born-electronic materials. With our agency's executive management team's support, an Electronic Records Workgroup of archivists and information technology staff undertook the challenge of making the Kaine administration's emails accessible in time for the 2012 election cycle. The sheer volume of emails, reductions in staff, and budget cuts at the library, coupled with unforeseen technical challenges, meant the 2012 election came and went with the Kaine emails still inaccessible to the public. But we soldiered on and finally released the first batch of the collection online in January 2014. Ironically, our release coincided with the inauguration of Governor Terry McAuliffe, a Democrat whose administration brought many familiar faces from the Kaine administration back to state government just as we were opening the books on their previous service in Virginia.

PLANNING

The library wrestled with a number of issues during the project planning phase, all of which affected our later approach to appraisal. First and foremost was the question of how the processed emails should be served to the public. The Electronic Records Workgroup explored two options:

limiting access to dedicated computer terminals in the library's reading room or allowing anyone with an Internet connection to view the emails through the library's online digital asset management system, DigiTool. Initially, the workgroup leaned toward providing in-house only access to the Kaine email via dedicated computers in the library's archives reading room. Under this option, state records archivists would minimally process the email, removing folders containing privacy-protected and restricted records. Researchers would access processed copies of the PST files using Outlook, recreating the look and functionality of each email box. In-house access would also mitigate any potential widespread release of privacy-protected materials missed during processing. Users of the collection would be required to sign the library's reading room agreement that requires researchers to refrain from disclosing any privacy-protected or confidential information they might discover.

However, upon closer examination of the transferred email, we discovered that our plan to conduct only minimal processing of them would not work due to the content and lack of organization in many of the PST files. The Library of Virginia provides in-depth records management training for more than 200 staff members of the Office of the Governor. We assist them with understanding their responsibilities under Virginia's Public Records Act and their records retention schedules, the definition of a public record, and managing their email for archival purposes. The library, with the assistance of the Virginia Information Technologies Agency, created PST folder templates for each office to help them organize their email. The template included folders for each office's records series. Despite our efforts, the email transferred to the library by the Kaine administration included personal material and non-permanent records. Additionally, restricted material, such as attorney–client privileged records and clemency files, was not handled uniformly by the record creators. While some Kaine staff members' boxes used our email template or a similar folder structure, others did not. Our initial processing plan had been based on the library's expectation of receiving well-organized email boxes with restricted items placed in separate folders for easy identification. Without that foundation, minimal processing was not possible.

We also discovered that the plan to provide public access to the records in our reading room had technical challenges. While it would lessen the risk of the accidental release of privacy-protected information, viewing the PST files in Outlook on public terminals—which would best simulate the original look and functionality of each email box—risked the authenticity of the email. We could not guarantee that a patron had not changed, edited, or deleted email messages and attachments from the PST files without each PST file being "refreshed" by our information technology department after each use. In addition, each in-house computer terminal would require the appropriate software (and maintenance) for viewing attachments in a variety of formats. Logistically this would be difficult, even if we had the staff to do it (which we didn't). The workgroup began exploring option two: online public access.

We were fortunate to have some of the key technology in place to provide online access to the email collection. Since 2007, we have provided online access to our digital collections through the digital asset management system, DigiTool. Our digital collections include both digitized materials, such as county and city records that have been scanned and ingested into the system, and born-digital materials, such as state publications that are electronically deposited by state agencies. The system has robust search capabilities and options for both downloading and emailing specific records. Give the logistical challenges associated with in-house access, these features easily tipped the scales toward the online access option, and the workgroup decided to move forward with putting the emails online. This meant committing ourselves to finding meaningful ways to deal with potential privacy-related concerns.

In order to ensure that privacy-protected records were excluded from the online collection, state records archivists decided that the electronic equivalent of item-level appraisal and review was warranted. Given the disparate organization of many of the PST files, we decided it would be irresponsible to release these records online without reviewing each email. In addition to the potential public relations fallout from a large-scale accidental release of privacy-protected information from the Kaine administration, we foresaw the possibility of damaging our relationship with the Office of the Governor for future administrations (and therefore acquisitions). As the official archive of the Commonwealth of Virginia, we hold in trust the records of our government. We could not risk this trust by being single-mindedly focused on public access to the exclusion of our professional responsibilities to protect confidential records.

IMPLEMENTATION

Our institution had never processed email previously, and we could not find any other institutions processing PST files with the goal of public access. Thus, we had to write appraisal and processing procedures from scratch. For the purposes of processing, we treated the Kaine email as a single collection (Governor Timothy M. Kaine Administration, Electronic Files, Email).[2] Each subdivision within the administration, such as the Executive Office, Policy Office, and every cabinet secretariat, is a series. The email of each person within an office is a subseries. Description is done to the PST file level (that is, to the individual message level). The processing archivist would note important subjects and correspondents and describe significant emails in detail. This approach also allowed for content and context analysis, which provided crucial descriptive information for the collection's finding aid.

The first step in creating a manual containing specific procedures for appraising and processing the Kaine email was reviewing the library's *State Records Procedures Manual* and *Guidelines for Restricting State Government Records*. These documents contain an overview of the specific types of records that are restricted by state or federal statute. The second step was reviewing the Office of the Governor's records retention schedule, which describes specific record types, retention periods, and any access restrictions. We quickly discovered, however, that these documents were woefully inadequate. The email contained a wide variety of record types and subjects not usually found in paper records or listed on the governor's office retention schedule, such as requesting and scheduling meetings, event invitations, conference information, event planning and logistics, and unsolicited resumes. To ensure consistent processing of all email, we created a list of record types that were not public records or that were non-permanent public records, along with the appropriate general retention schedule and series number for each record type, and added it to the Kaine email procedures manual.

After much trial and error, we used our manual to process 138,532 emails within the 15 email accounts from the Kaine Administration Executive Office and segregated the emails that did not qualify as public records or were restricted from public access. To do this, we opened a copy of each PST file in Outlook and created five subfolders within each file: *open*, *open-redact*, *restricted*, *Virginia Tech–review*, and *non-record/non-archival*. The *open* emails were those deemed ready for public access. The *open-redact* emails were those requiring the removal of specific protected information, such as personal cell phone numbers. The *restricted* emails were those closed to public access for a period of seventy-five years. The *Virginia Tech–review* emails comprised email related to the 2007 mass shooting at Virginia Tech; as described later in this case study, the Virginia Tech emails are a complex subset of the Kaine email collection and required their own set of handling procedures. The *non-record/non-archival* emails were those determined to be either not public records or not records requiring permanent retention. The library does not yet have formal policies or procedures for deaccessioning electronic records, so these emails remain on a server for the time being. After each email was reviewed, it was dragged into the appropriate subfolder.

The process was not strictly linear. Identifying restricted material, such as attorney–client privileged records was a huge challenge and created fits and starts in processing. These records were not treated consistently by the record creators. For example, while the counselor to the governor, Larry Roberts, created folders for attorney–client email, the recipients within the administration did not. In addition, Roberts acknowledged that he did not have time to review the content of each email to make a legal determination. He arranged his attorney–client email by subject and often included email that did not contain legal advice. In December 2011, the Library of Virginia asked the Virginia Office of the Attorney General for a clear definition of attorney–client and the application of the attorney–client relationship within the Office of the Governor. This advice was crucial to ensure these records were treated consistently across the collection by the processing archivists. All processing stopped until this issue was resolved.

The Attorney General's Office January 2012 opinion had a significant impact on processing. The opinion advised the library that attorney–client privilege did not attach to any of the counselor's communications with others in the Office of the Governor. The attorney–client privilege could attach to communications with the Attorney General's Office or properly appointed special counsel.[3] The result of this opinion meant that a large number of emails previously marked attorney–client and restricted for seventy-five years were not confidential by law and would be open to the public once processing was complete. Some records remained closed based on other provisions of the code, such as the Virginia Government Data Collection and Dissemination Practices Act and the Virginia Health Records Privacy Act. The Library conveyed this change in status of these records to Kaine's former counselors, and then we had to go back and reprocess the email boxes that we had already completed.

Because we were essentially creating policies and procedures as we went along, the processing was initially handled by only one archivist, Roger Christman. Once the written procedures were completed, we brought a second archivist, Ben Bromley, into the fold. A key test for the soundness of the procedures was whether someone who had not been involved in the project since the beginning could get up to speed and start processing in a timely manner. Training took approximately one week and involved walking Ben through the guidelines at a computer workstation with Outlook and an email box open. This was followed by assigning him a PST file to process and establishing an open-door policy for questions about types of records that may not have been explicitly mentioned in the guidelines. Then it was simply a matter of learning by doing, with multiple passes through the first PST file until a level of comfort with the procedures was established. We also decided to process each office's paper records alongside the email because it allowed the two different formats to inform the work on the other. It also helped inform consistent appraisal decisions.

Once the first batch of PST files had been appraised, our information technology department began to experiment with getting them online. We knew that we had to work within the parameters of DigiTool, but other than that, we had no real lead to follow. To our knowledge, no other state has made archival emails freely available online, so we had no prototype to learn from. Instead, we drew inspiration from the extremely resourceful 1980s television character MacGyver and improvised a solution.

Our first technical decision point concerned how to serve the email records online. PDF is the library's default "nonimage" format for delivery of digital content, and it is the format we chose for delivering the Kaine emails. We reasoned that users are familiar with the format, it is probably the most sustainable format that is widely used by the public, and it makes the emails look like emails. Additionally, multiple file formats can be converted to PDF, which meant we could theoretically include email attachments (such as Word, Excel, and PowerPoint) as additional pages in the PDFs we created from the email files as long as a conversion tool existed with that capability. We also liked that PDFs are full-text extractable and would make the emails full-text searchable. Additionally, Adobe Acrobat has easy-to-use redaction tools that could be employed for removing privacy-protected information from specific emails.

Once we knew that we wanted to create PDFs, we turned to finding affordable software for converting PST files into PDFs. There are numerous such tools available, but not all of them include the ability to convert email attachments into PDFs. We found two relatively cheap tools advertising that ability and downloaded trial versions for testing purposes. The first, PST Viewer Pro, was a breeze to work with and created PDFs that look just like a printed email, but it had one major limitation. The program cannot convert .msg attachments to PDF, meaning that if an email has an email attached to it, only the parent email is converted to PDF. Any attached email remains in the .msg format and requires the user to have the ability to open .msg files. The second tool, Total Outlook Converter, had the opposite problem. It crashed frequently and produced wonky-looking PDFs (e.g., with information missing from the email headers), but it could easily convert .msg attachments to PDF. Like Goldilocks searching for the perfect bed, we scoured the web for a magical third tool that made beautiful PDFs with .msg attachments converted and included, but alas, we could find no such tool. Instead, we compromised. All emails without .msg attachments were converted to PDF using PST Viewer Pro, while all emails with .msg attachments were converted using Total Outlook Converter. This decision necessitated a refinement of the archival processing step. The processing archivists were directed to create an additional subfolder called *open-w/msg* within the processed PST files and to drag any emails with .msg attachments there. Those emails were then converted to PDF separately from the bulk of the emails.

Processing decisions and technical hurdles were two of the main phases of implementation, but we juggled a third phase externally while dealing with the behind-the-scenes aspects of the Kaine email project. This phase consisted of building and maintaining a good relationship and level of trust with the record creators. In 2002, the Library of Virginia and former Virginia governor James Gilmore (1998–2002) had a contentious and public dispute over the disposition of his administration's records. When Gilmore's records arrived at the library in January 2002, staff immediately noticed that the volume of records was much less than they had expected. State records archivists surveyed the collection and realized that entire records series listed on the retention scheduled were missing. The library made several inquiries about these series, but Gilmore aides stated that the bulk of the administration's records had been transferred to the library. The dispute went to mediation in the summer of 2002. During one of those sessions, the library learned from Gilmore's representative that the former governor had 240 boxes of records in storage. The library and former governor Gilmore reached an agreement in November 2002, and more than 200 boxes were transferred to the library.[4] In the aftermath of this dispute, the library requested that each outgoing governor designate a post-administration contact in order to keep the lines of communication open. The Kaine administration designated Sherrie Harrington, confidential assistant to the governor, and Roberts, counselor to the governor. As we were processing the paper records, we found no issues about which we needed to consult. As a courtesy, we notified them when the library released processed paper records from the Kaine administration beginning in 2010.

When we informed Harrington and Roberts in the fall of 2011 that we were planning to release the Kaine administration emails online, they were understandably apprehensive about being the guinea pigs of open government in the electronic age. To allay their fears, we offered them the opportunity to review the processed email prior to its release. This was a courtesy to alleviate any concerns; the library retained authority over any final decisions on what would be released. We found that this simple gesture strengthened our agency's relationship not only with the Kaine administration but also with the Office of the Governor. It demonstrated that we are a responsible custodian and can be trusted with restricted records. Roberts took us up on our offer and reviewed most of the 66,422 emails in the first batch we processed. He flagged only a few attorney–client records that we missed during processing. Satisfied, Roberts did not request to review any of the subsequent Kaine email releases. In the same spirit, we notified each Kaine staff members prior to the release of their email files. This gave them an opportunity to review their records before we announced the release to the public. These notifications were greatly appreciated. Several staff members took us up on the offer, but no one questioned our appraisal and processing decisions.

Our relationship with Roberts was essential to processing email related to the April 16, 2007, mass shooting at Virginia Tech, a horrific event in which Seung-Hui Cho killed 32 people and injured at least 17 others before turning the gun on himself. On April 19, 2007, Kaine created the

Virginia Tech Review Panel, whose mission was "to provide an independent, thorough, and objective incident review of this tragic event."[5] The Kaine email collection contains more than 11,000 messages related to the aftermath of the Virginia Tech shooting. Subjects of these emails include the creation, work, and report of the Virginia Tech Review Panel, meetings and correspondence between Kaine administration officials and family members of those killed or injured during the shooting, mediation and settlement discussions and agreements, implementation of the settlement agreement, and privacy-protected material such as medical records. The correspondence between Kaine and victims' family members presented an enormous processing challenge. In the aftermath of the Virginia Tech shooting, Kaine met with family members of those killed or wounded. He also provided them with his direct email address. The collection contains dozens of exchanges between family members, Kaine, and Roberts. Many of these emails express raw emotion: anger, grief, frustration, incomprehension, and compassion. Based on the records retention schedule, Virginia statute, and our professional appraisal, these are public records and should be included in the online release. However, it is doubtful that the families who wrote these emails ever imagined they would be made public. We struggled with our professional code of ethics and our own emotions on this issue. As archivists, we are committed to providing open access to records except where sanctioned by law. But if we had written these powerful emails, we know that we would not have wanted them shared for the world to read.

We received a temporary reprieve in 2012 when the Virginia Office of the Attorney General advised the library not release any records related to the aftermath of the Virginia Tech shooting until final resolution of all litigation relating to the incident. (Two families did not take part in the 2008 settlement with the commonwealth and sued Virginia for negligence in its handling of the shooting.) Accordingly, we focused our efforts on the release of the other processed emails and waited for the final resolution of the litigation. This came in January 2014, at which time we sought Roberts's assistance in understanding the confidentiality issues related to the mediation and settlement process. As the Kaine administration's liaison to the Tech families, Roberts developed intimate knowledge of the administration's response to the tragedy and clarified which email records related to the shooting should remain closed to public view. He also agreed to help us reach out to the Tech families prior to the release of the emails that we cannot keep closed. As of this writing (September 2014), we are not yet ready to tackle that portion of the release. It is our hope that we can arrange for the families to view the emails before we put them online.

RESULTS

As of September 2014, nearly 562,000 emails have been appraised by two archivists working twenty to twenty-five hours per week on the project. While we have thoroughly documented our appraisal procedures, each individual email is a judgment call that the processing archivist has to make. In the time-honored tradition of archivists of all sorts, we tend to err on the side of keeping things rather than getting rid of them. At this time, the library has yet to decide on what to do with the more than 350,000 emails deemed non-records.

Another benefit of our item-by-item appraisal process is that we have strengthened our appraisal toolkit with a deeper knowledge about how the Office of the Governor operates and the types of records created by gubernatorial administrations. We have used this knowledge to appraise the records of Governor Robert McDonnell (2010–2014), Kaine's successor, as well as to influence records management in the administration of McDonnell's successor, Terry McAuliffe, through significant updates to the Office of the Governor's records retention schedule.

In January 2014, the Library of Virginia released the first 66,422 emails online via the Kaine Email Project @ LVA portal (http://www.virginiamemory.com/collections/kaine/). In addition to providing access to the email, the portal page includes a detailed finding aid, search tips, a brief overview of the functions and responsibilities of the Office of the Governor and cabinet, links to related paper and electronic records, and a project overview. We felt it was important to place the email collection within the larger context of Kaine administration records. A second batch of emails was released online in May 2014 and a third batch in July 2014, bringing the collection total to more than 130,000.

While it is too soon to fully evaluate the success of this project, we believe our outreach efforts via social media, as well contacting educators and members of the media, will encourage use of the collection. The main source of publicity for the collection so far has been through the Library's Twitter account and through our blog. We have written blog posts of a variety of topics so far, using them to highlight various emails and to link them to current events.[6] For example, in conjunction with Sunshine Week, we highlighted a series of emails that were part of a response to a 2008 Freedom of Information Act request submitted by Delegate Scott Lingamfelter. Lingamfelter wanted to know how much money was being spent by state agencies on publications; as a direct result of this request, the Kaine administration issued a near-total ban on publications, which ended up saving the state almost $8 million.[7]

Importantly, we have built and maintained relationships with former members of the Kaine administration. We have kept Kaine's representatives informed about our progress in processing his administration's paper and electronic records and our outreach efforts, especially social media, and called upon them for assistance with the Virginia Tech emails. As a result, we have built a foundation of good donor relations with the Office of the Governor, which, we hope, will be instrumental in future acquisitions. We have seen some signs that our approach has been effective. During the tenure of Governor Robert McDonnell (2010–2014), Larry Roberts championed the Library of Virginia as a responsible custodian of gubernatorial records. McDonnell was succeeded by Governor Terry McAuliffe, and many former Kaine administration officials, including Anne Holton, Kaine's wife, are part of the McAuliffe administration. We attended one of the first McAuliffe cabinet meetings and provided the cabinet with an overview of their records management responsibilities. We then had follow-up meetings with the deputy cabinet and individual records officers. Securing an administration's time to talk about records management is never a given, and we were thankful to see our good working relationships with Kaine staffers bear fruit in a subsequent administration.

Kaine representatives have offered to help in various areas, including helping to publicize the collection to educational institutions and navigating the eventual release of a particularly sensitive subset of emails. Former chief of staff Bill Leighty was instrumental in getting us a meeting at the L. Douglas Wilder School of Government and Public Affairs at Virginia Commonwealth University. We were able to address an audience of graduate students and faculty, many of whom had never thought of doing research at the Library of Virginia before. On an internal level, we now also use the collection alongside archival material from the eighteenth, nineteenth, and twentieth centuries in tours that we give. Normalizing this collection and other collections of digital records in the minds of archival researchers is now a key part of our outreach strategy.

The media has already begun to take advantage of the availability of the email collection, even after the initial flurry of articles subsided. The *Daily Press*, a newspaper in Newport News, Virginia, used emails from the collection to compare the Kaine administration's response to the 2006 budget crisis and possible government shutdown to the actions taken in 2014 by the administration of Governor Terry McAuliffe.[8]

LESSONS LEARNED

This project has revealed an archival catch-22 for us. Providing online access to government records raises the stakes in terms of appraisal. We do not want to release restricted records, and thus we believe item-level processing of government emails is warranted if the end goal is online access. However, in spite of our enthusiasm and carefully constructed procedure manual, we know that item-level processing of emails is not a sustainable method for our institution given limited staffing and the expected growth in electronic records. So we are taking a step back and examining our role earlier in the records lifecycle, well before government emails reach the step of being acquired and appraised. All indicators point to a need for further development of our relationships with the records creators.

Despite our best efforts at the time, we now realize that a different approach to records management for electronic records is required. People do not create and use electronic records in the same way that they do paper records. As of September 2014, of the nearly 562,000 emails we have appraised, more than 350,000 have been deemed either non-records or non-permanent records. If we have any hope of solving the catch-22, we must either make headway in how government officials manage their email or change expectations of what will happen to their email once we accession it. Tackling the problem from the email management side has proved daunting. Even with the best training, records creators by and large do not seem inclined to manage email like they manage paper, that is, by filing individual records in specific folders. While more sophisticated email management tools could streamline workflows and improve how electronic records are managed, the implementation of these tools within government agencies is largely out of our hands due to Virginia's centralized information technology structure. We, thus, are left with changing expectations about what happens to email once it is transferred to the Library of Virginia. One option we are considering is informing future record creators that their email will be made public "as-is." We could then, as a safety net, conduct item-level processing on only those email accounts that, based on job title or role, we expect would contain a significant amount of restricted material.

However we proceed, we will need to draw from, and continue to strengthen, our relationship with records creators. Public access to electronic records is still a novelty, which gives us an opportunity to shape expectations around the steps involved in acquiring, appraising, and eventually serving these records to the public.

CONCLUSION

We may not have found a permanent solution for dealing with email records, but we have completed the difficult first step of moving from theory to reality without alienating our donors in the process. From this project, we take away the knowledge that appraising and processing electronic records requires flexibility and creativity. Flexibility and creativity must go hand-in-hand, though, with diligent documentation of improvised appraisal and processing methods to both ensure consistency of application and assure donors that we remain responsible record custodians even in an age fraught with the uncertainties of electronic records management. We also take away the knowledge that carefully orchestrated incremental steps are the key to moving forward over uncertain terrain.

With that in mind, we hope that our public access project has opened a door for us on another fundamental chapter in electronic records management: preservation. Making the Kaine email records accessible online makes them visible beyond the institution's four walls and shines the spotlight on the value of archives. Shining the spotlight on archives, in turn, helps to lay the groundwork for an enduring electronic records program by engaging multiple stakeholders, including record creators, traditional patrons as well as new audiences, and, importantly, potential funders. As we work toward the completion of processing the Kaine email, we plan to simultaneously navigate the landscape of long-term preservation by exploring ways to develop a sustainable program around archival electronic material. Success on these fronts will mean that every minute spent item-level processing the 1.3 million Kaine email records was worth it.

Benjamin S. Bromley *is a development research analyst at Virginia Commonwealth University. Until October 2014, he was a state records archivist at the Library of Virginia.* ***Roger Christman*** *is the governors' records archivist, and* ***Susan Gray Eakin Page*** *is the digital archives coordinator at the Library of Virginia.*

NOTES

1. A Personal Folders file is a Microsoft Outlook data file that stores messages and other items on a computer. See "Introduction to Outlook Data Files (.pst and .ost)," Office Online, accessed July 25, 2014, http://office.microsoft.com/en-us/outlook-help/introduction-to-outlook-data-files-pst-and-ost-HA010354876.aspx.
2. Ben Bromley and Roger Christman, *A Guide to the Governor Timothy M. Kaine Administration Electronic Records, Email, 2002–2010 (Bulk 2006–2009)*, Library of Virginia, http://ead.lib.virginia.edu/vivaxtf/view?docId=lva/vi00993.xml.
3. Assistant Attorney General Carrie Nee, email message to John Metz and Roger Christman, January 10, 2012.
4. Conley Edwards, "'It Was a Dark and Stormy Night': A Saga of the Transfer of Gubernatorial Records," *Government Record News* 20, no. 2 (Summer 2004), http://www.archivists.org/saagroups/gov/newsletters/summer2004.htm#Stormy.
5. Executive Orders Digital Collection, Governor Tim Kaine, Executive Order 53 (2007), Virginia Tech Review Panel, 06-18-2007, Library of Virginia, Richmond.
6. *Out of the Box: Notes from the Archives @ the Library of Virginia* (blog), http://www.virginiamemory.com/blogs/out_of_the_box/category/state-records-blog-posts/kaine-email-project/.
7. Roger Christman, "Kaine Email Project @ LVA—Sunshine Week Edition," *Out of the Box: Notes from the Archives @ the Library of Virginia* (blog), March 17, 2014, http://www.virginiamemory.com/blogs/out_of_the_box/2014/03/17/kaine-email-projectlva-sunshine-week-edition/.

8. Dave Ress, "Kaine Emails Detail 2006 Plan to Avoid Budget Shutdown," *Daily Press*, April 9, 2014, http://articles.dailypress.com/2014-04-09/news/dp-nws-shutdown-kaine-20140409_1_house-republicans-kaine-state-budget.

FOUR

Hardware for SoftPoems

Appraisal and Acquisition of Vintage Computer Equipment

Will Hansen and Matthew Farrell, Duke University

At Duke University's Rubenstein Rare Book & Manuscript Library, recent acquisitions have included the papers of authors of electronic literature, defined by the Electronic Literature Organization as "works with important literary aspects that take advantage of the capabilities and contexts provided by the stand-alone or networked computer."[1] Hypertext fiction and poetry, allowing readers to click linked words or phrases to choose one of many possible paths through a work, is perhaps the best-known genre of electronic literature; however, hypertext is only one of many tools employed by practitioners in the field. Authors whose papers are now at the Rubenstein Library include Judy Malloy, who pioneered the use of hypertext in her 1986–1987 "database novel" *Uncle Roger*[2] and went on to incorporate visual art and email into works such as *Forward Anywhere* and *Its Name Was Penelope*, and Stephanie Strickland, who has explored the possibilities for digital "verse-scapes"[3] in works such as "Sea and Spar Between"[4] and "V: Vniverse."[5] Robert Kendall, whose papers were acquired by the Rubenstein Library in 2012, "has been creating interactive multimedia poetry since 1990."[6] He has also worked in a variety of genres, including works that combine digital photography with poetry and kinetic works incorporating animation and sound, dubbed "SoftPoems" by Kendall in the early 1990s.[7]

In collecting these authors' papers, the Rubenstein Library has occasionally acquired software used to create these works, which are often complex digital objects. Malloy's papers, for instance, included a version of Eastgate Systems' Storyspace application. Processing of the digital component of the Malloy papers is ongoing, and so a final appraisal decision has not been made. It is likely that Malloy's software will be kept, however, as a significant portion of the Malloy papers are works by peer authors and include unpublished and commercially published versions of their work. Although Storyspace is not required to access commercially published works, the application saves drafts in a proprietary file format. Files opened in Storyspace offer the user multiple views to assist in navigation of the works, including bird's eye maps. Similarly, the larger Duke University Libraries collected commercial titles released by Eastgate throughout the 1990s. In collecting the personal papers of other individuals, the Rubenstein Library has acquired desktop towers and laptops. In many of these cases, staff removed the hard drive(s) from a particular machine to create a disk image or otherwise extract born-digital materials. The remaining physical hardware has been dealt with inconsistently, partly because of space concerns but largely due to a lack of library-wide policy.

In the case of Robert Kendall's papers, an offer of hardware included a bulky touch-screen monitor, speakers, and hard-drive towers. These were used to display his works of interactive literature in the early 1990s; Kendall would transport the equipment to galleries and exhibitions, since some of his works like the "SoftPoems" required touch-screen technology and audio components not readily available with all personal computers at the time. Kendall also offered us suites of commercial software used to create his works.

How should institutions evaluate the research value, broader utility, and long-term preservation needs of such materials, either as part of specific archives or to repurpose for other uses? There is an emerging practice among archival institutions to acquire legacy electronic hardware, at least in some cases. The Maryland Institute for Technology in the Humanities (MITH) has collected vintage computer systems, both as artificial collections—such as their Vintage Computers collection, comprising hardware donated by Associate Director Matthew Kirschenbaum and former MITH staff member Doug Reside—and as part of personal archives like the Deena Larsen Collection. Similarly, the University of Texas at Austin's Harry Ransom Center, Yale University's Beinecke Rare Book & Manuscript Library, and Emory University's Manuscript, Archives, and Rare Book Library (MARBL) have accepted literary papers that include obsolete computer systems. MARBL designed a well-publicized program and exhibit around their acquisition of Salman Rushdie's papers and computer systems. Those acquisitions made sense for those repositories, but under what circumstances would it be appropriate for our archives to acquire vintage hardware and software? This chapter examines the steps we used to reach an appraisal decision about the equipment offered by Robert Kendall as part of his personal papers as well as some general reflections on how other archives might approach similar donations.

ANALYSIS

When at all possible, discussions between curatorial staff, staff with digital records expertise, and potential donors about their born-digital records should begin prior to signing a formal agreement. Before acquiring the Robert Kendall papers, Assistant Curator of Collections Will Hansen sent Kendall a brief survey to assess the amount and types of born-digital material in his papers. (See appendix 1 at the end of this chapter for an example of the survey.) Kendall reported on the survey that "one of my early pieces was a computer installation that was dependent on hardware for audio and touch-screen functionality. I still have the 486-based PC and touch-screen monitor that I used for interactive kiosk-type displays of my early work. I also have a second 486 PC from the same period that should also be able to run the audio hardware."[8] Kendall was not able to start either computer, but thought that this might be a matter of replacing system batteries or other, easily fixed problems, not completely nonfunctioning hard drives.[9] Kendall did not provide a detailed description of audio hardware, including speakers, which he had to offer; it was, however, included as part of his exhibition kiosk setup.

Kendall also reported that some of his works were created using obsolete multimedia software, such as IBM Storyboard Live! and Virtual Video Producer, as well as a variety of word-processing programs, such as Microsoft Word, WordPerfect, and XyWrite. For some of these, Kendall offered a suite of the original software on floppy disks or CD-ROMs, while he thought that other programs might still be installed on the hard drives that he offered.

It was not possible for us to visit and assess Kendall's materials in person, at his home in the northeastern United States, so based on the information provided in the survey, staff in the collection development and technical services departments sought to determine whether it would be worthwhile to have Kendall ship the hardware and software for further evaluation on site at the library. The decision was difficult: since we were not sure that we would be able to recover any of Kendall's files from either computer or whether the software media (CD-ROMs and floppy disks) would still be functioning, we needed to determine if we might want to retain the hardware and software themselves as part of the Kendall papers or for other uses. This involved a number of conversations about various potential uses of the equipment, strategies for its preservation and associated costs, and contingencies for return or retention depending on the condition of the materials. Throughout these conversations a number of questions recurred and helped to guide our decision-making process; what follows is a simplified and streamlined list of the questions and answers that were most useful in helping us to determine whether or not the hardware and software on offer might be worth examining.

Is the material within scope according to our collection development policy?

The Rubenstein Library's collection development policy did not formally address hardware and software. The Kendall papers had been deemed of interest for the library's American literature collections, within which the archives of authors of electronic literature were a new initiative. However, it was unlikely that vintage hardware or software would be of interest in their own right if they were offered outside of the context of a larger archival collection: the history of technology and, more specifically, of computers were not areas of strength or of focus for the library. So, while the hardware existed in a gray area vis-à-vis our collection development policy, there were other factors arguing in favor of accepting the hardware. If we could get either machine running, they could be useful in documenting the context in which Kendall worked. If neither machine was operational, we might be able to extract partial or full contents from the hard drives; the application of digital forensics to archival workflows was, at the time, a nascent area of interest for us and has since become part of our born-digital accession and analysis workflows. If neither scenario came to fruition, one might still argue that the specific computer setup was intrinsic to understanding how some of Kendall's early work was originally experienced.

What is the creator's view on the importance of the material?

As with many appraisal decisions, creators should be consulted for their input when possible. In this case, Kendall was particularly interested in the disposition of the hardware that was used in some of his early installations. The hardware had been an essential part of these installations, and he had hauled this equipment, including the early touch-screen monitor, sound module, speakers, and tower hard drive, to galleries and other spaces where his work was to be exhibited or presented in the 1990s. Kendall felt that the physical presence of the equipment might give researchers a better sense of the work involved in the creation and display of not only his specific works but also of some genres of early electronic literature in general.

Is the material likely to receive use by researchers?

The research value and potential for use of archival materials by scholars obviously remains a paramount consideration in an appraisal. In this case, it seemed unlikely that Kendall's hardware and software on its own would attract much traditional use in our physical reading room. However, some use of the equipment to run and view older works in their original environment seemed likely—if it worked. Scholars in fields such as the history of authorship, textual criticism, and the history of technology, in addition to those intimately interested in a specific creator's work, will also want to be able to experience such files under conditions as close to those in which the author created them (or intended for them to be viewed) as possible. For electronic literature, especially, the perceived success or meaning of a work could change dramatically depending on its presentation on different monitors or at different resolutions, the sound capabilities of the hardware used for its display, the speed and other technical capabilities of the machine used to run it, and the programs used for its display. Because "physical hardware components can be essential to understanding the affordances of an obsolescent system,"[10] even if access copies of materials will be made available on contemporary computers, the original hardware contains evidential value.

If one-on-one, in-person use in the reading room were the only type of use under consideration, we would likely decline the software as not having significant research value, decline all hardware except the three hard drives, and discard or return the hard drives after attempting to copy files related to his work. However, the library is currently undergoing a major renovation. Upon reopening in 2015, the Rubenstein Library will feature increased exhibit space. The likelihood of including artifacts from electronic literature collections meant that the traditional reading room experience was only one potential use of the items.

Would the material be useful in exhibitions, instruction sessions, and other public presentations?

Outside of extraction and preservation of the data held on obsolete media, the media itself might also be worth considering for its value as visually appealing material for exhibitions and other displays. For institutions with exhibition programs, it can be a challenge to make physical exhibitions focused on archival materials, and especially on digital materials, engaging or appealing. Hardware and packaged software can serve as physical "icons" that attract those interested in the history of digital media and might also be useful for classroom instruction on the history of computing, sessions for potential donors, and other topics.

In this case, the library was interested in the possibilities for mounting a physical and digital exhibition about the history of electronic literature. An early installation setup would be an excellent addition to such an exhibition.

Would the material be useful as part of a "digital workbench" for use with other accessions?

As more archival accessions include born-digital materials, the need for obsolete software and hardware to run files in their original environment grows. This is certainly important for internal use by library staff for the many cases where files cannot be adequately recovered or read in newer environments and also for the uses by scholars if feasible.

Of course, not every institution will want or be able to build such a suite of obsolete software and/or hardware. In many cases, migrating files to newer viewing environments, or using web-based or locally produced emulators of vintage software, may suffice. Migration to a newer or more stable format is often seen as easier or less resource intensive than emulation. While this may be true of documents created in office applications, complex or composite digital objects may pose challenges to migration. Creators may also have already recreated their works for access on newer systems themselves. For instance, Judy Malloy created web-based editions of her works that were originally available on floppy media. The differences between a work created in a DOS-based application and a later edition produced for a web environment are visually apparent to an end-user, to say nothing of the underlying code. Because archivists of literary papers are interested in unpublished draft materials and earlier versions of works, presenting such material in as close to the original context as possible is desirable in many cases.

The material offered by Kendall and others creators presented an opportunity to discuss the Rubenstein Library's current position regarding development of such a workbench. It was decided that this should not be a priority when considering donations of such material, but that staff should be opportunistic if particularly hard-to-find materials (or materials useful in preserving and making available complicated or problematic digital objects) became available.

Is the material rare or hard to find?

As mass-produced commercial products from the past thirty years, most personal computer (PC) equipment is unlikely to be genuinely rare. However, the present generation of researchers might struggle to find examples of particular hardware and software products that are available for use in institutions, as most computer museums and archives devoted to computing history are in their infancy. A researcher's only or easiest option might be to purchase a piece of used equipment, frequently for sale via an online vendor on eBay or similar sites.

The software on offer consisted of operating systems, system utilities and device drivers, and commercial applications used in the creation of Kendall's work. The operating systems and utilities appeared to be available for purchase, or emulators of their functions had been created. In many cases, the same is true of the commercial software, although it is interesting to note the code fixes and updates Kendall received from IBM alongside personal correspondence from the IBM project manager for Storyboard Live. It is also worth noting the variety of software versions Kendall kept of Storyspace, Storyboard Live, and Virtual Video Producer.

The hardware dated from the early 1990s and included two desktop PCs with standard consumer-level peripherals, a cathode ray tube (CRT) monitor, an early touch-screen CRT monitor, a MIDI sound generator, and transportable speakers. The two PCs were manufactured by popular business and consumer-grade companies—a Gateway2000 tower that Kendall used as his office machine and a Dell that Kendall used to present his works. Examples of many of the components appeared to be available for purchase online or otherwise documented. However, the touch-screen monitor and the MIDI sound generator were early examples of their kind. Although touch-screen technology had been in development by various parties for decades, the MicroTouch system being offered dated from the first five to eight years after the launch of the Hewlett Packard HP-150, generally considered the first consumer-level touch-screen system. During the early years of personal computing, developers pursued different methods to achieve a touch-screen product for consumers. MicroTouch was involved in resistive and capacitive technologies, as opposed to the infrared-based Hewlett Packard. In contrast to products produced and sold as touch devices, the Kendall monitor appeared to be an example of converting standard, noninteractive devices into devices that support tactile interaction with users. The MIDI sound generator was the first sound module to make use of the General MIDI standard. Although it is not particularly hard to find at present—units typically sell on eBay for less than $100—having the module along with the rest of Kendall's kiosk setup speaks to the opportunities associated with the field of electronic art in the early 1990s as well the limitations imposed by selecting one model over another.

While these are not "rare" in the same way that a sixteenth-century book might be rare, they could be seen as important artifacts that would become increasingly scarce and important for documentation of this period of rapid change in both electronic literature and PC use more broadly. Nevertheless, it seemed unlikely that the hardware or software would attract much use or require preservation based on its rarity, and it also seemed unlikely that the equipment would become impossible to find in the future, as activity in collecting and emulating such vintage products has developed rapidly in recent years.

Where and how would the material be stored?

Because the hardware would include bulky items such as speakers, a large monitor, and two computer towers, storage costs and capabilities had to be considered. The hardware was likely to require a special arrangement of deep, wide shelving, reducing the number of record storage cartons or other large items that could be held. For long-term retention, it might also require custom-made boxes or other enclosures to be made by Duke University Libraries' conservation technicians.

The Rubenstein Library holds some material in an off-site storage facility, the Library Service Center (LSC), but this material would likely require on-site storage due to the irregular size of the materials and their boxes. This consideration was further complicated by the library's impending renovation, which began in the summer of 2013. On-site storage was reduced to a minimal level during the renovation, so in the short term, the hardware would take up the only available range in the bay of shelving reserved for artifacts.

For long-term retention, depending on the use case, the software could either be boxed with the physical papers in the archival collection (if it were to be treated as part of the papers documenting Kendall's works and process) or installed on a library workstation and stored with other equipment used by Duke's digital records archivist (if it were to be included in a digital workbench or otherwise repurposed).

Under what conditions would use of the material be possible and permitted?

Since limited reading room use of the hardware and software was anticipated, we suspected that we did not need to address what would constitute an acceptable use of the hardware until a use case arose: for instance, we thought that we could defer a decision on whether we would allow researchers to use their own digital forensics tools in the reading room to examine Kendall's hardware. However, we anticipated restricting use of the original hardware and software if the contents were successfully extracted and mounted on the library's servers. If we were not able to successfully operate the hardware or extract files, researcher experimentation might be welcomed under certain conditions, for example with staff supervision, perhaps in a consultation room or other area outside of the reading room to prevent distractions to other researchers.

DECISION

To summarize, we concluded that the materials being offered by Kendall were not addressed in our collection development policy but likely in scope for our collections when considered as documentation of his work. Kendall believed the hardware used in installations of his early works was important for both his own work and for the history of electronic literature, but he was less concerned about the other hardware and software. A limited amount of research use of the materials could be expected but perhaps not enough to justify retention of most of the hardware and software. Some of the materials, especially the gallery installation setup, could be very useful for exhibitions and displays in the library. The specific materials offered here were not likely to be useful in a digital workbench or for use with other accessions of born-digital collections, and the materials were not especially rare or hard to find but might be important as contextual artifacts for the development of electronic literature. Storage would be mildly problematic in the short term and would continue to be an important factor in considering future offers but, in this case, not a major long-term difficulty, and implementation of a policy regarding use of the hardware could be deferred until a specific-use case arose, since limited demand was anticipated.

After considering all of these factors, we decided to incur the expense of shipping the hardware and software to allow us to attempt to recover files and programs from the hardware and to review the software for potential use with Kendall's own papers and other accessions containing born-digital materials. We felt that we could more easily appraise the hardware with an in-person review and could reassess whether or not to retain that equipment after attempting to extract files from the hard drives.

RESULTS

The materials arrived in two shipments. On November 6, 2012, the computer equipment and software arrived in seven boxes (see appendix 2 for a complete list). This was followed by the more traditional manuscript material, including electronic files on digital media, on December 26. Most of the hardware and software were received in their original packaging, which Kendall had retained. The equipment shipment consisted of two large Gateway boxes, a Dell box, two nested boxes housing the monitor, and a box containing the sound equipment and other peripherals. None of these were of a size that would easily fit on archival shelves (see figure 4.1). The hardware also appeared to be in excellent condition, at least superficially, given its age and use.

Upon arrival at the library, staff attempted to extract files from the three hard drives. The Gateway2000, the tower that was for Kendall's use at his home office, appeared to be completely nonfunctioning. Although initial signs indicated that the problem related to the system battery, replacing that battery did not result in a bootable machine. Efforts to recover data from either of the two hard drives in this tower using the Forensic Toolkit Imager also failed.[11] Because different forensics toolsets have different strengths and weaknesses, staff have made further attempts to extract contents as new tools become available. Similarly, efforts to boot the Dell tower used for installations of Kendall's works failed, as well as subsequent efforts to forensically recover data from the hard drive. Disk images were created from floppy media also transferred by Kendall. Data were extracted and appraised; those disk images that documented Kendall's work were accessioned and copied onto the library's preservation servers.

Kendall agreed that it was not worthwhile to retain the Gateway2000 tower from which no files could be recovered, so its specifications were documented for retention in the library's files on the Robert Kendall papers, and it was recycled. Retention of the Dell tower used in the installation of Kendall's works was considered in conjunction with the touch-

Figure 4.1. The Dell tower, touch-screen monitor, and sound equipment boxes. Not pictured: two oversize Gateway2000 boxes.

screen monitor and sound equipment. Though not outside the realm of possibility, it is difficult to test whether the monitor is fully functional as Rubenstein Library does not currently possess a working machine compatible with the MicroTouch drivers included. While emulation or virtualization is an option to test the equipment, our current ability to support such activities is limited.

Because the Dell tower was nonfunctional and would require significant staff time to repair, it was difficult to decide whether a full suite of the bulky installation hardware had enough artifactual value or display value in exhibitions and other public displays to retain and to offset the costs of storage and conservation. This was particularly the case given that the donor had expressed his preference to see the materials preserved as part of the record of his work. It was likely that the monitor and sound equipment, which appear to be in good working order, could be connected to a new computer to display the works in their original environment either through a virtual machine or emulated software.

Because some of Kendall's works, and most works of electronic literature more broadly, are sensory experiences of which particular digital environments are an integral component, the question of whether to preserve the hardware and software environment in which his early works were first experienced was particularly weighty. While discarding the hard-drive tower after extracting and uploading its data to library servers could save some storage space and conservation costs, it would reduce the visceral impact that the actual equipment hauled to exhibit Kendall's works might have on a researcher or exhibition attendee, especially as cultural memory of a time before ubiquitous digital access recedes. It seemed even less likely that the specific tactile, auditory, and visual experience of the touch-screen monitor would be easily replicated by emulation or virtual machines. For these reasons, we decided to keep the Dell tower, touch-screen monitor, and sound equipment.

The software that arrived with Kendall's papers has been retained with them at this time, but this decision may be reviewed in the future. When, for instance, staff attempt to connect the touch-screen monitor to a working computer, the MicroTouch device drivers will be required. The Storyspace versions may be required to access drafts of Kendall's writings as well. Since the papers are still actively receiving new accessions, the software may be useful for future accretions; if not, it may be discarded or repurposed, after appropriate documentation of the removed material has been made to retain with the papers. Kendall also sent some documentation, such as users' manuals for the hardware and software, he used to create his works. These used little space and were easy to file, and so they were retained as well.

LESSONS LEARNED

Overall, appraising the hardware and software in Kendall's papers has been a worthwhile learning experience, while also providing the opportunity for the Rubenstein Library to refine its general policy or, at least, a typical stance toward these kinds of materials. While we still have not developed any hard-and-fast rules or collecting policies for this kind of material, we have learned some essentials about how best to approach future offers of this kind.

Our experience reinforced for us that the process of appraisal of unusual material should always involve collaboration between staff in technical services, collection development, and conservation; in this case, it was also useful to discuss the matter with the Duke University Libraries' exhibits coordinator, to gauge her interest in using the hardware in future exhibits, as well as the Rubenstein Library director. This slowed down the process of making a final decision but allowed all of those involved to discuss the ramifications of accepting this kind of material. If we had not discussed the possibilities for future exhibits, our thought process around the kiosk equipment would have been very different, and we may have reached a different decision.

While we were able to take the time for consultation with our colleagues, we were not able to appraise the materials in the field before bringing them into the library because of the distances involved. This lack of hands-on appraisal of the materials before their arrival was certainly less than ideal. Accepting shipment of materials prior to making an accessioning decision can make it more difficult to decide that the material is not wanted; once it's in the door, it can seem like more work to remove it than to accession it. The decision, however, was ours to make: the official donor agreement had already been signed by both parties prior to any materials arriving. It transferred ownership of the materials to the library upon their arrival and gave us room to define what precisely would comprise the papers and remove and return unwanted materials to the donor. However, it is always in our interest to maintain a close, positive relationship with living donors and their families. Kendall had a strong desire for the library to retain the kiosk equipment but agreed with us about discarding the other desktop machine. Had we inspected the equipment prior to acquisition, the resulting conversation would likely have taken a different shape. Of course, appraisal in the field becomes very difficult with digital materials when they are not already on live machines, such as when digital materials exist only on legacy devices and media.

In the case of the Kendall papers, their status as an exemplar of archives of authors of electronic literature presented a set of circumstances that led us to decide to retain some hardware and software in this case. However, as a general rule, institutions may prefer other options depending on their goals or desired outcomes. If institutions seek to document a creator's digital working process or environment, they may want to collect metadata on the hardware and software used most often by the creator. If they seek to document the creation of a particular work or set of works, an oral history or interview about the creator's process might be a useful option. If the digital content still exists on a working machine, making a screencast recording with the donor prior to acquisition is worthwhile. If they have received obsolete or broken hardware or software with an accession and do not foresee any need for the physical items themselves but believe that researchers may wish to learn something about a creator's equipment, photographic documentation might be sufficient.

CONCLUSION

Hardware and software are media that blur the line between museum and archives. Do these components themselves contain sufficient documentation to receive archival processing and preservation, or are they only suitable for conveyance of documentation? Should they be entrusted to museums or find their place in archives and libraries as part of the documentation of individuals' careers, organizations' operations, and the like? In part, answering these questions may depend on changing perceptions of the nature of archives as places for interpretation of their holdings through exhibits, events, public programs, and classroom instruction. It will also depend on different organizations' available resources—human, technological, spatial, and other—to devote to such media.

The offer of hardware and software in the Robert Kendall papers provided an opportunity for the Rubenstein Library to begin consideration of formal policies on acquisition of such materials and on appropriate storage and preservation of them. Next steps for the organization will include drafting such policies, which will be useful for future offers of similar materials. As we continue to build our collection documenting the field of electronic literature, we will probably encounter these kinds of questions more often. It is likely that other institutions will as well as they begin collecting more complex collections of born-digital materials. Donations of vintage hardware and software should neither be accepted out of hand nor automatically rejected but given the same kind of thoughtful appraisal as audiovisual materials, realia, and other non-paper materials.

Will Hansen *is director of reader services and curator of Americana at the Newberry Library. Until May 2014, he was assistant curator of collections at the David M. Rubenstein Rare Book and Manuscript Library, Duke University.* ***Matthew Farrell*** *is digital records archivist at the Rubenstein Library.*

APPENDIX 1: SURVEY FOR BORN-DIGITAL MATERIALS IN INDIVIDUAL DONORS' PAPERS

1. What kinds of files do you have?

-What operating system(s) do/did you use?

-What software or other applications are/were used for your work? Please specify versions as needed (e.g., Microsoft Word 2000).

-Are any of these applications defunct, obsolete, homemade, or otherwise hard to find? If so, do you still have a copy of the application available?

-What file formats are represented (e.g., .doc, .pdf)?

2. How much file volume do you have?

-If possible, please provide an estimate in megabytes/gigabytes and/or number of disks for the amount of files you plan to transfer.

3. How are these files currently stored?

-On your computer's hard drive?

-In an external hard drive or USB flash drive?

-On CD, DVD, or floppy disk? (Please specify type/number of each.)

-On an institutional server or other local network?

-In a web-hosting, online storage service, or other web application? (Please specify sites or services used, including sites such as Flickr, Google applications, Basecamp, Facebook, etc.)

-Only in printouts or other analog manifestation?

-Do you know of any potential preservation problems with these files (e.g., corruption)?

APPENDIX 2: DETAILED LIST OF HARDWARE AND SOFTWARE OFFERED BY ROBERT KENDALL

Gateway2000 4DX20-66V – Intel 486 PC

- Two Western Digital Caviar hard drives: Caviar 31600 (1624.6 MB) and Caviar 2340 (341.2 MB)
- Removable storage: optical drive, floppy drives (3.5", 5.25")

Crystal Scan 1572 FS monitor (15" CRT)
Dell 466/LV

- Western Digital Caviar 2340 (341.2 MB) hard drive
- Removable storage: optical drive, floppy drive (3.5")

NEC Multisync 3FGX CRT monitor with MicroTouch layer added
Roland Sound Canvas Midi Sound Generator SC-55

Realistic Amplified Speaker System
Software: Utilities and Drivers

- Gateway system utilities (5.25″ floppies)
- Dell system utilities (3.5″ floppies)
- Chinon CDS/CDX (3.5″, 5.25″ floppies)
- PhoenixBIOS upgrade disk (3.5″ floppy)
- Soundblaster 16 (3.5″ floppy, CD-ROM)

Software: Operating Systems

- MS-DOS v5.0 (5.25″ floppies) and v6.0 install disks (3.5″ floppies)
- Windows v3.0 install disks (5.25″ floppies) and v3.1 install disks (5.25″, 3.5″ floppies)

Software: Applications

- MicroTouch Software: Drivers for various systems including Drive-Point for DOS and TouchWare for Windows (3.5″ floppies)
- MicroTouch Software: Pad Manager for creating touch-driven applications (3.5″ floppies)
- IBM Storyboard Live: v1.0 and v2.0 install disks (3.5″ floppies)
- IBM Storyboard Live: Drivers to interface with Roland MIDI sound module (3.5″ floppies)
- IBM Storyboard Live: Correspondence with and code updates from Storyboard project manager (3.5″ floppies)
- Virtual Video Producer: v3.0, v3.21, v3.25 install disks (5.25″ floppies)
- Virtual Video Producer: Font Factory disk (5.25″ floppies)
- Virtual Video Producer: Grab & Cut screen capture and sprite cutter disk (5.25″ floppies)
- Eastgate Systems Storyspace: Windows v1.0.3, v1.0.7, v1.0.9, v1.1.0, v1.2, and v1.75 install disks (3.5″ floppies)
- Eastgate Systems Storyspace: Mac v1.3, v1.5, v1.75 install disks (3.5″ floppies)
- Eastgate Systems Storyspace: Storyspace Tools disk (3.5″ floppy)
- WriteTrak v3.5 install disks (3.5″ floppy)
- E-Lit works by Kendall (published and unpublished) and others (published) (3.5″, 5.25″ floppies, CD-ROM)

Gateway2000 4DX20-66V – Intel 486 PC

- Two Western Digital Caviar hard drives: Caviar 31600 (1624.6 MB) and Caviar 2340 (341.2 MB)
- Removable storage: optical drive, floppy drives (3.5″, 5.25″)

Crystal Scan 1572 FS monitor (15″ CRT)
Dell 466/LV

- Western Digital Caviar 2340 (341.2 MB) hard drive
- Removable storage: optical drive, floppy drive (3.5″)

NEC Multisync 3FGX CRT monitor with MicroTouch layer added
Roland Sound Canvas Midi Sound Generator SC-55
Realistic Amplified Speaker System
Software: Utilities and Drivers

- Gateway system utilities (5.25″ floppies)
- Dell system utilities (3.5″ floppies)
- Chinon CDS/CDX (3.5″, 5.25″ floppies)
- PhoenixBIOS upgrade disk (3.5″ floppy)
- Soundblaster 16 (3.5″ floppy, CD-ROM)

Software: Operating Systems

- MS-DOS v5.0 (5.25″ floppies) and v6.0 install disks (3.5″ floppies)
- Windows v3.0 install disks (5.25″ floppies) and v3.1 install disks (5.25″, 3.5″ floppies)

Software: Applications

- MicroTouch Software: Drivers for various systems including Drive-Point for DOS and TouchWare for Windows (3.5″ floppies)
- MicroTouch Software: Pad Manager for creating touch-driven applications (3.5″ floppies)
- IBM Storyboard Live: v1.0 and v2.0 install disks (3.5″ floppies)
- IBM Storyboard Live: Drivers to interface with Roland MIDI sound module (3.5″ floppies)
- IBM Storyboard Live: Correspondence with and code updates from Storyboard project manager (3.5″ floppies)
- Virtual Video Producer: v3.0, v3.21, v3.25 install disks (5.25″ floppies)
- Virtual Video Producer: Font Factory disk (5.25″ floppies)
- Virtual Video Producer: Grab & Cut screen capture and sprite cutter disk (5.25″ floppies)
- Eastgate Systems Storyspace: Windows v1.0.3, v1.0.7, v1.0.9, v1.1.0, v1.2, and v1.75 install disks (3.5″ floppies)
- Eastgate Systems Storyspace: Mac v1.3, v1.5, v1.75 install disks (3.5″ floppies)
- Eastgate Systems Storyspace: Mac Storyspace Tools disk (3.5″ floppy)
- WriteTrak v3.5 install disks (3.5″ floppy)

E-Lit works by Kendall (published and unpublished) and others (published) (3.5″, 5.25″ floppies, CD-ROM)

NOTES

1. "What Is E-Lit?," Electronic Literature Organization, accessed May 20, 2014, http://eliterature.org/what-is-e-lit/.
2. Judy Malloy, *Uncle Roger*, World Wide Web edition, accessed July 14, 2014, http://www.well.com/user/jmalloy/uncleroger/partytop.html.
3. J. R. Carpenter, "Sea and Spar Between," on Stephanie Strickland's website, accessed July 14, 2014, http://www.stephaniestrickland.com/sea.
4. Nick Montfort and Stephanie Strickland, "Sea and Spar Between,"*Dear Navigator* 2 (Winter 2010), accessed July 14, 2014,http://blogs.saic.edu/dearnavigator/winter2010/nick-montfort-stephanie-strickland-sea-and-spar-between/.
5. Stephanie Strickland and Cynthia Lawson Jaramillo, "V: Vniverse," on Stephanie Strickland's website, accessed July 14, 2014, http://www.stephaniestrickland.com/vniverse.
6. "About," on Robert Kendall's website, accessed July 15, 2014, http://www.wordcircuits.com/kendall/#!about.
7. "SoftPoems," on Robert Kendall's website, accessed July 15, 2014, http://www.wordcircuits.com/kendall/#!poetry/softpoet.htm. A later example, "Faith," requires the use of Flash and is accessible at http://www.wordcircuits.com/faith/.
8. Email from Robert Kendall to Will Hansen, October 1, 2012.
9. See appendix 2 for a detailed list of hardware and software offered by Kendall.
10. Matthew Kirschenbaum, Erika L. Farr, Kari M. Kraus, Naomi Nelson, Catherine Stollar Peters, Gabriela Redwine, and Doug Reside, "Digital Materiality: Preserving Access to Computers as Complete Environments," accessed June 10, 2014, http://mkirschenbaum.files.wordpress.com/2009/10/digitalmaterialityipres2009.pdf.
11. For a detailed description of the Rubenstein Library's digital forensics workflow at that time, please see pages 44–48 of Martin J. Gengenbach, "'The Way We Do It Here': Mapping Digital Forensics Workflows in Collecting Institutions," accessed June 10, 2014, http://digitalcurationexchange.org/system/files/gengenbach-forensic-workflows-2012.pdf.

FIVE

From Projects to Policy

The Evolution of a Systematic Reappraisal Program

Tina Lloyd, Library and Archives Canada

In 2006, Library and Archives Canada (LAC) realized we had a problem: we had too many records. With a mandate to preserve both the government and private records of Canada, our holdings had grown much faster than anticipated from the 1970s into the new millennium. By 2005, we found the vaults in our new state-of-the-art storage facility, only opened in 1997, were full. Although the building was designed to physically stand for 500 years of service and had more than 150 kilometers of shelving, we had filled it in less than 10 years. This realization made us consider more than just the challenge of running out of storage space. We began to look at why we had the problem of too many records coming in and asked if perhaps we weren't capturing the best archival record of Canada's history. We also knew that all too often our valuable records were buried in piles of records that weren't as useful and that many of our holdings were not as accessible as we wanted.

While LAC has seen expansion of its collections of private records, it was the government records that were the cause of our collection's enormous growth. We often talk about post–World War II as the period of rapid growth in government bureaucracy and records, but based on the volume of our holdings, it seems to have escalated faster in the 1970s with a sudden explosion of government programs and then in the 1980s and 1990s when word processing and computers took over, resulting in multiple versions and copies of documents showing up in files. Archival practices in Canada changed as well during this time period. In response to the 1985 Deschênes Commission,[1] LAC had developed a corporate practice of taking more records to provide a margin of safety, as well as to enable the possibility of facilitating the study of different types of history, and to provide records for different types of researchers, including social historians and public investigations. Though the commission eventually determined the archives was not responsible for any unauthorized destruction, the question itself seemed to change the culture of archivists at LAC for a generation, making them more cautious and less willing to destroy records. It's also possible that macro-appraisal, which was developed and implemented at LAC partly in order to try to deal with the government records explosion, may have contributed to the records glut; the focus of macro-appraisal, with its top-down approach, was an analysis of the three elements of function, structure, and citizen that resulted in governance. Though case files on "citizen–state interaction" were never explicitly mentioned as the target of macro-appraisal, it was often interpreted that way, and millions of case files were retained as a result. This, combined with the growth in the output of records created by the government, contributed to the rapid expansion of LAC's holdings.[2]

To address the problems created by the growth in our collection, over the past decade, LAC has initiated a series of initiatives to explore reappraisal, moving from a small project-based effort to implementing a policy of systematic reappraisal. Ranging from groups exploring high-level theoretical and policy issues to teams actually digging into specific records series, we've attempted to marry strategy with practicality, theory with action. I have been involved in all of these efforts, usually on the side pushing for practicality and immediate action. I've experienced firsthand both the need for reappraisal at LAC and how challenging it can be to implement.

From the outset in exploring a reappraisal program at LAC, we were concerned with the archival correctness of what we were doing and began to investigate the legitimacy of reappraisal, its history, and the theory and writings that discuss it. The archival literature in the Unites States has seen considerably more discussion of reappraisal, with archivists like Leonard Rapport and Karen Benedict arguing the pros and cons of reappraisal.[3] In his seminal 1981 article, Rapport writes, "Every repository of public records has on its shelves records which, if offered today, we would not accept. If we wouldn't accept them today, why should we permit these records to occupy shelf space? For such records there should be no grandfather clause."[4] He also posits the idea of thinking of archival records not as having "permanent value" but rather as worthy of "continued preservation," arguing that this distinction "implies that some accessionable records may be less than eternal. It permits us more easily to entertain the thought that appraisal standards can change, [and] that an appraiser's evaluation may be less than infallible."[5] He suggestes reappraising records already held by archives by the modern rigorous criteria used to appraise outside records, noting that it would result in lots of useful internal disposal. Despite the arguments of archivists like Karen Benedict, reappraisal became an increasingly legitimate collection management activity. Mark Greene has a more recent series of witty and intelligent articles advocating for reappraisal.[6] So our review of the literature gave us confidence that we could move forward with reappraisal on solid archival ground.

Although there were procedures for the deaccessioning of government records from the early days of the program,[7] they weren't actually applied often. Until about 2009, LAC did not have a policy on reappraisal, and in this we were not alone. Barbara Craig's survey of Canadian practitioners[8] indicated that 70 percent of institutions had no formal policy on reappraisal. Craig's study also showed that, like LAC archivists, many in the profession held reservations about reappraisal. This case study will review the major reappraisal projects LAC undertook between 2007 and the present and provide a detailed example of how our current reappraisal policy was applied on one problematic group of records.

CLEARING THE PATH PROJECT (2007–2008)

LAC's first step toward systematic reappraisal was the Clearing the Path project, initiated as a short-term effort to deal with an acute problem. It was charged with ensuring that LAC acquired, preserved, and made available only the best archival materials. The project gathered a team of interested people and began to look at possible targets for review. Reappraisal had always been possible within our government archives control procedures, but it wasn't encouraged; the goal of this project was to begin changing that perspective. At the same time, LAC also saw deaccessioning as a way to improve the accessibility of all its collections. Reducing unwanted holdings would enable LAC to continue bringing in valuable records and dedicate more resources to making the records that remained more accessible, by creating better finding aids and better metadata for them.

The initial scope of the project was to destroy between 1,200 and 1,500 meters of non-archival records, freeing vault space for more desirable ones. The group began by assessing a number of possibilities that had been identified by creating a system report for series previously identified as needing review. However, our best successes were series identified by other archivists as good reappraisal targets. We also discovered early on that some of the records that had the least value had no finding aids or no useful finding aids. The project focused on those government records accumulated by LAC over time—in other words, records in our existing holdings. Many were acquired through the process of selective retention, which allowed archivists to transfer records while delaying the final archival review to occur later. Various weak disposition tools, such as inadequate, misinterpreted, or out-of-date records authorities, resulted in the acquisition of many records of no permanent value.

Clearing the Path identified and analyzed these records in our holdings, reviewing them in light of our available disposition tools, including more recent authorities and generic tools. By disposing of records that were not useful and spending resources on creating better finding aids for those that we determined we wanted to keep, we could improve the accessibility of the materials for the public. We began to develop some best practices as well, such as guidelines about how much documentation was required and when to communicate with records creators and earlier appraisal archivists.

As our first foray into reappraisal, Clearing the Path gave us many useful lessons. For example, the power of the anecdotal approach in identifying targets has proven to be surprisingly consistent. While we have tried to be strategic and systematic about out initiatives, we found here (and in later projects) that our most effective reappraisal projects have often come through word of mouth. Because reappraisal was an activity new to most of the participants, the learning curve was fairly steep. We struggled with everything from becoming familiar with the types of records we were reviewing to the responses of other archivists (not positive or encouraging) and the variable responses of creating departments (thrilled, indifferent, and hostile) and the levels of authorization and layers of process required within LAC to actually get the records off the shelves. At times our efforts seemed to be a comedy of errors as we made all the mistakes we possibly could, though we did learn as we went. As a result, we changed, adapted, persevered, and were able to accomplish a lot of disposition in a fairly short period of time, and our successes were more visible than our failures.

To some extent, the name "reappraisal" is a misnomer to describe what we have done at LAC. We were never actually appraising these records, never researching and crafting an appraisal, but simply applying appraisals that already existed at LAC more appropriately. Our most common reappraisals have involved identifying records series where there were errors in original filing or selection or where there was a more recent or better disposition authority that could be applied.

Clearing the Path was able to identify more than five kilometers of non-archival records for deaccessioning, thus freeing up valuable space for the acquisition of information assets of higher potential for use and leading to significant annual savings. We also processed the records selected for retention, making them more accessible for researchers.[9]

THE LEGACY PROJECT (2008–2009)

LAC management liked what had been accomplished with seemingly apparent ease, and so they initiated a follow-up project that enlarged the mandate to include dealing with "legacy records" both within our holdings and in the storage repositories of the government in general. These were records that we didn't know very much about, often without finding aids of any kind, without good descriptions, only partially managed or in some cases completely unmanaged. It included file rooms and storage warehouses full of undescribed records. The Legacy Project tried to take some of the things we had learned about reappraising our own records and apply it to records before they were transferred to us and became part of our backlog. It was a sign of LAC moving away from straight focus on archival value and more into involvement in the information management of the government of Canada.

The results were mixed. Review of records outside of LAC's holdings in the Legacy work called for us to create guidelines for departments to apply to mitigate the risks of them not having maintained effective accountability for their records. We developed guidelines based on risk mitigation that could help with this and were able to test them with by applying them to some small projects, but there wasn't much acceptance of the low-risk tools by the client departments we needed to work with. In retrospect, the Legacy Project may have been too preliminary and too tentative to convince client departments we knew our business. One of our successes was with a fairly messy group of records in LAC's own records office that had resulted from a physical move of office space as well as the amalgamation of the National Archives and National Library. This project destroyed a large number of legacy boxes on shelves in the records office, as well as in the warehouses, and allowed us an avenue to develop some preliminary theory about dealing with legacy records, most of which involved ways of mitigating risks, determining where risk would be acceptable and where it wouldn't.

THE MII4 PROJECT (2010–2011)

The next effort was MII4, the reappraisal component of a series of Modernization Innovation Initiatives. Over the course of a year, the initiative conducted pilot projects to explore what kinds of projects worked, examining a variety of challenges in different media and different areas of responsibility including published and unpublished records, government and private, records at different stages of acquisition, and touching on most of the types of media that LAC holds. Pilot projects included large government records series with very low archival value, special media registration vaults, and a duplicate series of Japanese Canadian Redress

Files, which we tried to offer to other agencies with no luck.[10] We also worked with published material, removing series from our holdings and offering published material that was not in our mandate to other agencies. In addition, we targeted some holdings based on preservation concerns, including removing a large collection of decaying newspapers from our holdings.

By the end of the year, as a result of the pilots, we concluded that reappraisal may be done for valid reasons beyond freeing up collection storage space, and the cost effectiveness of a project should not be assessed solely on the extent of holdings disposed. Reappraisal objectives may include removing blocks of nonsignificant holdings, gaining better control over unmanaged records, solving preservation concerns, and addressing duplication among the multiple copies and formats in our holdings. The reappraisal process also gave us opportunities to increase discoverability of holdings, enhance relationships within the community, and prepare relevant holdings to move to a new facility.

The report also concluded that large government series or fonds are typically the best candidates for reappraisal that has as its objective the removal of significant extents of records from holdings. Appraisal decisions in these cases must be clear and easily applicable, preferably at the box or series level. Where detailed finding aids do not exist, archivists must seriously consider what kinds of metadata we need to produce in order to document and be accountable for records destruction. An important recommendation was that the future of reappraisal at LAC should target those records that are least discoverable, in an effort to increase their value to Canadians. Specifically, reappraisal efforts should focus on government textual records (by far the most voluminous holdings of LAC), examining the records that have not yet been incorporated into our holdings or that have no finding aids. The report also made recommendations about being more selective (or "turning off the taps") with new acquisitions.

The project resulted in a successful level of progress in the pilots and a final report that asserted that moving forward LAC's reappraisal program must:

1. Be systematic, policy based, and evidence driven, with clear and documented rationale for how decisions are made.
2. Be cost effective.
3. Use appropriate tools that assess holdings for significance, sustainability, sufficiency, suitability, or use by society, to allow LAC to make consistent decisions.
4. Ensure holdings are relevant and discoverable and that this process integrates elements of preservation.

5. Support the development of the archival community in Canada to enable cooperation for activities such as transfer of title or long-term loans.

All of these recommendations are still in use in the reappraisal program today.[11]

AN ONGOING REAPPRAISAL PROGRAM (2011–2014)

After recent changes at LAC, we found ourselves still with an important job to do—attempting to reexamine all our government holdings in a systematic fashion—but also needing to prioritize what we assume to be some of the best returns on investment. This was the first time that LAC really began to talk about reappraisal as an ongoing activity that needed to continue indefinitely and not a short-term solution to a crisis. We were asked to present a strategic approach to the challenge and to develop a plan for continuing and effective reappraisal. This has allowed us to refine the criteria for reappraisal that we had at our disposal from our previous projects.

Our recent attempts to review our government holdings systematically use the criteria established by MII4, which we've turned into best practices. While a reappraisal program could start with one part of LAC's holdings and systematically work its way through the entirety of the collection, there are also many potential triggers for the reappraisal of intellectual content or a review of the form and function of holdings, such as unappraised or unprocessed holdings, collection move preparation, preservation concerns, public demand for holdings, or new valuation criteria. As recommended in the MII4 report, we are also focusing on government fonds with broad scope for reappraisal deaccessioning.

Problems in government record groups become apparent in several different ways, but one of the most typical is when record groups have substantial backlogs indicating that either there are more records coming in than anticipated or that there is some reason the archivists are leaving them in the backlog. Other indicators that reappraisal may be needed include no finding aids available, records with large amounts of case files, or records at selective retention. As a result of this new systematic approach, the records of Public Works and Government Services Canada were identified as one of the targets for reappraisal.

REAPPRAISAL OF RECORDS FROM THE PUBLIC WORKS AND GOVERNMENT SERVICES CANADA

In 1997, LAC had appraised the records of Public Works and Government Services Canada (PWGSC), identified a subset of records in the

Architectural and Engineering Branch as having archival value, and established terms for the transfer of those records. PWGSC agreed and signed the transfer. Over time it became apparent that there was a problem. LAC had identified specific files in one area as being of archival value; however, rather than the limited number of boxes of records the archivist anticipated receiving, we received about 10,000 boxes of records, many filled with records of little or no value. Identification of this problem took a while because the appraising archivist had moved on and was no longer responsible for these records, so successive archivists didn't realize there was a substantial difference in extents expected and received. Also the records arrived in facilities across Canada, not just in one central repository, helping to mask identification of the problem. And of course, we are used to large extents of records at LAC, as we try to document the machinery of government.

Initial identification of the reappraisal problem came from the Legacy Project team in a Regional Service Centre in Edmonton in 2009, which raised a flag about numerous boxes of records without much obvious value. As we researched it, it became evident that there were many similar boxes across the country. However, as archivists, even reappraisal archivists, we tend to assume that the records do have value but that we simply have not yet figured out what the appraising archivist saw in terms of enduring value. However, with these records, that was stretching things.

The Legacy Project team examined the records authority, which identified that these records had archival value because they could provide information on heritage buildings, historic sites and monuments, and major renovations to these sites. But it was clear that we were receiving more than that. The boxes were filled with a jumble of documents on fairly minor activities in fairly minor buildings. We were not inclined to keep them, but it is always a bigger undertaking to get rid of things than to just hold on to them, and after some research, we eventually concluded that it was too complicated to pursue, and we abandoned them for simpler projects. We returned to the question of these records time and again over the next four years but without success. It was clear that the records were problematic and were going to remain so, as records continued to pour in but there wasn't a simple solution that could be applied at the series or box level. We thought that with enough perseverance we should be able to find a long-term solution, but we didn't know what it was.

From 2009 to 2013, we had researched the problem. We discovered that the initial appraisal had been done hurriedly, without all the information that the appraising archivist had hoped for. The archivist had requested more time and more information but was told to proceed with the information available. He complied, completing the appraisal as well as he could, given what he understood about the records system and what he wanted to acquire. As a result, his terms and conditions directed the transfer of specific file blocks that gave information on heritage sites. The specified file blocks contained documents related to the construction of significant original structures (not built from standard plans), executive correspondence, particularly documents relating to policies, and major renovations or changes made to historic sites and heritage buildings that alter the monetary value, visitor experience, and/or the aesthetic or symbolic meaning of the site.

But we were receiving a lot of other, far-less-worthy records in the transferred boxes as well. In fact, the records we thought we wanted were about 5 percent of what we were receiving in the transfers for this authority. So why were we getting so many more records than we had expected? Although the boxes did contain some seemingly valuable documents on the heritage buildings, there were a lot of other records included too. It became evident that the creating department was filing all kinds of things in these files, seemingly anything related in any way to building and renovating and repairing any property operated by PWGSC, which included most federal government structures. Eventually we began to think that the records staff at PWGSC had begun to use the file blocks as kind of a "junk drawer" where they put all the records they didn't immediately have a home for. Further investigation revealed that there had been some staffing turnover issues in the department and then some training problems as well, which no doubt was contributing to the misinterpretation of the records authority.

Clearly our problem had arisen because of inexperienced archivists at our end and inexperienced records managers at the other end who all assumed the status quo must have been intended by their more knowledgeable and experienced predecessors; the tendency to assume that decisions made in the past are always right in archives is a pervasive one. Setting aside the problem of how to stop the incoming flow of incorrect records, we had to decide what to do with the large volume of materials that we now had in our custody. We interviewed media experts and archivists who had been responsible for the PWGSC records, and their advice ranged from "destroy all" to "keep all." An architecture specialist suggested we select based on significant architectural aspects, which seemed like a reasonable approach and in keeping with the original appraisal decision.

In the spring and summer of 2013, we decided it was time to try to work from the boxes themselves. To this point, we had been working primarily from the agency-created finding aids and accession and registration records. We knew what kind of records were in the accessions in a general way but not the specifics of how we could work with them. We planned this effort to be the point where we went through the boxes, file by file, and tried to really understand better what they were and to find solutions for them. Before we started, our hypothesis was that we could efficiently select the records that had the desired content identified by the records authority by viewing the actual files.

We requested an accession to work with and got started. In the first accession, we found many records about buildings that weren't considered "heritage," and lots of files on irrelevant changes to the buildings. It was easy to determine that the records we were looking at had little or no archival value. This was an encouraging sign, and we continued. The critical element was whether the buildings were important or not. The original accession we were working on was a relatively recent one of buildings in the national capital region, and we were relatively familiar with them, so we knew whether they were old or new, different or standard. We compiled a set of databases to use as resources to help with contested cases.[12] The one we ended up using the most often was the Canadian Register of Historic Places.

We were aware the finding aids didn't provide much information. Presumably they were useful for the creating department, but they identified buildings by an internal numbering system, so we needed information we didn't have in order to use the file lists. We requested a copy of the list linking numbers and names from the creating department, but we never received it. However, because the buildings were in our local area, we could skim files to find the name or address of the building, and in most cases, we knew right away whether it was "important" or "heritage." If we weren't sure, we could check it against the databases of historic buildings. We worked in groups of three to process boxes, so two of us could be checking boxes and calling out names and addresses to a third who could check the databases. We assumed that later accessions would include more regional records, but this was actually fairly rare for the boxes transferred to us at headquarters; most of the records we saw were from the national capital region.

The contents of the files also came under scrutiny. We were able to identify by sight which files represented important renovations and which were minor repairs or renovations. Sometimes it was possible to determine the importance from titles, and there were keywords that usually indicated minor or major projects. For example, "replace (item)," "modifications," "repair," "resurface," "install," "correct water leakage," "caulking," "improvement," and "tenant services" were all indicators that the repairs were minor, even if relating to heritage structures, and could be removed. Even in files on historic buildings, records on certain rooms could usually be rejected, so renovations to machine rooms, washrooms, kitchens, and staff spaces usually had low enduring value, as they typically did not significantly alter the monetary value or visitor experience of the site. Such minor projects for non-heritage sites could typically also be rejected.

Later accessions had more records that LAC clearly had never asked for, and we could identify blocks of records with file numbers that were not archival, and after some examination, we determined that there were no extenuating circumstances and they could be rejected as a group.

The next step was a regional implementation; there were records in the same series across the country in records centers in Vancouver, Winnipeg, and Halifax. Regional archivists took the report we had prepared, which outlined our criteria and process,[13] and adapted it to their specific circumstances and needs. One significant modification to our process dealt with buildings pertaining to First Nations and most especially to Indian residential schools.[14] When we did the pilot project in Ottawa, we realized we had no files on these buildings, so we knew this was one place where regional archivists would have to lead the way. They developed criteria that identified all such files and put them into separate accessions. Officially, the appraisal has not been changed, and these records were not initially identified as having archival value, though they have clearly become more politically sensitive since then. It seemed evident to all that these records should not be destroyed and that, if we did identify them for destruction, it could stall the whole project. So we moved them into new accessions and created more-detailed finding aids to highlight them. It is not clear whether they will have much value to future researchers, but Truth and Reconciliation Commission researchers are expected to look at these records. If they are judged over time not to have any archival value, they may yet be disposed of under the existing authority.

As of October 2014, we have processed about a kilometer of records in this PWGSC effort. We retained and described about 10 percent of that extent, arranging for destruction of the rest. There are still many similar records from PWGSC left in our holdings, but we are confident now in our ability to deal with them using the system we have developed. With the agreement and help of the creating department, we have changed our documentation on the records disposition authority to reflect these changes. It is our understanding that PWGSC have also changed their documentation on how to implement the authority at their end, though it is not really clear yet whether this will really change what they send us, and there are a lot of records currently in the system that will probably be sent to LAC. Also in the works is a new appraisal at the departmental level that will evaluate all the records of the department. This is expected to change the appraisal decisions and terms and conditions for these records, though that will not come to pass for at least a year or two.

While we have reported these promising findings, there has been such change at LAC that they have gone relatively unnoticed. And although the extents we disposed of are fairly large, LAC's collection of government of Canada records is vast, so in comparison this is relatively small. However, the records we now hold are the important "heritage" records initially identified in the records authority, and we have created better finding aids for them than they came with so they are easier for researchers to find. Our work also resulted in a new a series for buildings related to First Nations with a good finding aid to which researchers will have access, and that should enable us to better serve the Truth and Reconciliation Commission as well. While it may be only a drop in the bucket for LAC overall, our work on this group of records is a good demonstration that our new policy allows us to free up shelf space while making valuable records more accessible and can also result in changes that help us "turn off the tap" for incoming records we don't actually want.

CONCLUSION

Over the past seven years, in a progression of reappraisal projects and efforts across the organization, we have succeeded in the most basic and tangible goal: we've removed a lot of records from the holdings of LAC. Some have been returned to creators, some transferred to other organizations, and many were destroyed. We have also processed the records we've decided to keep and created better finding aids as we went, making records we hold more accessible. Through our experience, we have identified triggers for reappraisal and process improvements and are making reappraisal a systematic part of the operations at LAC despite a corporate culture that often disapproves of the activity.

While we have removed records and improved documentation, in most cases the actual records authorities under which we receive the records have not been changed. Much of time we do still need to change the appraisals, which are often out of date or too vague to be useful. We need a working feedback process where reappraisal is more able to influence both current appraisal and the updating of older authorities. Our decisions are well thought out and based on clear problems in our holdings, but it is difficult for us to influence appraisers. However, unless we find ways to stop unwanted records from coming in to us—either because of outdated appraisals or incorrect application of authorities in departments—our reappraisal burden will continue to increase.

One of the key lessons we've learned about reappraisal is that it's often difficult to sell the idea to archivists. Anytime we talk about this project, no matter how black and white the decisions are to us, someone invariably says the records sound "good" or "valuable" or they aren't sure that removing them from our holdings is the right thing to do. We've found that once they actually see the records they are less enthusiastic about keeping them. So when the specifics of the case are made more tangible, the archivists tend to come over to our side and support what we are doing. However, we need to work to establish a culture in which our colleagues have as much trust in our reappraisal decisions as they seem to have in their colleagues' original appraisal decisions or in the random acts that lead to non-archival records ending up on our shelves.

The issue of trust and respect for the professional judgment of others is sometimes at the heart of the reappraisal work we've done. I personally struggle with telling anyone else that the decisions they made were wrong. I am more comfortable with the idea that they made the best decisions they could under the circumstances at a given time, and decisions may have been implemented badly. Our view of the results of their decisions is very much a result of our time and circumstance. But sometimes, after appropriate review and analysis, we need to do things differently.

Fortunately, with recent changes in senior management at LAC, there is a new determination to address backlog issues of various kinds as backlog reduction is one of the overarching priorities of the new head librarian and archivist. Whatever that includes will include reappraisal; this inclusion is a new way of thinking for LAC and a very encouraging one. Hopefully this is just the start of making the observations Leonard Rapport made decades ago part of our everyday thinking: appraisal standards can change, and an appraiser's evaluation may be less than infallible, and older records should have to meet the same critical standards we would use to evaluate records today. It's an exciting time as we move toward actually applying our reappraisal thinking to improve our existing holdings.

***Tina Lloyd** is a member of the Strategic Backlog Disposition and Discoverability Task Force at Library and Archives Canada.*

NOTES

1. In 1985, the Commission of Inquiry on War Criminals, known as the Deschênes Commission, investigating the destruction of immigration case files dealing with war criminals, required testimony from archivists from the Public Archives to speak to records retention and disposition practices of the archives and the government in general. The specific decisions by the appraising archivist and the overall practices of the archives fell under public scrutiny and made it very evident that the archives was and needed to be accountable to the public for its decisions and that they might sometimes be called upon to explain and defend their appraisal decisions. For a full description of this, see Robert J. Hayward, "'Working in Thin Air': Of Archives and the Deschênes Commission," *Archivaria* 26 (Summer 1988): 122–36; and Terry Cook, "A Monumental Blunder: The Destruction of Records on Nazi War Criminals in Canada," in *Archives and the Public Good: Accountability and Records in Modern Society*, ed. Richard J. Cox and David A. Wallace (2002), 37–65.

2. Terry Cook, "Macroappraisal in Theory and Practice: Origins, Characteristics, and Implementation in Canada, 1950–2000," *Archival Science* (2005): 101–61.

3. Leonard Rapport, "No Grandfather Clause: Reappraising Accessioned Records," *American Archivist* 44, no. 2 (Spring 1981): 143–50; and Karen Benedict, "Invitation to a Bonfire: Reappraisal and Deaccessioning of Records as Collection Man-

agement Tools in an Archives—A Reply to Leonard Rapport," *American Archivist* 47, no. 1 (Winter 1984): 43–49.

4. Rapport, "No Grandfather Clause," 143.

5. Ibid., 148.

6. See, for example, Mark A. Greene, "I've Deaccessioned and Lived to Tell about It: Confessions of an Unrepentant Reappraiser," *Archival Issues* 30, no. 1 (2006): 7–22.

7. Sheila Powell, in writing about reappraisal, notes the idea of reappraisal existed at LAC. See Sheila Powell, "Archival Reappraisal: The Immigration Case Files," *Archivaria* 33 (Winter 1991–1992): 104–16.

8. Barbara Craig, "Doing Archival Appraisal in Canada: Results from a Postal Survey of Practitioners' Experiences, Practices and Opinions," *Archivaria* 64 (Fall 2007): 1–45.

9. Library and Archives Canada, "Clearing the Path to More Accessible Records," final report, Library and Archives Canada Government Records Branch Recordkeeping Assessment Projects Initiative, 2007–2008, accessed October 13, 2014, http://www.collectionscanada.gc.ca/government/news-events/007001-6308-e.html.

10. We evaluated these records as having no value to LAC since they were duplicates of another series of records we held. But because it seemed they might have value to other archives or to researchers, we looked for other institutions we might transfer the series to. However, this proved unsuccessful, as there were issues of the fairly large size of the series as well as concerns about the Canadian Access to Information and Privacy Legislation, both of which would pertain in this case.

11. Library and Archives Canada, "Modernization Innovation Initiative 4: Reappraisal, Draft Final Report," June 22, 2012, internal files of Library and Archives Canada.

12. The databases consulted included the Canadian Register of Historic Places, the Directory of Federal Real Property, the Federal Heritage Buildings Review Office, Parks Canada Directory of Federal Heritage Designations, and the Heritage Canada database.

13. Lauren Markewicz, "Reappraisal of Public Works Report," August 2013, unpublished report in the files of Library and Archives Canada.

14. The Truth and Reconciliation Commission (TRC) was an element of the Indian Residential Schools Settlement Agreement between the Canadian Government and First Nations to investigate and inform all Canadians about what happened in Indian residential schools. There is a current large research project under way into the archival holdings of LAC by the TRC, which is expected to look at these records.

SIX

Terabytes from Far-Off Lands

Acquiring Records of the Ford Foundation International Fellowships Program

Jane Gorjevsky and Dina Sokolova,
Columbia University

Launched in 2001 with the largest single grant in the history of the Ford Foundation, the International Fellowships Program (IFP) developed a novel and promising approach to leadership education and training. Between 2001 and 2013, the program offered fellowships for post-graduate study to more than 4,300 people from underserved communities—women, indigenous people, people with physical limitations, and residents of remote rural areas—who strived to become social justice leaders in their countries but lacked regular access to higher education. The IFP operated in 22 countries in Latin America, Europe, the Middle East, Africa, Asia, and South Asia with a secretariat in New York setting policy guidelines and providing overall program management and coordination.

This innovative program was based on an inclusive higher education model that prioritized social commitment over traditional selection criteria. It provided remedial academic preparation and language instruction as part of the program, to prepare fellows for their further academic training in their chosen fields, frequently in foreign countries. The vast majority of IFP alumni returned to their home communities after their fellowships and reported positive local impact from their work.

Once the Ford Foundation decided to wind down the program, the IFP chose Columbia University as the permanent home for its archives, both paper and digital. In 2012, Columbia University Libraries / Information Services (CUL/IS) received a $1 million grant from the IFP for the purpose of preserving the archives and making them accessible to researchers. IFP program directors Joan Dassin and Mary Zurbuchen believed that the experience in using international education to promote community development and social justice documented in the records could be beneficial to generations of future scholars and policy planners all over the world.

This extensive archive also supports a ten-year longitudinal tracking study that aims to examine the impact of IFP on the lives and career trajectories of its grantees. The assembled data and future results of this study will be added to the archive as well.

An important secondary objective of the grant was to assist Columbia University libraries in building up its technology infrastructure and designing a workflow model for the growing number of projects with born-digital or digitized content. The Ford Foundation IFP records were Columbia's first organized and deliberate acquisition of born-digital materials. Their volume and hybrid nature provided us with a perfect opportunity to rework our archival acquisition process—that is, selecting, physically acquiring, and ensuring administrative custody of the materials—as it applies to modern institutional records. Traditional considerations of storage space and processing expenses were complemented by new problems of overabundance and duplication of information, typical for the large modern collections.

As of January 2014, the acquisition phase for both digital and paper components of the collection has been completed. The Ford IFP archive is now in custody of the Columbia University Rare Book and Manuscript Library (RBML). Its contents include administrative documents, website content, audiovisual materials, theses, master papers, academic records of the fellows who passed through the program, as well as raw data and output of studies conducted on behalf of IFP by Center for Higher Education Policy Studies based at University of Twente in the Netherlands.

In this case study, we will focus on challenges of the selection, appraisal, and acquisition of the born-digital part of the IFP archive and discuss the evolution of our application of these traditional archival concepts, as we applied them in the digital realm.

PLANNING

Columbia University's Rare Book and Manuscript Library serves as the repository for a number of large-scale institutional archives. The work of the unit includes many ongoing partnerships with philanthropic and nonprofit organizations engaged in promoting education or protecting human rights worldwide, such as Human Rights Watch, Carnegie Corporation of New York, and many others. History of education and history of philanthropy are major collecting areas for RBML, so the Ford IFP collection fits well into our mission and collecting policies.

The appraisal process for traditional paper files from such institutional archives was well established at Columbia and followed recognized best practices in the archival community. The process starts with working with the officials in charge of the organization's records to identify the materials of permanent value. In addition, acquiring modern institutional records always includes discussions of possible access restrictions and privacy issues. The RBML staff often perform on-site visits in order to appraise and select records of enduring value from a large diverse group of paper documents; they frequently presort and pack the material themselves. The expense and effort of moving paper records makes these pre-acquisition trips worthwhile. RBML curators or archivists then work with donors on arranging onetime or periodic shipments of agreed-upon materials. Due to these preliminary efforts, files are likely to arrive already broken down into tentative groups, in folders, and accompanied by a basic inventory.

Once these materials arrive in the RBML, their content is compared against the inventory (mostly at the box level), and their description, quantity, and new location are recorded in the departmental accession database. The collection can now wait, sometimes for a number of years, for its turn to be processed.

Some additional appraisal activities can take place at the processing stage, such as occasional deaccessioning of out-of-scope materials or separating sensitive information either for deaccessioning or to be closed for a specified period. These decisions could be made at the box or folder level, depending on size, relative importance, and use pattern of the collection. The nonrestricted materials are arranged and described, then made accessible as all analog collections are, on-site in the RBML reading rooms.

In order to acquire and process the IFP archive, we needed to update these acquisition routines to accommodate our first genuine, large-scale born-digital acquisition. Our plan was to build on our previous experience with analog collections and, at the same time, address the new challenges presented by the electronic nature of the material.

However, the first of these challenges was not directly related to the electronic nature of the collection; it was managing the entire process of donor communication remotely, since we were working with offices all over the world. The only entity we could (and did) visit was the IFP secretariat's office in New York City. The IFP program staff had included a trained archivist, Alan Divack, who, early in the course of the IFP program, provided international partner offices with electronic records guidance, indicating the key document types, their relative importance, and respective retention periods. Alan has continued to play an immensely helpful role in planning, communication with partner sites, and clarifying project and policy objectives. Due to his preliminary work, it was easy for us to establish the tentative overall organizational structure for the combined digital and paper archives, even prior to the arrival of any actual records. The records for each office were expected to fall into three general content categories: organizational records, fellows' records, and email correspondence.

Prior to the beginning of the IFP archiving project, the Columbia University libraries already had a Fedora-based institutional repository for storing digital assets, a robust digitization program, a variety of digital projects and exhibits, and a large number of EAD-based or scanned archival finding aids available online. However, until 2012, born-digital materials within these special collections had only arrived on an ad hoc basis, either on legacy media packed into boxes with paper materials or as email attachments.

At the very start of the project, a digital preservation working group was formed, bringing together the libraries' digital program division's director Stephen Davis, digital preservation librarian Dina Sokolova, and special collections analyst Terry Catapano, as well as the RBML's digital assets archivist Jane Gorjevsky. The group began meeting once a week to coordinate interactions with content donors, discuss the next steps, and map out the interdepartmental workflow for preserving born-digital materials.

Our original plan was to use the expertise of the content providers (IFP partner offices) to appraise, select, and sort the materials as much as possible prior to acquisition. We realized that we would be unable to manually review every file upon receiving it, and so we had to depend on sorting decisions made by the content creators.

A core objective of the project for both the IFP and Columbia was making the archive as accessible for research and scholarship as possible. This objective, however, made it imperative to identify and segregate content that needed to be restricted for reasons of privacy and confidentiality. The digital nature of the materials allowed us to make them instantly available to researchers all over the world but also magnified the consequences of unintentionally publishing someone's personal information. To address this issue, the decision was made that the IFP digital archives would have three levels of user access: publicly accessible online, viewable on-site in our reading room, and closed to general public until 2075. Guidelines were prepared and provided to the IFP partner offices asking them to carefully organize their files into those categories.

The secretariat had conducted a preliminary record survey of the international partner offices in 2010; that survey had estimated the size of future digital acquisition from those offices at 194 GB. After examining the results of the 2010 survey, we decided that we needed to update this data as well as ask several additional questions and perform a preliminary records assessment for all the offices. In the beginning of 2012, we distributed a new survey to the partner organizations. In addition to asking for new size estimates, the survey included questions about special privacy considerations, the software environment of the offices (e.g., any non-Microsoft products), and the staff's ability to run a simple software program creating an inventory of their files.

All the offices were in the process of closing down in 2012–2013, and in order to submit the most complete possible record of their activities, they needed to transfer their files to us very near their actual closing date. In most cases, we had an extremely short window of time to communicate with donor offices after receiving their final transfer, so we had to make sure the procedures worked correctly on the first try. To help ensure a successful final transfer, we decided to ask each office to create and send us a sample of their content for analysis several months in advance.

Several different approaches to the physical transfer of files had been explored and discussed with the partner offices, including FTP and the use of a file hosting service such as Dropbox. Privacy and confidentiality concerns finally led us to choose shipping the files on portable hard drives, rather than transferring them electronically over the Internet. For the submission of sample data, we asked that samples on smaller USB drives be shipped in exactly the same way as the final shipment would be. Each sample was to contain approximately 10 percent of each partner's electronic records selected randomly from all content categories and software formats used in the particular office.

In addition, prior to shipping us their samples, the partners were asked to run a simple software program we developed, which created an inventory of all the files and their corresponding checksums. Once the files arrived, we ran the program again to make sure that the checksums were identical and no files were corrupted during transfer.

With analog materials, after receiving the files and making sure they arrived safely, an archivist can just put the container on the shelf and record its location. With our digital acquisition, the content had to be validated and ingested, using specialized hardware and software tools. We acquired the FRED (Forensic Recovery of Evidence Device) workstation to work with various Windows-based media. After testing several types of software, we finally decided on using Forensics Toolkit (FTK) as a key element for our born-digital materials acquisition. (FTK generates low-level technical metadata and enables searching, reviewing, and labeling files for further processing.)

Clear communication with donors as well as between various departments involved in the project was essential for moving forward. Besides email correspondence, the team also set up a publicly visible project website,[1] where we published instructions and software download links that pertained to all the donors. In addition, we created an internal IFP project wiki site, which contained the project's logs, inventories, working group's meeting minutes, and emergent policy documents, as well as assumptions and decisions we made along the way.

IMPLEMENTATION

The first set of electronic IFP materials arrived from the Russian office in June 2012, since this office was the first to close down. This early closing date gave us no opportunity to ask for the preliminary sample, and the Russian office accession essentially served as a pilot case to establish and start documenting our acquisition workflows. These draft workflows were posted on our internal wiki site, along with the survey results and analytical reports on the data samples from other offices.

The Russian files were also the first to present the challenge of a non-Roman alphabet used in many file and directory names. We initially considered converting them to Roman character set equivalents for storage but ultimately were able to save them in their original format and addressed transliteration at the later processing stage.

We also found corrupted items, most prominently the cluster of website-related files. After considering this problem, we subsequently decided to exclude web files from our international partners' office acquisitions, since the IFP-related online materials were being collected separately via the existing CUL web archiving program (utilizing the Internet Archive's Archive-It service). The principal Ford IFP website and twenty-two partner websites were captured quarterly until the offices closed in 2013; since then, five sites for IFP alumni have been added to our web-collecting profile and will be captured successively on a quarterly schedule.

Responses to our new survey from most international partners arrived between June and November 2012. They confirmed that the bulk of our acquisition consisted of images, audiovisual materials, office files, databases, and emails. Among other things, the surveys indicated that the aggregate size of all the digital materials to be transferred into our custody (not including the web-harvested materials) comprised about 2.95 TB, the bulk of which (2.25 TB) would come from the secretariat in New York City.

The requested sample transfers were received from all offices between August 2012 and February 2013. Obtaining these samples gave us an opportunity to develop and refine workflow documentation for accessioning the transfer media, validating materials, and moving them to the storage server. Following the same procedures as those used for regular paper shipments, digital media were sent directly to the curatorial unit (RBML) and accessioned there—that is, entered into a database, put into an appropriate container, and labeled by Jane, the digital assets archivist. Original media was to be retained as part of the archive in our off-site storage facility, but first the materials had to be delivered to our digital preservation librarian, Dina, for checking, stabilizing, and transfer to replicated storage. All of this had to be done quickly upon receipt so that we could provide feedback to the content providers in case files or disks were unreadable for any reason.

For Windows-based media, the initial procedures were performed on the FRED workstation. In addition to the means for reading external drives, CDs, DVDs, ZIP disks, and 3.5-inch floppy disks, the workstation is equipped with a built-in write blocker, which ensures that the media-processing programs do not modify the original disk contents in any way. We started processing each media item with a virus check using ClamWin open-source antivirus software. The results of the virus check were saved into a text file and were subsequently included in the submission information package (SIP) that contained the files to be archived along with all supporting metadata.

The next task included creating archival copies of the transfer media. In conformance with the IFP records transfer agreement, all digital materials acquired from the partner offices had to be preserved at the bit level, regardless of their current research significance. This decision was made because most of the data would never be available from any other source and might be of great informational value in the future. Originally, we intended to create and preserve a disk image of original media in all cases but quickly discovered that this practice led to a huge waste of preservation storage space, since most transfer drives were far from full. Instead, it was decided to preserve a faithful copy of the data itself.

The next important step in our acquisition workflow was to create file inventories of the media and compare them to inventories provided by the partner offices. Most offices were able to create their inventories using our program and included them with their final set of materials. In all such cases, the comparison showed no changes; the files arrived uncorrupted. For the small number of the offices unable to submit their inventories, the inventories that we created upon intake were taken as a basis for further reference in ensuring file integrity. Then, we used FTK to view and evaluate the files and assign labels determining the further course of action. FTK also detected duplicate, system, backup, and password-protected files that we decided to exclude from SIPs. In addition, the software was able to repair certain corrupted files that could have been lost otherwise.

Our assessment of sample records quickly revealed several specific issues, and, based on these findings, we provided additional instructions to the partner offices. As we discovered from the samples, the partner offices took a variety of approaches to collecting and organizing data and were on different technological levels. Our new set of instructions provided additional guidance on creating inventories, file-naming, handling email and databases, and deleting transient and sensitive records. When feasible, the donors were also asked to provide the actual software programs needed to open and use uncommon file formats.

As expected, we discovered a significant variability in the email programs used by the partners. In most cases, they used MS Outlook, so we also created and disseminated simple step-by-step instructions for creating archival versions of Outlook email files, thus shifting to the donor partial responsibility for pre-acquisition reformatting.

Rearranging the content into appropriate access categories and removing transient and sensitive materials proved to be the greatest challenge for the international offices. Our project was taking place during the rapid shift from a paper-based to a digital world. It was originally assumed that the bulk of our digital acquisition would consist of organizational records and various promotional and publicity materials, while the files pertaining to the actual program fellows would arrive in paper format. In the samples, however, we discovered a large number of digital files related to fellows and thus were subject to privacy and confidentiality restrictions. Our post-sample instructions particularly stressed the need to sort the materials into three user access categories ("embargoed until 2075," "onsite access," and "online access") at the top level and reviewed the criteria for inclusion into each category.

Thus, the test phase of the IFP archives' acquisition involved collaborating with twenty-two international partners to address their particular concerns and occasionally adapt our requirements, workflows, and policies to their specific situation.

In July 2013, we started receiving the partners' full digital archives on external media. The bulk of the materials were sent on portable hard drives and flash drives. Several offices had problems shipping the materials and were only able to hand over the final sets to us personally when visiting New York for the celebration of the IFP program closing in the spring of 2013.

As the transfer drives arrived, we realized that we were going to face more challenges than we had anticipated. For example, despite several rounds of guidelines, some offices were using non-Roman character sets for file and folder naming. In the Windows environment, non-Roman characters turned into questions marks, underscores, and other unrecognizable characters. Fortunately, our file inventory program and FTK were able to recognize and retain the file and directory names in their original character sets as metadata. However, for further processing and especially file transfer, we had to take into account that most Windows programs were not able to recognize the non-Roman characters in file and directory names, so transfer of the files to the preservation server had to be performed on the Mac workstation.

Extremely long filenames and file paths were the second issue that, despite all the guidelines, we were unable to avoid entirely. File paths occasionally exceeded the maximum number of characters allowed by

Windows (260). In some cases, we were not even able to transfer the files from the original drive to the processing station and had to truncate the file names. Since the file paths and file names were the only descriptive metadata we had for the individual items, we manually reviewed each problematic case in order to ensure that the meaning of each file name was preserved as much as possible.

Database and email files also continued to present challenges. Many MS Access databases were blank, duplicate, and, in some cases, password protected. Luckily, we caught this problem in time to obtain the passwords from the corresponding offices and unlock the databases. MS Access databases that had no password protection were converted to XML format using Database Preservation Toolkit[2] and were preserved in both original and XML format. Conversion to XML format failed for formerly password-protected MS Access databases, so we had to preserve them in their original MDB format. Other databases were preserved in their original formats, since, as we requested, they came with the corresponding database software, so we felt confident that they could be opened and used at any time. In one case, a database (ACT! 2000) was saved as an Excel spreadsheet.

Email came in multiple formats: eml, mbx, msg, pst, and Pegasus Mail files. In accordance with the current best practices for email preservation, all email was converted to an open mbox format. After testing several email migration tools, we finally decided to use Aid4Mail software because it was able to convert all the email formats we received from the offices to mbox.

We also developed a content weeding policy that defined our rules and procedures. The policy defined several categories of files that needed to be weeded out: duplicates, system files, temporary files, and files containing personal information not relevant to the project's goal. With FTK, it was easy to identify the first three categories and mark them for deletion, but weeding extraneous materials and assigning desired level of end-user access was more challenging. The level of access was a crucial metadata element that needed to be associated with each file prior to ingest, since the final access rights and restrictions information is encoded into SIPs. We had been hoping to receive materials from each office already presorted into our three "buckets" or top-level folders ("embargoed until 2075," "onsite access," and "online access"). However, not surprisingly, despite all the record management guidelines, we discovered that the number and variety of files, as well as the pressure of office closing deadlines, in many cases didn't allow the partners to devote much time and attention to sorting of the archival files. Most offices attempted to sort materials into the three requested categories, but once we started examining the unrestricted and on-site files more closely, we found many items that raised privacy and confidentiality concerns.

We realized that the IFP's (and our) initial access assumptions were problematic. For example, the initial plan was to provide open online access to the majority of organizational records and to make email available on-site. We eventually realized that all the "online access" materials for various offices had to be handpicked at the item level, and the organizational records should be mostly accessed on-site (if at all). Most email accounts had to be relegated to the "embargoed" category.

Continued concerns prompted us to resort to manual content appraisal, albeit to a limited extent. Fortunately, we were able to retain Alan Divack as our consultant on this project. Alan looked over the FTK-generated file and folder lists for the international partners and examined the online and on-site access categories to decide whether the suggested level was appropriate. In dubious cases, he also opened actual files. Given the number of files in the acquisition, we decided that if a file was found to contain confidential information and had to be closed until 2075 then its entire containing folder was to be moved to the "embargoed" category. This decision was consistent with the practice for analog documents, where the restrictions on a folder are same as the restrictions on the most restricted document in this folder. Taking out isolated files could also remove important contextual information. However, to a certain extent, we had to violate this principle when selecting files for our "online access" category. It turned out that documents accessible for the whole world to see had to be handpicked in much smaller numbers than initially anticipated, and we couldn't necessarily make the rest of the contents of their associated folders available as well.

Unexpectedly, as the paper files for the IFP program began to arrive, we also discovered a number of floppy disks, CDs, DVDs, ZIP disks, and even mini-DV tapes sent along with the paper records. We are currently in the process of outsourcing the transcoding of materials received on video DVDs, audio CDs, and mini-DV tapes to preservation formats, and, once received from the vendors, they would be added to the corresponding offices' digital content. These unforeseen additions were responsible for the difference between the estimated size of our acquisition from the secretariat (2.25 TB) and the 3.43 TB we actually received.

Appraising and ingesting about 2 TB of video became one of our most time-consuming endeavors. Most of the video content came from the secretariat media library on a Mac external hard drive. So we had to develop a modified workflow for processing Mac drives and find corresponding firmware and software for reading the drive content, virus checking, file inventorying, and, finally, transferring the files to the PC-based processing area and long-term preservation storage. After files had been successfully transferred to preservation storage, we started examining videos for any formats that needed transcoding to preservation or access formats and for duplicates or multiple copies of the same video content in different formats. We found all these variations to be present, and hundreds of files turned out to be complete duplicates. Once again, FTK was extremely helpful in identifying and removing duplicate content. We are still in process of resolving several policy issues before deaccessioning possible redundant video materials, and many answers depend on whether we consider time, money, or storage to be our most crucial asset.

RESULTS

The library received a total of over 350,000 files from 24 organizations: 3.6 TB of electronic materials in 245 separate file formats, 10 languages, and 7 non-Roman character sets. All content has been validated and prepared for ingest into our Fedora repository. In the course of the project, we also developed a full set of policies for content weeding, access restrictions, and ensuring privacy and security of personally identifiable information (PII).

The partner surveys and instructions created in the course of the IFP acquisition also served as a basis for developing general donor questionnaires, digital archival materials transfer instructions, selection strategies, and so on. Throughout the last two years, accession tools and guidelines developed in the course of the project have been used for other digital acquisitions. The IFP project was so large and complex that it allowed us to work through multiple scenarios and issues of a large hybrid archive. Most other digital acquisitions require only a subset of the knowledge and tools acquired in the course of the IFP project.

Researchers will have online access to only a relatively small number of IFP files, selected at the item level. Overall, access restrictions had to be tightened for most document categories due to PII. The majority of unembargoed files will become accessible in our reading room in late 2014 via dedicated laptops; any copying will only take place upon permission from the digital assets archivist.

LESSONS LEARNED

Based on our experience, we firmly believe that some selection and arrangement tasks can and should be relegated to donors and take place prior to accessioning. However, the results are often highly uneven and require quality control and possibly remediation. The ease of creating and storing digital objects leads to presence of numerous extraneous files and the efforts undertaken by the donors to clean them up prior to archiving do not, in our experience, achieve the desired result. In the future, we are planning to insist that all the records that are intended to be viewed over the Internet go through an item-level audit. It is preferable to conduct this audit post-acquisition, and plans and budgets for future projects need to take this step into account.

Digital forensics tools greatly facilitated our post-acquisition selection, sorting, and weeding of materials. When used to review materials soon after the acquisition, FTK (our digital forensics tool of choice) allowed us to identify potential technical or content problems and go back to donors for rectifying them. In the future, we should advise donors not to spend their time on rectifying problems that are best addressed by FTK (such as weeding out all the duplicates or files with certain data patterns); their time and efforts might be better spent on defining formal exclusion criteria, which we can use for batch deaccessioning.

The completed surveys and record samples we received from the partner offices were extremely useful in testing the workflow and assumptions and allowed us to plan ahead, customize instructions, and refine our selection criteria. Working on the samples made us confident that we were ready to receive the final transfer of the partners' digital archives. We now knew that shipments could be successfully delivered, and our workflow has been tested and adjusted. In one particular case, the sample proved to be of even greater use. We ended up never receiving the full set of data from one of the offices, and so their sample, received earlier, provided us with at least a subset of their files. After this incident, we decided that sample files should be kept until the end of the project, rather than discarded after the testing.

We found out that many of our assumptions about this project's digital content were inaccurate, and our requirements had to be further refined. We eventually had to deal with a much greater variety of file formats and media types than any surveys indicated (or the donors themselves were initially aware of). Our initial assumptions about access levels also proved to be insufficiently protective. In the end, we were obliged in many cases to manually select content that could be made public. We now believe that donors and repositories should not commit to publishing any set of born-digital documents on the Internet, particularly correspondence and administrative records, without investing in a thorough item-level review.

Our acquisition/ingest process involved a set of tools that allowed us to deal with records in multiple languages while retaining most of file and path names that constituted the only source of descriptive metadata. Now we are confident in our ability to take in a great variety of digital files. On the other hand, in our future projects, we also expect the need to make manual changes in challenging cases of overly long or otherwise problematic filenames.

In many questionable cases, such as the restricting access to whole folders rather than single documents, we turned to the library's treatment of similar analog materials for guidance. In addition, legal issues relating to privacy and confidentiality concerns determined our choice of "onsite access" as the default level. Our setup for electronic access in the reading room is designed to mimic access to non-digital documents, thus allowing us to abide by the precedents and better-established legal framework developed for analog materials.

CONCLUSION

Evaluation and selection of digital materials occurs at multiple stages, both pre- and post-acquisition, and in addition to their content and context, it also has to take authenticity, stability, and reproducibility of the materials into consideration.

In addition, archiving digital materials blurs the lines between pre-acquisition selection/appraisal and post-acquisition arrangement and weeding. The relative ease of transferring digital objects makes pre-acquisition site visits less important, but a number of selection and appraisal steps still need to be taken both pre- and post-accession in continuous communication with record creators or donors. As the traditional stages of the archiving process become blended, selecting materials of permanent value, physically acquiring them, and ensuring administrative custody becomes spread out in space and time. Properly speaking, "digital acquisition" starts with record retention schedules and other instructions to the donors and ends with ingesting SIPs. It includes examining, validating, and stabilizing the content soon after its arrival, as well as auditing and frequently revisiting the donor's assumptions prior to ingest.

Interestingly, deeds of gift for digital materials, signed prior to any attempts at data transfer, cannot account for many unforeseen technical and content issues that may arise during the acquisition process. It is to be expected that some files are unreadable or can only be preserved in formats different from the original. All agreements made prior to actual file ingest need to be flexible enough to take these possibilities into account.

The ease of shipment and relatively low prices of computer memory create a temptation to transfer materials to the archives without much selection or attrition. Some kinds of selection processes lend themselves easily to automation, and so they are best performed by archivists post-accession. On the other hand, extraneous materials or documents with sensitive information are much harder to detect automatically and frequently require the expertise of the content creator to identify. Unlike analog materials, digital materials require that the restrictions information be associated with files early on. Donors' content expertise makes them natural authorities on making these decisions. However, there are limits to what can be delegated to donors, and in a complex archive, additional efforts are unavoidable and need to be included in plans and budgets.

Even after physically receiving digital materials, a repository still has not fully acquired them if the data is impossible to access. There is a need for a period of continuous communication with donors to address issues relating to passwords, providing additional software or sending material in alternative formats. Only at the moment the set of files is ingested into a repository can an acquisition be said to have fully taken place.

Jane Gorjevsky *is the digital assets archivist and* ***Dina Sokolova*** *is the digital preservation librarian at Columbia University.*

NOTES

1. "Ford Foundation International Fellowships Program," Columbia University Libraries, accessed October 23, 2014, https://library.columbia.edu/bts/ford-ifp.html.
2. "Database Preservation Toolkit," GitHub, accessed October 23, 2014, http://keeps.github.io/db-preservation-toolkit/.

SEVEN

So Much to Do, So Little Time

Prioritizing to Acquire Significant University Records

Laura Uglean Jackson, University of Wyoming

Acquiring substantive records documenting a university and its history presents many challenges for archivists. Many university archives have never benefitted from adequate resources to properly manage and appraise the sizeable amount of material that falls under their collecting mandates, including official university records, faculty papers, and student organization records.[1] Additionally, university archivists may be placed in an awkward position when refusing material from departments, senior administrators, and faculty members, as these individuals are often the repository's resource allocators and best potential allies.[2] On many campuses there is also a lack of effective policies for what and when to transfer.[3] These problems can and do contribute to the acquisition of insignificant records, large amounts of administrative dross, secondary research material, and useless ephemera. All too often these factors can result in university archives becoming little more than what Aaron Purcell terms "storage units for unwanted materials."[4]

Of course, these problems do not necessarily stop records of historical importance from being acquired by university archives; after all, many university collections contain historically valuable records despite being understaffed and operating without policies. However, the digital age only exacerbates these problems. Continuing to operate in a world where the records are unorganized, not clearly described, and easily destroyed or rendered inaccessible will bring an end to the serendipitous acquisition of historical records useful to patrons that was possible with non-digital material. Today, even the most understaffed university archives must attempt to address these challenges if it wants to acquire records of historical importance and usefulness.

The University of Wyoming (UW) University Archives and Records Management Program was a repository experiencing these problems. The university archives was an unofficial program within the American Heritage Center (AHC), the university's repository for manuscript collections and rare books. Despite long-standing efforts to create a formal unit with a full-time university archivist, the university archives had been overseen in a part-time capacity since its formation in the mid-1990s. In 2010, I had responsibility for the program as 25 percent of my position as a processing archivist. Although severely under-resourced, the program aimed to assist the entire university with records management support and transfer of permanent records, creating state-approved records retention schedules, facilitating the donation of faculty papers and student organization materials, making large and complex collections available for access, and contributing to the overall goals of managing born-digital records. No policies existed to guide me in acquiring records or managing workloads. After two decades of the university administration denying extra funding and stronger mandates that would give the university archives more leverage, there was little hope for additional resources to help with the problems.

One way to make this unmanageable job more manageable and address some of the problems was to prioritize and focus collecting efforts. To help me concentrate my limited time on activities that would result in acquiring university records of value, an AHC task force created a list of twenty-five units on which I would focus my efforts. This chapter explains how we developed the list, subsequent effects of the policy, and lessons learned from the entire process.

PLANNING

Recognizing the challenges we faced due to our limited resources, in early 2010 AHC director, Mark Greene, developed a plan. He appointed a task force charged with developing a list of twenty-five units to which the archives would offer prioritized records management support and assistance with transferring records.[5] We hoped the prioritization list would help address spotty, inefficient collecting and gaps in the historical record that might be corrected with better application of resources. While the number of units on the list was chosen arbitrarily, the idea was to provide enough units to guide the university archives' active solicitation work for five to ten years. The three members of the task force included the university archivist (me), a reference archivist (Shannon Maier), and the collections manager (William Hopkins).

We began our work by searching for similar documents at other institutions. Even though the units would likely be different at another institution, we hoped to find some kind of similar priority list, whether for manuscript collections or university archives, from which the procedure for creating our list could be borrowed. Thorough online searches and posts to archives listservs revealed that no comparable efforts existed. Instead, we found most university archives' collecting policies matched what Helen Willa Samuels described in 1992 as "vaguely worded, open-ended statement of goals that are not specific enough to guide selection or documentary activities."[6]

Without a template to recycle or procedures to borrow, we began researching appraisal theories applicable to university archives collections. We reviewed black box theory, macro-appraisal, documentation theory, functional analysis, and the Minnesota method.[7] While many of the theories offered a way to appraise university records, the Minnesota method, which outlines a process for prioritizing records creators, became the basis for our process. Mark Greene and Todd Daniels-Howell developed the process to aid the Minnesota Historical Society in the acquisition of the records of Minnesota businesses. It incorporates most of the other appraisal theories we considered and has been used to develop faculty papers collecting policies and as an approach to documenting the 2012 Olympics.[8] Although we deviated from the full method (as others have also done due its complex processes), it provided the necessary template to develop criteria and to score and rank the units.

Prioritizing twenty-five university units meant choosing from hundreds of departments on campus. With much difficulty, we set out to create criteria to determine which units would make the cut. Although the task force was small, the ideas were numerous, broad, and sometimes vague. Over a dozen ideas were suggested and debated, including the relationship of the department to the teaching and research mission of the university, the relationship of the unit to our manuscript collecting areas, the existing holdings within the university archives, and the uniqueness of the unit to UW. We had even briefly discussed using negative factors to eliminate possible units from the list, such as if a unit was likely to have cumbersome restrictions on its records; however, this was deemed unnecessary and too complicated to incorporate into the process.

In the beginning, discussion and debate over the criteria did little to move the prioritization list toward completion; instead, it only generated more ideas rather than narrowing them down. To assist us in coming to an agreement, we employed a few simple methods to help assess the options and make some decisions. We described each criterion as specifically as possible, so that we understood exactly how the criteria would be applied and what they would include. Then we categorized them into three groups: use, maybe use, and don't use. With most of the criteria ending up in the "maybe use" category, we each took a turn determining which units might score highly in those criteria and then researched the units to ascertain what types of records they had, if they had an existing retention schedule, and if the AHC held an existing collection for them. We reviewed collections in our holdings because we wanted to see if any units likely to be on the final list were already regularly transferring materials and using a current retention schedule, which would make further outreach efforts unnecessary. Going through this exercise helped us determine which criteria would ultimately identify the most significant units.

After multiple meetings over several months, we agreed on the following six criteria: political importance, position in hierarchy, relationship to manuscript collecting areas, sociocultural and economic impact, influence or impact on other units, and recognition. For each criterion we developed a definition, rationale for including it, point value scale, and explanation for determining the score for a given unit. In addition to the criteria, the policy document we delivered included background information on how the prioritization list was created.[9]

Despite several disagreements over the other five criteria, everyone easily agreed on the first criterion, political importance. It was an obvious one to include because it would assist the university archives and the AHC in building strategic relationships with other units on campus. Although Aaron Purcell makes the point that "taking in random collections from faculty and administrators for political or strategic reasons should be avoided," we would not be acquiring records haphazardly or for external political factors but rather working with units beneficial to the university archives.[10] When trying to establish a complete archives program, using any angle you can to show your significance and value is vital. Political importance was defined as the impact that working or not working with a given unit might have on the university as a whole or on the AHC. Examples of this impact might include setting a positive precedent for future collecting endeavors, enriching already-established relationships with units on campus, providing records management services for essential records, and raising the visibility of the AHC among influential constituencies. Basically, if it was advantageous to work with a unit, then the unit would receive a high score under this criterion. Units that scored high in this area included the President's Office and the Office of Government and Community Relations.

The second criterion, position in hierarchy, was meant to place value on units that were likely to hold records from subdepartments and therefore assist the archives with efficiently acquiring records of permanent importance. As we explained in the policy:

> Like all large organizations, UW has a hierarchy that defines to whom units report and the scope of authority of each unit. This criterion refers

> to the relative prominence of a given unit vis-à-vis its peers, the other units reporting to it, and the unit(s) to which it reports.

The higher a unit was in the hierarchy, the more likely it was to have records funneled up to it. However, we were concerned that this criterion would cause exclusion of units lower on the hierarchy. It was important to us that the prioritized list include units in the upper echelons of the hierarchy, those in the middle, and those at the bottom as well.

Influence or impact on other units was specifically placed in the policy to balance the top-down approach. The prioritization policy states that this criterion "allows for the recognition and documentation of units that, despite their low positions in the organizational chart, have widespread effects on the smooth functioning of the University." Units would receive a high score in this area if they had a significant impact on other units, not necessarily if other units reported directly to them. Certain offices, such as those of the president and provost, would likely receive a high score in both this and the former criteria. But groups such as the Staff Senate and Faculty Senate, which have no units reporting to them but have an impact on academics, administration, and governance, could receive a high score in this area. Including these units would not only balance the list but also diversify the types of functions and people represented.

The most debated criterion was relationship to our manuscript collecting policy. In documenting university history, there is typically either a vague or absent relationship between the university archives and the repository's manuscript collecting endeavors. Although university archives collections can be built based on the university's academic strengths, normally university records are evaluated independently of the manuscript collecting policy. We took a significant departure from this typical relationship and decided to strengthen the connection between our manuscript policy and our priorities for the university archives. The final policy document includes a lengthy rationale for this particular criterion because this decision did not come easily and was questioned by senior leaders when we presented our findings. In particular, one archivist was concerned that by incorporating a relationship to manuscripts the primary focus of collecting university records would shift toward the manuscript collecting areas and that documenting the university would become a second priority. While this might be a valid critique for a full-fledged university archives program, the task force disagreed with the opinion that we would end up acquiring only university records that corresponded to manuscript collecting areas. We reasoned that university archives collections were more likely to be processed and used if they aligned with manuscript collections because the manuscript collections make up the bulk of the AHC's holdings and are the AHC's primary focus for grant funding, strategic planning, and special projects. We believed that associating these two separate collecting areas would lead to an increase in the inclusion of university archives in such endeavors. By working with departments whose missions or functions aligned with manuscript collecting areas, we were more likely to acquire records that would be used.

The fifth criterion was sociocultural and economic impact as related to Wyoming. UW is Wyoming's land-grant university and the only four-year public university in the state. Several of UW's departments and programs reflect Wyoming's distinctiveness. The definition from the prioritization policy explains:

> The unit's mission and programs relate to the challenges that Wyoming faces as a predominately rural state. These challenges include, but are not limited to, the dissemination of scholarship regarding agriculture, ranching, and land management, the delivery of health care to a widely dispersed population, the prevalence of first-of-the-family college students among UW's undergraduates, and the lack of access, in general, to college preparation during high school.

We wanted to document the unique aspects of UW and also provide information on topics likely to be of interest to researchers. The taskforce was cognizant that university records reflect more than just university history; they also document issues of concern to the state and region. Units that would receive high scores under this criterion included Family and Consumer Sciences and Cooperative Extension. While these units did not in fact make the list, they are both units within the College of Agriculture, and this unit (at the dean's office level) was made a priority.

The sixth and last criterion was recognition, meaning an award or special accolade received by a unit from an external (non-UW) entity. Grants, significant rankings (i.e., top one hundred departments in the country), and other citations conferred on the department were taken into account.[11] This was included so that the university's high ranking and prestigious units would be documented.

Every criterion was given a numerical range with which to score individual units: political importance, 0–4 points; position in hierarchy, 1–4 points; relationship to manuscript collecting areas, 0–3 points; socio-cultural impact, 0–3 points; influence/impact on other units, 0–4 points; and recognition, 0–3 points. The point system was created somewhat arbitrarily, that is, no mathematically sound principles were applied to determine the value range of each criterion. The ranges were based on common sense and overall significance. For example, every criterion except position in hierarchy has a range beginning with zero points, but because every unit has to have some sort of position in the hierarchy, it would rate at least one point. If a unit could receive more points with a certain criterion, such as political importance, which can be up to four points, then that generally meant the task force determined the criterion to be of more significance and therefore more value.

IMPLEMENTATION

After the descriptions, rationales, and value ranges for each of the six criteria were finalized, we divided the work of scoring every administrative unit on the organizational chart, eighty-five units in total. While this sounds like a lot of work, it took less time to score the dozens of administrative units than it did to agree on and describe the six criteria. At this point, we made a decision to exclude academic departments (such as philosophy, chemistry, or civil engineering) in the priority list. This was done for several reasons. First, it would be too time consuming. There are over eighty academic departments and interdisciplinary programs within seven colleges. Scoring the administrative and the academic units would take too much time, and by this point, we were behind schedule. Second, we did not want academic departments to overwhelm the list. While a university's academic departments arguably represent the primary functions of a university (teaching and research) and undoubtedly hold records of historical importance, the types of materials tend to be similar and may not warrant a great deal of individual attention in order to collect. Although individual departments would not be ranked, the seven colleges overseeing all academic departments and programs would be, and it was likely that working with units at the college level would still yield permanent records such as academic plans, accreditation records, and department head correspondence, for individual departments within the colleges. Based on these reasons, we decided that academic units could be ranked separately at a later date, perhaps after demonstrated success of the administrative unit prioritization policy.[12]

Our approach to dividing the work was straightforward. The University of Wyoming's main organizational chart contained six vice presidents each overseeing a function of the university. Each task force member was responsible for scoring all units under two vice presidents. Eight units including the board of trustees and president's office were organizationally situated at the top of the organizational chart and, because of the assumed importance of these units, were scored by all task force members.

To assist us in scoring units consistently, we created a measurement scale for each criterion. As an example, a unit should have received zero points under political importance when "choosing to collect the unit's records would have no positive effect on the university, the unit, or the AHC. Conversely, choosing not to collect the unit's records would have no negative effect." The full amount of points would be awarded when "working with the unit to schedule their records is likely to have a positive impact on the university, the unit, or the AHC. Not working with the unit is likely to impact the university, administrative unit, or AHC negatively." We also included a mid-range point value and explanation. The most subjective categories to judge were political importance, relationship to manuscript collecting area, and sociocultural impact. These were judged and scored according to the best of our abilities with the information at hand but were impossible to score precisely. All of the information about the units came from their webpages and, when possible, previous knowledge about a unit. We discussed creating a survey to better gather information about each unit, but assumed the information on the website would be adequate for our purposes.

Perhaps not surprisingly, we discovered at this stage that our criteria and scoring methodology were extremely subjective and based on our individual perspectives. Despite our common experience working at the university and our long discussions about what we were trying to achieve, all the task force members had a different sense of what kinds of records we wanted to make sure we collected. Therefore, after we scored our respective units and reviewed our lists, we realized that some small reassessments were needed. If a unit of seemingly high importance did not receive a high enough score to qualify for the initial top ten, then the responsible task force member rescored it based on feedback from the other task force members so that it would appear on his or her top-ten list. This led us to change rankings for three or four units. Units from the three members' top-ten lists were then scored by the other task force members, and the average from the three scores was taken for a final score. The total possible highest score that a unit could receive was twenty-two; the lowest was one point. We then had a list of thirty units, in the order of priority in which the task force had ranked them.

In analyzing the list of thirty units, we found that our carefully crafted criteria and scoring system couldn't be used in vacuum. Our numbers needed to be balanced by looking at the rankings holistically. So after the initial scoring was complete, the group analyzed the ranked list of thirty units and made changes where necessary. Specifically, we were concerned that none of the seven colleges within the university made the cut. So we reviewed the rankings to see if any units could be replaced by some of the colleges. One such unit was the Executive Director of Resident Life, Dining Services, and Wyoming Union, which oversees residence halls and dining facilities. Although important to student life and the campus in general, its administrative records were unlikely to be of much historical value. Replacing this unit with a college, which holds much more administratively interesting and historically important documents, seemed more logical. Thus, the list was fine-tuned and the rankings adjusted by agreeing to change one person's given score for a unit.

Throughout the creation of the policy and the rankings, the AHC director was consulted, and he approved the policy in stages. However, as the final step in the process, the Director's Advisory Group had to approve the entire policy document. This group consists of the director, associate director, department heads, business manager, university archivist, and a representative from the nondepartmental heads and is consulted on high-level decisions, such as reviewing policies and setting goals. We presented the policy, including the final list, to this group after concluding the entire process. Although most of the group's comments and concerns required only minor changes, as I described previously, some expressed concerns about the relationship to manuscript collecting policy criterion. After we provided more rationale for the criterion, the Director's Advisory Group approved the policy. It was then largely kept internal and made available to AHC staff and others by request. It was also shared with the provost in the hope of receiving top-level support, such as a signed letter from him to the high-priority departments. This did not happen even though the provost expressed support for the policy.

RESULTS

The priority list included the following units, in order of their final scores:

President's office (15.6)
UW trustees (14.6)
Vice president for academic affairs (14)
General counsel's office (13.6)
Athletics, director's office (13)
School of Environment and Natural Resources (12)
Office of Government and Community Relations (11.3)
School of Energy Resources (11)
Facilities Planning Office (10.3)
Faculty Senate (10)
Vice president of institutional advancement (10)
Office of Student Education Opportunity (10)
College of Agriculture (9.7)
Wyoming Technology Business Center (9)
Vice president of student affairs (9)
College of Business (8.3)
Associate vice president / dean of students (8)
Office of Corporate and Foundation Giving (8)
Vice president of administration (8)
Experimental Program to Stimulate Competitive Research (EPSCoR) (8)
Assistant vice president for budget and institutional analysis (7.6)
Vice president for information technology (7.6)

Staff Senate (7)
University Counseling Center (7)
Vice president of research and economic development (7)
College of Arts and Sciences (7)

The first thing to note is that there are actually twenty-six units rather than twenty-five. Because of the large number of ties, we felt it was easier to just add one more unit rather than figure out which one to remove. Overall, the list is representative of the diverse units and functions of the University of Wyoming. It includes all six of the vice president offices but only three of the seven major colleges. Two schools that are independent of a college easily made the list with relatively high scores: the School of Environment and Natural Resources and the School of Energy. Both of these units have a working relationship with the AHC, cosponsoring symposia and working jointly on various projects, and scored high in political importance. They also both relate to the AHC's manuscript collecting areas of conservation/environmentalism and economic geology and scored high in that criterion. Smaller units such as EPSCoR, which supports and facilitates research, and the University Counseling Center, also made the list. As might be expected, units such as the president's office, board of trustees, and provost's office received the top three scores. This may have been an indication that the scoring was at least somewhat accurate because these units were the most obvious in terms of importance.

The prioritization list for administrative units proved effective in that it gave me, as the quarter-time university archivist, a way to determine which departments to work with at length. Because UW did not have a mandate or university regulation requiring units to create or use a retention schedule or transfer permanent records to the archives, efforts made by the archives to reach out to units were often futile. The only productive way to work with a unit had been if they had a reason to work with me and initiated the process. The prioritization allowed me to know who to reach out to and then when to persist with outreach efforts. If priority units did not respond to communications or the effort did not produce immediate results, then the priority list provided a rationale for persisting in outreach efforts, such as attempting different modes of communication, directing efforts to different staff members, or using new tactics.

Second, by using the list, I would know which unit to prioritize if and when multiple units contacted me at the same time. For example, after the approval of the priority list, both the vice president for student affairs' office and the music department contacted me for assistance with their records at the beginning of the summer. Because it was important for us to continue creating positive relationships with units not on the list, I had to develop strategies for assisting them while still having time for the high-priority units. With the list in hand, I felt justified in spending much less time and effort on the music department. I asked the unit's staff to do much of the work that I typically did, such as identifying record groups and summarizing the content of materials. Other strategies included offering other resources that would be of assistance and doing all of this through email or phone calls rather than on-site visits. I spent much more time assisting the student affairs' office, where I spent one afternoon a week for the entire summer at their office meeting with staff, appraising records, and creating a retention schedule.

Units such as the music department were not informed of the priority list or that they were receiving a lower level of service. It seemed unnecessary and would send the wrong message. The issue was not that I did not want to work with them or didn't want their records; it was just that I didn't have the time! However, I told units on the priority list that they were considered a priority in the hopes that this would encourage them to work more with me and transfer their records.

Although no formal assessment was done, there are a number of ways in which one could determine if the list was an effective tool for collection development of university records. The most obvious way to assess this would be to review responses and actions that came from contacting the units. How many units responded to outreach efforts? How many collections came in or retention schedules were created? How many units actually received assistance? Our goal was not only to acquire records but also to raise the visibility of the university archives and help units with their records needs. So simply tallying the amount of interactions with units on the list would help determine if it was effective. One could also track the amount of time spent on outreach efforts and compare that to the amount of material received or number of positive outcomes from a consultation, such as creation of a retention schedule, improved file organization, or positive feedback. Unfortunately, the limited time I was able to spend on university archives left me no time to undertake these kinds of assessment activities.

LESSONS LEARNED

As with anything, hindsight is 20/20, and certainly, developing collecting policies is never a perfect process. Looking back now, there are several things I think we could have done better or at least differently. First, creating and agreeing on which criteria to use was difficult and required both creative thinking and a systematic process. Many more criteria were suggested than the six implemented, and, looking back, perhaps other criteria would have made more sense to use. One example of this is the criterion that measures the amount of awards or recognition of a given unit. After the scoring began, we found that most units had not received any type of outside recognition. This is a much more useful determinate for individuals or even academic programs, but administrative programs of colleges are not often nationally ranked or awarded. Had we ranked the academic units, then this criterion may have been much more applicable. We decided too late that academic units would not be included, but when we did so, we didn't consider whether this would mean we should reconsider the criteria.

Not scoring the academic units also lead to problems after the scoring was complete, when we realized that documenting some of the colleges was a higher priority than some of the units that originally scored high enough to be prioritized. Although these minor adjustments were not part of the original plan, it was simpler to simply replace some units so that we would not have score all of the units again. This problem in the methodology may, in part, be attributed to the subjectivity of measuring the criteria. This method may work better with more objective criteria and definitive scoring measurements. Additionally, there are some units that are, across every university, a high priority. Units such as the board of trustees, president, and founding colleges will automatically be on such a list. If this was assumed from the beginning, it may have prevented us from having to tweak the results to include the colleges and freed up time to analyze the more debatable units.

Perhaps the biggest and most important lesson learned was that the prioritization list was not a surefire method to acquire substantive and valuable materials. Rather, it was a way to prioritize and focus efforts that might result in new accessions or, in other words, a tool to focus my time. Acquiring the actual material was still a challenge. An implementation plan would have been a wonderful complement to the prioritization list, as there was little support and time to implement the list after its completion. Once the policy was official, I sent letters to the top-five units on the list, but nothing much came of it. I think I had high expectations that the provost would assist us with contacting units. Once it was clear that this was not in the cards, it was discouraging. An implementation plan could have provided concrete ideas for incorporating the other task force members (or their departments) into outreach or collecting efforts to supplement the quarter-time allotted to my role as university archivist.

CONCLUSION

The prioritization list was a start to solving the problems of properly managing and appraising records, refusing low-value materials from other departments and senior administrators, and acquiring records of substance. Rather than sitting back and passively accepting whatever came our way, we had units that we knew were important and that we should try to work with. Creating the prioritization list identified which units were too important to say no to or for which tactfully declining the old artifacts found in their basement closet would be appropriate.

With archivists struggling with limited resources in all aspects of their jobs, prioritization can be a useful tool. A similar method could be employed in other areas of archives work, such as working with and prioritizing a large number of units for a university anniversary or records retention overhaul. Hopefully this case study will give others a plan from the start rather than spending valuable time trying to figure out the plan, as we did. Our main objective was to prioritize units for general outreach and acquisition of records, and I believe that through the method outlined in this chapter we did reach this goal. The university archives now has an approved list of units to focus on for years to come. As with any policy, the criteria and list of departments will need to be revised periodically. This would not only be to address any problems with the rankings but also to incorporate newly formed units and recognize changes in activities of the existing ones. Developing and incorporating an assessment plan would be ideal.

Creating the priority list was just a first step, and unfortunately, the AHC is still a long way from having a well-staffed and well-resourced university archives. However, an organizational goal during the upcoming years is to create a university regulation that would give recognition, authority, and mandate to the university archives. Achieving this would increase the success of working with priority units, but the AHC also hopes to receive more resources for university archives and create a full-time university archivist position. Although creating this prioritization list demonstrated that prioritizing outreach efforts doesn't necessarily lead to acquisition, our effort to appraise records creators gave us a way to prioritize my very limited amount of staff time, which was an important step to carrying out all of the functions of a university archivist within our challenging situation.

Laura Uglean Jackson *is archivist for University Archives at the Special Collections and Archives department, University of California, Irvine. Until May 2014, she was the university archivist at the University of Wyoming.*

NOTES

1. Bessie Schina and Garron Wells, "University Archives and Records Programs in the United States and Canada," *Archival Issues* 27, no. 1 (2002): 35–51; Lisl Zach and Marcia Frank Peri, "Practices for College and University Electronic Records Management (ERM) Programs: Then and Now," *American Archivist* 73, no. 1 (2010): 105–28.

2. For more about the challenges of acquiring faculty papers, see: Maynard J. Brichford, "University Archives: Relationships with Faculty," *American Archivist* 34, no. 2 (1971): 173–81; Jane Wolff, "Faculty Papers and Special-Subject Repositories," *American Archivist* 44, no. 4 (1981): 346–51; Tara Zachary Laver, "In a Class by Them-

selves: Faculty Papers at Research University Archives and Manuscript Repositories," *American Archivist* 66, no. 1 (2007): 159–96.

3. According to a survey on electronic records management programs in college and university archives, there is a lack of general policy for transferring records: "Thirty-two percent of the institutions (40 of 124) reported having no consistent guidelines and that records were transferred to the archives unsystematically, if at all." Zach and Peri, "Practices for College and University Electronic Records Management (ERM) Programs," 116.

4. Aaron Purcell, *Academic Archives: Managing the Next Generation of College and University Archives, Records, and Special Collections* (New York: ALA Neal-Schuman, 2012), 139.

5. The task force was also charged with creating collecting policies for faculty papers and student organization records, but those will not be discussed here.

6. Helen Willa Samuels, *Varsity Letters: Documenting Modern Colleges and Universities* (Metuchen, NJ: Society of American Archivists and Scarecrow Press, 1992), 2.

7. Frank Boles and J. M. Young, "Exploring the Black Box: The Appraisal of University Administrative Records," *American Archivist* 48, no. 2 (1985): 121–40; Terry Cook, "Macroappraisal in Theory and Practice: Origins, Characteristics, and Implementation in Canada, 1950–2000," *Archival Science* 5, no. 2–4 (2005): 101–61; Helen Willa Samuels, "Who Controls the Past?" *American Archivist* 49, no. 2 (1986): 109–24; Samuels, *Varsity Letters.*

8. Mark A. Greene and Todd J. Daniels-Howell, "Documentation with 'An Attitude': A Pragmatist's Guide to the Selection and Acquisition of Modern Business Records," in The Records of American Business, ed. James M. O'Toole (Chicago: Society of American Archivists, 1997); Tom Hyry, Diane Kaplan, and Christine Weideman, "'Though This Be Madness, yet There Is Method in't: Assessing the Value of Faculty Papers and Defining a Collecting Policy," *American Archivist* 65, no. 1 (2002): 56–69; Matt Phillpott, "The Olympics, Documentation Strategy and the Minnesota Method," *History SPOT* (blog), May 17, 2012, http://ihrprojects.wordpress.com/2012/05/17/the-olympics-documentation-strategy-and-the-minnesota-method/.

9. Copies of the full policy can be requested by contacting the author at lugleanj@uci.edu.

10. Purcell, *Academic Archives*, 161.

11. The AHC itself received a high score in this area because it was a recipient of the 2011 Society of American Archivists' Distinguished Service Award.

12. At the time of writing, there were no plans to create a prioritization list for the academic units that were excluded.

EIGHT

The Studio Theatre Archives

Staging an Embedded Appraisal

Leahkim A. Gannett, Vincent J. Novara,
Kelly J. Smith, and Mary Crauderueff,
University of Maryland

The archive of a performing arts organization is a complex entity—one-half corporate archive documenting the administration and daily operations of the organization as a business, one-half archive of artistry and creative production. Theater companies are especially complex. Their records contain evidence of every component of a theatrical production: the director's vision, stage directions, scenic, lighting, sound, and costuming designs and technical documentation. Often in the case of theatre, the final product—the performance—is not captured, and it is the materials documenting the lengthy creative process that too often serve as the only record of a finished artistic work. Adding to the complexity is the fact that these records come in a wide range of physical media types, each with unique preservation challenges, to say nothing of the increasing born-digital formats in theatre design.

Beyond the challenges of managing diverse materials from a wide range of functions and origins, performing arts collections have another layer of complexity: as with many creative endeavors, the record creators may hold intense emotional connections to the archival material, as it is the physical manifestation of their life's work. Appraising such collections requires not only an understanding of arts organizations and performance creation and documentation but also an awareness and sensitivity to the emotional investment the record creators may have in the material. The appraisal and acquisition of the Studio Theatre Archives at Special Collections in Performing Arts at the University of Maryland exemplifies these challenges.

The Studio Theatre was founded in 1978 in a former hotdog factory on the corner of 14th and P Streets in Northwest Washington, DC. Specializing in contemporary drama and performance, the company has grown to become an anchor for both the DC theatre scene and the surrounding neighborhood. The 14th Street corridor has undergone great transformation and revitalization in the thirty-plus years the Theatre has resided there—a transformation that is closely linked to the Theatre's presence and the company's growth.

In the summer of 2009, the Theatre's founding artistic director, Joy Zinoman, announced she would retire in 2010 after thirty years at the helm. Leahkim Gannett, then assistant curator for Special Collections in Performing Arts (and wife of the Theatre's staff carpenter), reached out to Joy at a Theatre staff event to gauge her interest in finding a permanent home for the company's archives.

Special Collections in Performing Arts (SCPA) specializes in building, preserving, and providing access to performing arts collections. Holdings include archival collections in music, theatre, and dance that preserve performance, creativity, education, and scholarship. Leahkim naturally saw SCPA as a good fit for the Theatre's records. Joy embraced the opportunity to secure a permanent home for the company's history and a dialog began.

PLANNING

While we might not have recognized them clearly at the time, three primary needs emerged during the planning phase: (1) trust needed to be built between the Theatre and SCPA, (2) a mutually agreeable memorandum of understanding needed to be designed, and (3) a records aggregation and archival appraisal plan needed to be created and implemented. The Theatre and SCPA worked together to creatively address these needs, and this collaboration and creativity is largely responsible for the success of the project.

Leahkim's earliest conversations with Joy Zinoman centered on trust and permanence and reassurance that the Theatre's archival legacy would be secured. This reflected Joy's deep personal connection to the company and perhaps also some understandable anxieties that come with facing retirement. For example, Joy's investment and hands-on involvement in the Theatre was demonstrated in something as seemingly minor as the storage of props. All props were stored in the theatre building, in a miracle of organization and efficiency highly unusual for any performing arts company. In order to maintain the small storage footprint, Joy personally identified and priced extraneous props for the Theatre's annual garage sale.

Another early step during the planning phase was to begin negotiating a memorandum of understanding that took the form of a deed of gift. At this phase, Vincent (Vin) Novara, curator for SCPA, became more involved in the cultivation effort. Though both curators were working closely with Joy, who was still the company artistic director, negotiations for the deed were ultimately conducted with the company's board of trustees. This board is composed of some of the luminaries of DC's performing arts community, as well as local business leaders with considerable political influence. Ultimately, the chair of the board signed the deed in October 2010. In the final version of the deed, it was stated that Joy would maintain possession of her production books, as well as her personal papers. An unusual component of this deed was the explicit statement that Joy would bequeath her materials to SCPA in her will. As the project progressed, and the archives interns earned Joy's trust, she chose to release the production books to SCPA in the second installment of materials.

Typical of our deeds of gift at this time, a transfer of copyright was not essential; the primary purpose of the deed was to transfer physical ownership. At first, the Theatre proposed that SCPA merely have the right to possess the collection, but as that constituted more of a deposit arrangement, and given the considerable resources and efforts this collection would require, all parties agreed to physical ownership. It seems likely that not seeking transfer of copyrights sped up the process of appraisal and acquisition, as neither side had to devote any energy to contemplating restrictions related to intellectual property concerns.

Additionally, in the deed, SCPA requested a loose commitment from the Theatre pertaining to financial support. Though the deed included our standard request that the Theatre only agree to "cooperate with the university to identify and maintain funding," the company actually went above and beyond all expectations in their financial support of the project.

In the initial months and meetings, it became apparent that the volume, diversity, and distributed nature of the Theatre's thirty-plus years of records would require a great deal of time to aggregate and appraise. Though the Theatre had been founded in 1978, an acting conservatory predated it by a few years and had run parallel to the company continuously. Consequently, more than three decades of records consisting of many material types from diverse records creators (including administrative records, production records, pedagogical materials, personal papers, and architectural records) were disbursed in multiple locations throughout DC. Altogether, records potentially totaling three hundred linear feet were in need of appraisal and weeding prior to transfer to the archives. Additionally, the lines between the Theatre and Joy's personal records were not always distinct, and there was considerable personal investment from many other staff members in the company's records.

Conducting archival appraisal of the records in situ was beyond the abilities of the Theatre's staff but also required a level of support that was beyond SCPA's resources to perform within the necessary timeframe. Joy was anxious that the transfer be completed before her official retirement in 2010, immediately after which she would be leaving the country to travel for a year. But the "take it all and sort it out later" approach to acquisition was also not desirable as Joy had concerns about how her legacy and the legacy of the Theatre would be represented in the archival collection. She needed a granular knowledge of which materials would be transferred for her peace of mind. "Take it all . . ." is also rarely good for the archives, as context and original order is easy to muddle in such a large, unorganized transfer, and often, "all" can include a high percentage of duplicate material.

The SCPA curators, Vin and Leahkim, proposed an unorthodox solution: the Theatre would fund an archival internship position that would run for twelve weeks over the summer of 2010 with the curators serving as co-supervisors. The Theatre had a previously established and long-running internship program, filling multiple administrative and production internships every summer, so this position fit well into an existing organizational structure, and Joy and the Theatre staff supported the idea.

The Theatre not only agreed to pay for the intern's wages but also offered to provide for his or her housing. Providing local housing was well beyond the level of support any archival institution could hope for, and this not only demonstrated the Theatre's commitment to the project but also ensured that the curators could recruit and attain the best interns from a national pool.

Additionally, a dedicated liaison within the Theatre was assigned to assist Vin and Leahkim in designing the internship and in supervising the intern, once hired. Chloe Schama, a development associate, was the initial liaison. The curators worked with Chloe to write the job description and then posted the position in the appropriate venues. The curators also conducted the first round of applicant reviews and suggested a short list of candidates to Joy. The final interview panel consisted of Joy, Chloe, Vin, and Leahkim. The ideal candidate had a performing arts background and was pursuing an MLS in archives or had recently attained the degree. Kelly Smith, a recent graduate from University of Pittsburgh's iSchool, was the successful candidate. Kelly had a background in dance and had also recently interned in the archives of the Jacob's Pillow Dance Festival.

IMPLEMENTATION

The internship was initially designed to run for twelve weeks through summer 2010 with a goal to completely survey records located at the Theatre building on 14th and P Streets NW, Joy's home in Northwest, DC, a nearby storage facility personally maintained by Joy, and possibly the homes of other pertinent individuals connected to the Theatre. After a brief training and orientation period, the intern would begin inventorying and appraising the company's records, with weekly check-in meetings scheduled with the curators and with Chloe at the Theatre. All parties agreed to meet together periodically to discuss the project's progress and make decisions as needed.

Orientation was done in two parts: orientation to SCPA, which involved a tour and meeting with the curators, and orientation to the Theatre, which also consisted of tours of the various departments and meetings with key staff members. Once orientation was completed, Leahkim, Vin, and Kelly began working with an existing records retention policy put in place by the Theatre's accountants. Leahkim and Kelly developed survey criteria with an eye toward archival value, physical condition, and recommending accession strategies. Materials were anticipated to include manuscripts, paper and electronic office records, photographs, scripts, prompt books, three-dimensional scenic models, costume renderings, and a wide array of ephemera. This became the first phase of the project.

As the work progressed much to the satisfaction of all parties involved, two more phases were added, which the Theatre continued to fund. Phase two was devoted to scanning photographs and duplicating other materials, so that copies of essential items could be retained at the Theatre for continued use, and then facilitating the first transfer of materials to SCPA. Phase three was devoted to inventorying the Theatre's cofounder and resident scenic designer Russell Metheny's materials that had not yet been transferred to SCPA, reaching out to other scenic designers via a survey to determine if they had relevant materials, and facilitating another transfer to the university.

Phase one ran for the initially planned twelve weeks. During this time, Kelly surveyed the materials in each area of the Theatre's building, systematically working her way through the various administrative divisions and departments. She began by talking with department managers and staff to discover what kinds of records they created and the locations of the materials. The Theatre's positive corporate culture and buy-in for the project facilitated Kelly's work. These informal interviews, along with the Theatre's organizational chart and records retention schedule, served as a guide for how to proceed with the inventory and as a basis for eventual series.

The administrative records, portions of the production records, and most of the photographs were already well organized, and similar materials were frequently collocated. This made inventorying the bulk of office records fairly straightforward. Most of the physical records, and some of the digital files, were well organized, including those records relocated from the founder's home. Most departmental materials were stored together, and prior to the start of the project, archival materials that were in the basement props storage area were brought upstairs in order to decrease the locations in which Kelly would need to look for materials. Filing cabinets throughout the administrative area were numbered, which made it easier to identify the location of materials. Also, the staff worked to assist Kelly by making themselves available when she had questions, and shortly before phase one ended, one staff member volunteered to organize the digital production files.

The most challenging part of inventorying the physical materials was the sheer volume and time constraints. Kelly, under the curators' advisement, created a preliminary inventory spreadsheet for physical materials, which included the following fields: record group, drawer or box label, assigned box number, item description, date range, size, physical location, arrangement, value, condition, preparation work required, send to UMD, and notes.

Born-digital materials and three-dimensional objects were more challenging. The Theatre's digital files were inconsistently organized with some departments arranging files by production and others either topically or by year. Many digital folders contained no files, something that did not occur with the physical folders. Some document files were named but did not contain information. The born-digital inventory was created on a separate spreadsheet that included similar information as the primary inventory but included file type since software obsolescence required consideration. Inventorying the digital files was more painstaking than the physical files because it often required item-level examination to determine a file's contents. This was certainly not the approach taken with the files of papers, but it did prove necessary for digital files and three-dimensional objects.

Although there were three-dimensional objects located throughout the building, those of highest archival value were the scenic models: scaled renderings of the production sets. There were forty-seven models in varying condition, stored in multiple areas of the building. Because of space constraints and preservation concerns, SCPA only committed to acquiring a small selection of the models, but as the first phase of the project drew to a close, Joy became increasingly concerned that the information and artistry conveyed by the models that were not accessioned would be lost.

During a meeting with Kelly, Leahkim, Vin, Chloe, and Joy Zinoman, a decision was made to document all of the models with photography. As a result, Joy personally selected eight scenic models that were most significant and best represented the Theatre's work for transfer to SCPA. For the rest, SCPA would acquire copies of the photographs of all forty-seven models.

Then resident scenic artist Luciana Stecconi was tasked with cleaning and restoring the models in preparation for photography. All of the models were moved to a central location in the Theatre to be labeled, and Joy personally provided Kelly with metadata for each one. The Theatre contracted professional photographer Scott Suchman to shoot the models in one day. All parties were satisfied with the outcome, and photographs for all forty-seven models are available for viewing through University of Maryland Digital Collections and are linked from the collection's finding aid.[1] This level of effort exerted for the models was an outstanding gesture of commitment by the Theatre to the burgeoning archives program. It was above and beyond, especially the resources devoted by Joy.

The survey of the storage unit took one day and resulted in the relocation of materials into the Theatre's building on the same day. Most of this material appeared to be personal papers, records, and artwork belonging to Joy and Russell Metheny, and it was decided that they should be set aside initially for review at a later date.

Kelly spent two days in Joy's home surveying personal documents related to the Theatre. Items were stored in filing cabinets, on shelves, and in boxes. Priority was directed to Joy's production books, annual company retreat materials, and her daily calendars. Most of the boxes from the apartment were transferred to the Theatre's building before phase one ended. In this case, Joy self-selected much of the material that would be transferred as part of the collection, with a mind that her own personal papers might come at a later date and form a separate collection.

Phase one was a great success. Intellectual control was gained over the Theatre's records, and appraisal decisions were made in mutual agreement between Joy and the curators ahead of her retirement. For selection decisions, the curators adhered to recommended appraisal practices: acquiring no more than two copies and only accepting items possessing an identifiable degree of informational, historical, or aesthetic value or items that must be legally kept for the long-term based on the Theatre's existing record retention policy. Leahkim and Vin also took into account the intended scope for the collection, thus excluding any personal items that had mixed in over the years, such as diaries, correspondence, and photographs that did not relate to the Theatre. Condition was also a factor, and SCPA regretfully had to pass on nearly thirty posters and promotional graphics due to extensive mold and water damage.

Some series were identified as being of core importance to daily operations but were also of high archival value. It was agreed that these materials would be duplicated at the Theatre before the originals were transferred to SCPA. To complete this task, a second phase was added to the project. At the end of phase one, Chloe left the staff to take a new job, and the liaison role was taken on by Sarah Branzelle, then the Theatre's director of administration.

Phase two ran for six additional weeks, ending in late October 2010. The goals for this phase were to create digital surrogates of the publicity photographs and duplicate other materials as needed for the Theatre's retention and to complete the first transfer of materials to SCPA. Kelly scanned more than two decades' worth of publicity photographs and created copies of images that were stored on compact discs for the Theatre's future use while transferring the originals to SCPA. She also labeled and created a list of the boxes for transfer. Kelly continued to meet frequently with Leahkim and Vin to plan the transfer but less so with the Theatre's staff as this phase was concluding.

Joy had officially retired by the time phase two began, and though the project had been given her final blessing, staff anxiety surrounding the removal of the company's historic records was evident during the first transfer of materials. On that day, one of the company managers said that he had not authorized the transfer of his own materials. He quickly looked through the boxes of his records, which Kelly previously had inventoried and met with him about, and decided to keep some of them at the Theatre to go through at a later date. These files are still with the company.

A third phase was added, scheduled to begin in January 2011 and run for eight weeks. This period was dedicated to following up with Joy and Russell Metheny on their personal materials, working with Joy to survey designers and other people who might have relevant material in their personal possession, and continuing to facilitate transfer of materials to SCPA. However, in the time between phases two and three, Kelly was offered and accepted full-time employment in Pittsburgh. Both the Theatre and the curators felt that another intern should be recruited to continue the project. For the sake of expedience and maintaining momentum on the project, rather than initiate another national search, the curators recruited Mary Crauderueff, a former graduate assistant at SCPA. Mary had a background in theatre, an MLS with a concentration in archives and records management, and was already familiar with SCPA. Joy and Sarah Branzelle met with Mary and agreed that she would be a good fit for the internship. Luckily, Kelly was able to visit DC for one day in January for a torch-passing and orientation.

As Mary met with Leahkim and Vin and various Theatre personnel and got to know the project, the goals of phase three expanded somewhat as other loose ends were identified, mostly pertaining to other series that required targeting. The series pertaining to the board of trustees and renovation records needed special attention. (The Theatre's physical space had undergone a great deal of transformation over the years, and Russell Metheny, a cofounder of the Theatre, personally designed much of the renovation and architectural work. This gave the renovations and the records surrounding them a special meaning to the Theatre.) The duplication of publicity materials Kelly had begun in phase two still needed completion, and a plan for future accessions and procedures also needed to be developed. Coming into the project as the second intern, Mary also had to earn new trust from the staff and maintain their confidence in the archives project, as it had been several months between Kelly's departure and her arrival.

During Mary's two months in the project, she met with many helpful staff and volunteers, as well as current and former board members, conservatory teachers, and others who had worked for the Theatre in an artistic manner. She utilized the results from a questionnaire that Kelly and Leahkim developed and administered during phase one for designers, teachers, and other people related to the Theatre. The questionnaires revealed that there were paper and audio materials in homes and studios, but surveying or transferring these materials were not part of the project's goals. Mary also incorporated the results of the surveys into recommendations for future actions in a final report presented to the board.

The Theatre staff stressed that they needed to maintain access to some of their materials, especially public relations files, and this was borne out as Mary observed the day-to-day functions of the organization. Mary spent time with the head of public relations to establish what could be done to meet the needs of both the Theatre and the archives. We needed to maintain access to materials of immediate need in the offices but also enable transfer of select materials to SCPA for processing, storage, and scholarly use. Mary was able to finalize photocopying and scanning materials so that there would be two copies of public relations materials: one for the Theatre to keep and use and one for SCPA. Three administration interns were assigned to assist Mary with photocopying thirty years of public relations materials and completing the scanning of twenty years of production photographs started by Kelly. This included advertisements, reviews, and press releases, among other materials. In the end, the photocopies went to the archives, unless multiple originals were available, in which case one original went to SCPA. The Theatre retained a set of digitized photographs for their own use. This was not the curators' preferred arrangement, but it was a compromise that ensured that the material would be available at both the Theatre and the archives.

Mary gathered materials collected from many different departments and people, including development, production, administration, and the conservatory. The materials included but were not limited to: annual reports, independent audits, board minutes and retreat information, conservatory materials, prompt books, production books, costume renderings, lighting plots, and scenery plans. While most people involved in donating were very eager to get the materials out of their personal storage and into the collection, there were some who were more apprehensive.

When Mary initially met with Brandee Mathies, one of the main costume designers at the Theatre, he was hesitant about sending his materials to SCPA, as he uses older designs to influence new work. Mary spent an afternoon with him describing the type of access he would have to his materials. Once he felt ready, Mary worked with him to organize the materials for the transfer. At the same time, Mary was able to create an inventory of the materials on the spot, which was a part of the documentation sent over to SCPA. The inventories of the works Mary gathered were distributed both to the Theatre and to SCPA for their respective use. This is one of the many instances Kelly and Mary encountered that underscored of the importance of recognizing and honoring human emotion in the archives.

Mary's work concluded with the second major transfer of materials from the Theatre to SCPA in March 2011. Upon her departure, a transfer schedule for records was established, and a wish list was created for expanding specific kinds of records.

RESULTS

The most tangible results of this process were the pre-appraised accessions. In October 2010, SCPA acquired forty-five boxes constituting sixty linear feet of paper materials and eight representative set models. This was followed in March 2011 with another fifty-five boxes of eighty linear feet of paper materials, including twenty-five years' worth of prompt books (highly valuable primary source material for the study of theater productions) and nine boxes of Joy's professional papers. Soon after in May 2011, Keith Alan Baker, managing director and artistic director for the Theatre's 2ndStage performance series, transferred a newly collected box of records gathered from one of the 2ndStage directors. (The 2ndStage series is a sandbox and showcase for young, emerging artists.) Baker's eagerness to transfer the records of the latest production to SCPA work further demonstrated the organization's commitment to the archives project.

It is also interesting to note that when reviewing the accession records and control file now, a few years removed from the acquisitions, there is no evidence of deaccessioning any material once it reached the archives. For more than 140 linear feet of new material, that is quite remarkable and facilitated efficient processing and description, as no re-appraisal was necessary.

While researchers use this collection at the same rate as any other in SCPA's holdings, Theatre staff members have thus far been the primary users for their own administrative purposes. Their questions ranged from asking if certain records were already transferred, to asking curators to consult plans of prior productions, as well as for copies of slides for use in promotional material. These reference consultations also provide an opportunity to demonstrate our good stewardship of the collection, as our detailed description makes the questions easy to answer.

Appraising materials and creating an inventory while the collection is still in its original order and location, and in some cases still active, allowed us to discuss the materials and their uses with the people who actually created and used them. Having the luxury of time and access allowed us to create better intellectual and physical control. This was particularly helpful with the complex administrative files that required division into eight subseries to represent the ways the company used them. Similarly, this input was vital for the records of the acting conservatory, which would not have stood out to the interns and curators as a distinct set of records if the people most familiar with them were not on hand for consultation.

A major benefit of this approach has been the diminished degree of effort and time expended on archival processing. The bulk of efforts have gone into sorting materials into their respective series in those cases when items arrived separated or not in good order. This has enabled SCPA staff to focus entirely on archival processing and expanding description after the materials were transferred. Furthermore, we were able to devote more energy to grappling with some formats that were unfamiliar, particularly the larger architectural drawings and scenic models.

Embedded appraisal also created opportunities to build a significant relationship with the entire donating entity, which resulted in more effective and efficient transferring of documents and enabled a long-term partnership toward future accessions, as well as mutually beneficial interpretive initiatives like exhibitions or publications. The interns embedded at the Theatre were able to interact with company staff regularly and allay their fears, allowing the staff to focus on the benefits of placing their materials with the collection in our custody.

The Theatre and SCPA have mostly kept to the records transfer schedule created during the planning phases for the appraisal project. Since the initial accessions, sixteen linear feet of materials have been acquired, including more than 2,000 slides and photographs of productions and gala events, public relations files, office records, and other items. This process is organized from the Theatre's perspective and was approved by all involved. This established transfer schedule distinguishes between materials that will be transferred on a yearly basis and materials that will be transferred on a five-year rolling schedule. Additionally, other materials may be transferred on an occasional as-needed basis determined by the material's function and usefulness to the company. This flexible transfer arrangement has also mitigated any residual concerns staff held pertaining to letting go of active materials prematurely.

The outcomes described here demonstrate the benefits of including apprehensive donors in the archival appraisal of their collections, as well as the benefits of deploying archivists for embedded appraisal prior to acquisition. SCPA has referenced this endeavor numerous times when cultivating new donors, and most find the idea attractive. Furthermore, it is easier to request funding support for such a scenario when the curator can demonstrate first-hand that this method works.

One last result is the corollary benefits of having the Studio Theatre Archives at SCPA. This collection solidified SCPA's position as a serious, well-rounded performing arts repository and helped bring our overall offerings more in balance after decades of emphasizing music collecting. Furthermore, it complements other previously established SCPA collections that already include materials pertaining to the Studio Theatre. These include the Stanford Barouh Collection of performing arts photography, which documents several of the Theatre's productions, the James J. Taylor Collection of the Washington Area Performing Arts Video Archive, which offers performance documentation of more than forty productions by the Theatre, and the Potomac Stages Collection on DC theatre criticism, which features fifty-four reviews of the company's work. Lastly, when SCPA is ready, we will certainly refer to this collection when we pursue the papers of other major theatre companies in the DC area.

LESSONS LEARNED

This experience was instructive for the curators in terms of donor relations, building relationships, and managing human resources. Archivists must remain aware that appraising collection materials in the presence of the donors, while also implementing a new transfer protocol for the records managers, might elicit a wide range of complex emotional responses. In such circumstances, archivists need to acknowledge that different people respond differently under stress, and these kinds of emotions can even be contagious. There might not be ways to completely alleviate the stresses brought on by sending material off to an archive, but sensitivity to the emotional implications for the stakeholders will be helpful, as will not interpreting their stress as a reflection on the archivist's work or intentions. Both Kelly and Mary were wise to recognize that any emotional situation they encountered was not to be taken personally.

Conveying clear expectations for the donor and of the materials' future is important, not only for gaining trust and navigating emotional situations but also for maintaining professionalism and for gaining physical control of the materials. Knowing when to be flexible and when to be firm is important as well. For instance, if the SCPA team had been firm and not taken any intact scenic models into the collection, there may have been negative relations with the donor, and the collection would not be as rich. However, the team did have to be firm in the number of models we could take, and by utilizing digital photography, the complete record of models is far more accessible for all parties. The final results are a benefit to the company, SCPA, and the scholarly community.

Flexibility is also needed in building new working relationships while concurrently selecting records. The more Kelly and Mary worked at the company appraising the collection, the more collection materials were discovered either by them or the company staff. There was no initial cap placed on what would transfer in the first shipment, and this left the project too open-ended. Though the interns were trained to identify materials based on information, historic, or aesthetic qualities, the curators began the project with an exploratory mindset and elected to not dictate any firm parameters, perhaps being overly cautious to accommodate for the unforeseen. Fortunately, additional funding was provided by the Theatre to continue to employ the interns beyond the original project.

And while we learned the value of considering the emotions of the people at the donor organization, we also learned some lessons about our own as well. Kelly and Mary were both surprised that when their role in the project ended so did any formal communication from Leahkim or Vin about the collection's progress. This was not a consequence of their performance; indeed, all measurable objectives were met, and they had done very good work. It was just that the curators naturally turned their attention to processing the materials with the preexisting SCPA staff at UMD, as well as to their other responsibilities, and so became unintentionally inattentive to the personal investment the interns may have held for a project on which they both expended tremendous energy. While this chapter has provided an excellent chance to reconnect as coauthors recollecting our respective roles in the project, there was clearly a missed opportunity to further mentor the two interns in relation to the outcomes of the collection and toward their professional development. At the very least, a post-project performance evaluation would have served all involved.

CONCLUSION

In the end, the pre-custodial and embedded appraisal approach informed every aspect of this collection's acquisition, including outreach, donor relations, and, predictably, the archival processing. The strong relationships that were forged during our time working at the Theatre's offices resulted in greater investment by the staff, who became eager to identify and release materials to SCPA, including key materials that would have otherwise been delayed or perhaps held back. Truly, the interns earned the trust of the staff through their performance. This aspect of appraisal proved essential in the successful development of this collection.

The four archivists involved agree that this is a model that works as it allows the donating organization to maintain focus on their core mission without getting tangled up in the web of their history. By embedding a project archivist at the theatre, the company can advise as necessary and learn about the archival appraisal process with minimal interruption to regular operations. Funding such a position, or even just permitting volunteer interns, should be negotiated on a case-by-case basis. We benefitted from the fundraising savvy employed by the Theatre under Joy's direction and were fortunate that she was able to make arrangements so quickly to fund—and continue funding—interns for this project. However, with enough advance planning, outside grants may be able to support such an endeavor. (And, of course, free housing for our interns in Washington was something we couldn't have anticipated!)

This is only one experimental model.[2] While this degree of personal investment by records creators may be more likely to occur in the creative and performing arts, and perhaps other branches of the humanities, there is good reason to propose this model for any organization in any field inclined to preserve their legacy. Ultimately, the Studio Theatre was documenting corporate activities, administrative and business operations, as well as its rich history of artistry and creativity.

***Leahkim A. Gannett** is the librarian for communication, film and media studies, theater and dance, and the writing program at the University of California, Santa Barbara. **Vincent J. Novara** is the curator for Special Collections in Performing Arts at the University of Maryland. **Kelly J. Smith** is the project archivist at the Rauh Jewish Archives at the Senator John Heinz History Center. **Mary Crauderueff** is the owner of Organize. Preserve. Simplify!*

NOTES

1. The Studio Theatre Archives, Special Collections, University of Maryland Libraries, Series 5.2, Production Records, 1970–2010 and undated, http://hdl.handle.net/1903.1/19638.

2. Any archive interested in collecting materials from active performing arts organizations should also review the work undertaken by the Dance Heritage Coalition (http://www.danceheritage.org/, last accessed September 29, 2014) and the American Theatre Archive Project (http://americantheatrearchiveproject.org/, last accessed September 29, 2014).

NINE

Making the Bulb Want to Change

Implementing an Active Electronic Records Appraisal and Acquisition Program

Brad Houston, University of Wisconsin–Milwaukee

Q: How many psychiatrists does it take to change a light bulb?
A: Only one, but the bulb has to want *to change.*

The electronic records program at the University of Wisconsin–Milwaukee (UWM) Libraries' Archives Department is, like many other similar programs, of relatively recent vintage. When I arrived in 2007, the archives had been accumulating a small number of electronic records since about 2000 but had been doing so without any real systematic approach. In most cases, electronic records were accessioned as physical items within larger analog collections, with the decision of whether to separate them from the physical materials largely left to the accessioning archivist. We rarely removed the records from their original media (or the media on which they arrived), so as a result, formatting issues rarely arose. Our treatment of these electronic records was in keeping with the standard practice in most records management settings: that we ought to consider content versus format. In an archival context, of course, this dictum is less applicable because of the preservation, access, and storage implications of digital files.

More challenging than the technical issues facing the electronic records program, however, were those of public perception. In general, most offices and employees on campus were not treating electronic records as an official copy worth sending to the archives. The accessions I processed from 2007 to 2010 suggested that most offices were already conducting business electronically—for example, many folders created after 1995 included printed copies of emails and webpages as documentation—but for whatever reason, offices did not appreciate the value of the records in their original, searchable electronic contexts or else did not know how to transfer them to the archives in a form we could use.

More alarmingly, the presence of printed born-digital documents in accessions also implied the existence of electronic records that would not transfer well to paper format, such as databases and audiovisual materials. Perhaps some of these records were being retained by the offices of origin, but digital preservation was certainly not on the minds of the records creators. It was very likely that electronic records of historical interest were being destroyed, or at the very least, they were not arriving at the archives for administrative or researcher use.

The dwindling size and amount of physical transfers to the UWM archives in my first three years as university records archivist (2007–2010) suggested a need to grapple with these issues of electronic records appraisal and acquisition head-on. The archives needed to make university offices aware of their electronic records responsibilities and establish itself as a responsible keeper of those materials or risk losing its relevance as the institutional records repository. Fortuitously, a transfer of electronic records from the Office of the Chancellor in 2010 provided the framework for our eventual strategy. To appropriately appraise and accession the campus's electronic records, we would need to develop the technical infrastructure for appropriate e-records review and ingest while also training records creators on the best way to transfer those records in digital form. To these two elements we would eventually add a third meta-strategy: make transfer to the archives and access to electronic records as easy as possible for the creators and archivists alike. In many cases, this third approach led to eliminating the need for transfers at all, allowing us to create a hybrid post-custodial electronic archives environment.

The road to creating such an environment, of course, was not quite as smooth as the neat summation above implies. Much of this case study will actually be devoted to our initial failures to effectively develop and implement our acquisition and appraisal strategy—and to be sure, there were many! In this case, however, we were able to turn our setbacks into successes, and so both are presented here as an indication of how far it is possible to progress, even with limited tools and training. As is often noted in regard to electronic records, the perfect should never be the enemy of the good; this case study will detail our path toward the perfect to, at least, the "good enough."

PLANNING

The relative dearth of electronic records in the archives at the beginning of this process—and the low levels of electronic records expertise among archives staff—meant that as we began to move to a more aggressive appraisal and acquisition approach, we were effectively starting from scratch. While such a blank state was daunting, it also gave us an opportunity to begin planning less encumbered by legacy policies and procedures. Even in those early days, it was clear that developing an overarching strategy first would help us answer potential donors' (and other staff members') questions down the road.

As we began planning our electronic records strategy, we were significantly helped by Wisconsin's tradition of strong records laws and policies. Chief among these is the Wisconsin Public Records Law (Wis. Stat. 16.61), which provides a legal mandate for records management in state agencies, including UW-System schools. More pertinently, the definition of public records in the statute makes several references to format neutrality, noting that records include:

> all books, papers, maps, photographs, films, recordings, optical disks, electronically formatted documents or other documentary materials, *regardless of physical form or characteristics*, made, or received by any state agency or its officers or employees in connection with the transaction of public business.[1]

As this statute mandates management of electronic as well as physical records, this aspect of e-records training could be folded into general records management training. This tactic would, however, prove difficult to implement at first.

More directly related to electronic records in particular is Wisconsin Administrative Rule 12, developed in 2000 to define electronic records and the qualities required to manage them appropriately in conjunction with the Public Records Law. According to this rule, electronic records must inherently possess six key characteristics to be considered as the official copy of record in Wisconsin:

- Accessible: information arranged, identified, indexed, or maintained in a manner that permits the custodian of the public record to locate and retrieve the information in a readable format within a reasonable time.
- Authentic: retained electronic record correctly reflects the creator's input and can be substantiated.
- Accurate: all information produced exhibits a high degree of legibility and readability and correctly reflects the original record when displayed on a retrieval device or reproduced on paper.
- Reliable: the electronic record produced correctly reflects the initial record each time the system is requested to produce that record.

- Legible: the quality of the letters, numbers, or symbols can be positively and quickly identified to the exclusion of all other letters, numbers, or symbols when displayed on a retrieval device or retrieved by device or reproduced on paper.
- Readable: the quality of a group of letters, numbers, or symbols is recognized as words, complete numbers or distinct symbols.[2]

These principles are pretty good for establishing electronic records guidelines in general, but having them written into an authoritative source definitely helped our outreach efforts. Parsed into digital preservation and archival functions, the final four qualities put the impetus on records creators and archivists to protect records from obsolescence, bit rot, or other preservation hazards, in order to ensure that records can be rendered as originally intended. The "accessible" quality pointed us toward developing training on effective file organization and naming, which had been part of our records management training materials in any case. For working with authentic records, we relied heavily on the advice of the InterPARES project, in particular the "Requirements for Assessing and Maintaining the Authenticity of Electronic Records." In the absence of an enterprise content management system, we knew that we would have to rely heavily on the presumption of authenticity as dictated by that report's "Benchmark Requirements" and began developing forms and procedures for documenting the relevant attributes.[3]

Focusing on records management in our particular institutional context also helped us to refine our outreach and acquisition strategy for e-records. The push to develop electronic records training and infrastructure coincided with a move toward a more functionally based retention schedule for UWM and the other UW campuses with which I work on records management issues. By working with multiple offices developing general schedules for broad functional areas of records, such as administrative and student services, I was able to approach transfer of archival records (and disposition of temporary ones) as a fait accompli for most offices, rather than having to develop specific schedules for individual units as had been done in the past. The general schedules gave the archives a "foot in the door" to appraise records of archival value in offices that hadn't transferred records in years; during these appraisal visits, I was often able to discuss or infer electronic file structures and broach the subject of electronic transfer with records creators.

While this expansion of e-records appraisal via developing new schedules was going on, I was still cognizant of the need to have a technical underpinning to the acquisition process. The accession from the Office of the Chancellor we had received in 2010 underscored the importance of combining records management with this technical expertise: the records were transferred on the actual computers in use by the outgoing chancellor, and each contained thousands of files of varying utility and record value. I was helped in developing a systematic acquisition model through lessons taken from a number of SAA's Digital Archives Specialist courses. Most notably, the Arrangement and Description of Electronic Records course introduced me to the Open Archival Information System (OAIS), which informed my planning for additional technical appraisal and metadata control.[4]

I was also fortunate to be able to work with two interns[5] from UWM's School of Information Studies, both of whom during the 2012–2013 academic year helped me test ingest and descriptive tools, work through appraisal and acquisition scenarios, and create a workflow for electronic records from transfer to preservation. With this workflow in place, I felt much more prepared to tout the UWM Archives as an active collector, and trusted custodian, of born-digital materials created by university offices.

IMPLEMENTATION

Armed with updated schedules, a better understanding of how e-records were being created in offices, and some understanding of key electronic records principles and practices, I was ready to begin putting the new policies into action. Sadly, the early stages of implementing our e-records acquisition process can in many ways be seen as a case study in how not to approach the problem. By this time I had already facilitated a number of records management workshops through UWM's online professional development tool, and so I offered a series of workshops on managing electronic records through that same tool. The workshops drew heavily on the continuum model of records management, encouraging users to create records in sustainable file formats, put records in folders according to retention schedules, and apply tags and other metadata to make electronic records more searchable for both active and archival use. As suggested by the Wisconsin Public Records law, the emphasis of these workshops was on the equivalency of electronic and paper records in employee's records management responsibilities.

Response to these workshops was disastrous. Where workshops on particular functional general schedules or legal issues in records management typically drew twenty to thirty attendees per session, the electronic records workshops drew an average of six. As might be imagined, these workshops had a negligible effect on either the amount or quality of electronic records that were transferred to the archives. Eventually, it occurred to me that if employees did not recognize that e-records management applied to them, they would not consider an electronic records workshop relevant to their needs. I was effectively making offices come to me to find out their electronic records responsibilities; I needed to figure out a way to bring knowledge to them.

In this new, active mode, I employed both top-down and bottom-up strategies. For the top-down, I began developing my relationship with the campus chief information officer (CIO) and other members of University Information Technology Services (UITS), most notably the communications liaison. While I had received a frosty reception from the CIO when I advocated for an enterprise-wide records management system, he was much more receptive to working with me on educational approaches. I once again presented my electronic records workshop, but this time in the context of the CIO's monthly open forum, attended by IT professionals and other leadership from across campus. Presenting in this capacity increased my exposure and provided my content with the legitimacy added by the CIO's implicit approval. Records management and archives content was added to UITS-produced presentations and handouts as a standard section, further promoting the relevance of electronic records management as part of technology use in general.

Beyond working with the CIO directly, collaboration with other technology subunits further increased my electronic records reach. Information Security was the most prominent relationship developed among these; by couching records management as a security measure, we were able to raise awareness of electronic records as an issue and encouraged people to think of their archival and temporary records alike as the copy of record. Also around this time, I was elected to the campus Information Technology Policy Committee (ITPC), where I kept records management and electronic archives issues in the consciousness of committee members and meeting attendees. The work at this level also led to me being asked to participate in a number of school- and college-related e-records activities, including creating e-records policies that specifically established procedures for archiving materials.

These top-down activities promoting good records management and treating electronic records as records helped with my credibility with the bottom-up strategy, that is, personal contact. When conducting records surveys for physical materials in campus offices, I now invariably also discussed the offices' electronic files as a key component of their records. As my work with the CIO and the ITPC progressed and my recognition on campus as an archivist working with digital records increased, office managers and division heads became more comfortable with the concept of electronic records and thus more receptive to transferring those records to the archives directly. I had, by this time, prepared a series of online resources for more information about records management, to which I could refer employees in these circumstances. Having this information at my fingertips proved extremely useful in gaining the trust of employees and assuring them that the management and archival transfer tips I provided were appropriate. In many cases, I was invited to departmental or even school-wide staff meetings to talk about records management in general and electronic records in particular, which further increased comfort levels with sending series of electronic records to the archives. The effect on the rate of transfer was almost immediate: whereas the records from the chancellor's office was the first major accession of e-records since 2006, we received six major transfers of born-digital material in the first half of 2013 alone.

Once the records arrived, of course, it was not always clear from the perspective of a processing archivist what to do with them. Here again, early acquisition practices were embarrassingly inefficient, which in my own defense was at least partially attributable to the novelty of the medium in the archives. The records of the chancellor, for example, were split across three computers and existed in various states of organization. Files on one computer were in folders by project or record series, but in other cases, documents were kept unorganized in the "My Documents" folder, with only the filename occasionally providing a clue as to the document's content. As a result, the first attempt at appraisal below the series level involved opening every document on all computers to manually inspect each file.

Our approach to the 2010 accession from the chancellor's offices was clearly not scalable moving forward. Fortunately, after extensive testing of tools and processes, and with the significant assistance of fieldworkers from UWM's School of Information Studies, we developed a workflow that reflected an appreciation of scale and common sense. In most cases, files received from campus offices in subsequent accessions were organized well enough to determine from folder and document titles the series to which documents belonged and whether that series was truly permanent. For additional granularity, and to assist with those records that came to us in a more disorganized state, we introduced tools into our accessioning workflow that automated processes we worked on by hand with the chancellor's records:[6]

- A random number generator for sampling. Many of the accessions we have received include large numbers of files that are considered archival by strict adherence to record schedules, but in practical terms, not all the files need to be kept in order to adequately represent the historical record (for example, photographs of campus events grouped by event but with no identifying metadata attached to the image files). To minimize selection bias as much as possible with these records, we used a random number generator (in this case, NARA's File Analyzer) to assign each candidate for weeding a number, then chose an appropriate sampling rate and selected accordingly. Regular expressions can be a big help with this step to allow the archivist to select more efficiently.
- A de-duplication program or script. This was a relatively late addition to our workflow but would have helped immensely in scenarios such as that of the chancellor's records, where the same files

appeared on two or even all three of the computers we received. Simple versions of these programs, such as the free version of Fast Duplicate File Finder, compare the checksum values of two files and flag exact duplicates for the archivist to weed as space requires. More sophisticated tools use algorithms to detect files with similar names or even similar content. We decided to forgo the latter functionality, however, due to the high probability of false positives.

- A feature identifier for personally identifiable information. At their most basic a hard-coded set of regular expressions, these tools allow the archivist to quickly identify files with confidential information and weed or restrict them, as appropriate. Simple programs of this type, such as Firefly SSN Finder, search for nine-digit (Social Security numbers) or sixteen-digit (credit card numbers) strings, but programs such as Bulk Extractor can search files for email addresses, telephone numbers, and other common features. Programs of the latter type can usually also be customized to look for files with other key identifiers of personal information, greatly reducing the risk to the archives of inadvertently releasing this information. This tool was a relatively late addition to our process, since we are providing access to our non-web records in the reading room only, and therefore the risk of inadvertent disclosure of restricted information is relatively low. However, "low" is not the same as "nonexistent," so we (and our legal department!) were happy to be able to add this first important step to our workflow. Moreover, as we explore ways of making our records more accessible to a general audience, the issue of privacy will become more important, so it is useful to have a foundation to build from.
- A file format identification and validation tool. In addition to the above processes, which are essentially automated analogues of traditional archives activities, it quickly became obvious that we would also have to take our ability to manage, preserve, and provide access to the files as electronic files into account during appraisal. For some accessions, such as the collection of digital photographs we received from University Communications, file format was relatively homogenous across the entire collection, making this step of appraisal relatively simple. For collections such as the chancellor's office records, a more diverse collection of file formats and genres made it necessary to use a tool such as DROID to identify and report on the file formats present in the accession. Once this step was accomplished, we used a modified version of the Digital Preservation Coalition's decision tree for selection of digital materials for long-term retention to help determine whether files requiring extra work to preserve long-term were significant enough to put in the effort of migrating them to preservation formats or extracting the data within. If, after following this interactive flow

chart, it was not deemed possible or practical to reformat the obsolete file or files, we weeded them from the collection.[7]
- A basic metadata harvester. As Neil Beagrie and Maggie Jones note in their digital preservation handbook, accurate documentation "provide[s] not only essential details for managing the resource over time but also information on context without which there may be little point in preserving the digital object itself even if it is technically feasible to do so."[8] As with paper collections, contextual documentation is generally derived from conversations with the records creator and recorded in accession reports and finding aids; the metadata harvester provides the implicit documentation required for maintaining authenticity, of which the creator is often not even aware. As of this writing, no one tool has served our metadata needs for all of the formats that are part of the collection, but we have used a suite of tools that gather basic information such as dates created and modified, the hardware and software environment used to create the records, the author of the document (as applicable), and any subject or keyword tags embedded in the files. In addition to maintaining this documentation for preservation purposes, extracting it at point of transfer serves as a first line of quality control. If a field doesn't match up with expectations (e.g., if the "date created" field indicates 2014-11-01 for a document dated 2010 in the text), we can contact the transferring office and seek clarification/replacement of the affected documents.

With an improved outreach strategy and more established technical expertise in place, we were now ready to look at the third and final aspect of our more aggressive e-records acquisition implementation, web archiving. This collection development strategy was not originally intended to fit into our wider plan, but found its way into our strategy almost as a happy accident. As originally envisioned, we planned to use our web archiving program, facilitated by the Internet Archive's Archive-It service, primarily to take "snapshots" of UWM's web presence as a record itself. To this end, we chose as our main points of access the home pages of the main nonacademic divisions, the academic schools and colleges, and a few other key units such as the Alumni Association and the athletics department. In contrast, individual offices and academic departments would not receive their own "catalog entry" from our landing page on the Archive-It site but would be captured by the crawler and could be discovered through searching and browsing of the entire collection.

Once the first annual capture took place, we performed a quality control inspection to determine where portions of pages or sites had not been captured, attempted to resolve display issues from the standard web archives preservation format, and so forth. To our surprise, we discovered that many of the static electronic records we had been chasing for years had been captured along with the websites that housed them. For example, departments regularly posted meeting minutes, newsletters, unofficial photographs, policy documents, and other public records to their websites, very often in directories effectively organized by records series and academic year. In many cases, we had had no luck in getting these kinds of materials for the archives, but by capturing them in our web crawl, we have been able to preserve access to the authentic record. Given the constant threat of content purges or reorganizations on the live web, being able to harvest these records while they are still available means that they live on even after they are deleted from departmental web servers. Recently, the archives has also started providing links in our finding aids to select captured records series in our web archives, giving researchers another access point to these documents.

It is worth noting that this serendipitous post-custodial approach has not been a panacea for our active acquisition of electronic records. For one, our web crawls do not capture the confidential or semipublic electronic records of departments, such as internal planning documents or email correspondence; solicitation of "traditional" electronic records must continue. Additionally, during quality control of our initial crawl, we found records in various states of accessibility. Some documents were IP-restricted to campus computers only, meaning the (California-based) crawler could not access them; others were managed in a complex database-driven system, which the crawler could not "read" without also picking up millions of blank pages. These challenges prompted additional rounds of outreach to department webmasters and communications professionals about setting robots.txt exemptions and creating organized file structures within their web directories. The fact that these harvested materials are hosted on Archive-It servers also complicates the long-term fate of these records; our exit clause with the service provides return of our data but not necessarily the software or expertise needed to keep that data accessible. These caveats aside, the ability to ingest copies of previously unavailable records, even indirectly, has greatly expanded the scope of the university's post-2000 documentation.

RESULTS

As with most practices in the digital archives realm, our appraisal and acquisition practices are constantly evolving, and it is difficult, if not impossible, to declare a given set of procedures "complete." That said, by a number of metrics and intangible results, I am prepared to declare at least partial success, particularly in the absence of an integrated records management system. Most visibly, the raw amount of electronic records received from UWM and other sources, including a number of professional organizations for whom we serve as the archival repository (the Society of American Archivists and the American Academy of Allergies, Asthma, and Immunology are among the largest) has risen dramatically in the two years since beginning active solicitation of electronic records, from 39 GB (mostly digitized copies of analog records) to 273 GB (mostly born-digital materials). Certainly part of this rise is a natural effect of more records being created, used, and stored entirely electronically, but I believe the efforts to change people's perceptions around these records has also helped.

For example, in 2012, when I processed a larger accession of electronic records from the chancellor's office, I had to couch acquisition of these materials to my administrative contact in terms of an index to potentially related paper files. By May 2014, however, my outreach to campus units had apparently borne fruit; my discussion of transferring documents in the same series as the 2012 accession was treated as a natural, common occurrence. Even more excitingly, archival series from other offices, such as course syllabi, are being transferred to the archives electronically by department managers' own initiative. In cases such as these, the responsible parties in the offices have expressed appreciation of the archives' commitment to preserve records while also allowing copies to remain on-site for internal reference.

To be sure, UWM's electronic records acquisition program has many areas for potential improvement. Email appraisal and acquisition in particular has been a difficult nut to crack locally thus far, though we are examining a modified version of NARA's Capstone approach to capture emails of key officials as we transition to a new email system.[9] I am also aware that faculty and staff are maintaining official records in unofficial and unsecured locations, such as cloud services, which makes those records invisible to traditional systems methods of appraisal and acquisition while still vulnerable to discovery under the Public Records Law. I ultimately hope to work with UITS to help develop storage and collaboration infrastructure that is attractive enough for employees to actually use, thus keeping those records on-site (and, ideally, providing a pipeline to the archives for records with permanent retention). The outlook for installation of such systems is unclear, but increasingly, records creators and IT staff alike are aware that they are needed, which is in itself a huge step forward.

LESSONS LEARNED

As this account of it reflects, my work with electronic records has resulted in the steady learning of new skills and concepts, although perhaps many of those skills and concepts are known in the field. What may be in some ways innovative, or at least new to some readers, is how I approached putting those skills and concepts into practice. And in the course of putting them into practice, I have learned some lessons that I think may be useful to others.

As noted, when we received our first real accession of born-digital records, the novelty of the medium led to some questionable appraisal methodology, which in turn were enabled by an overly close inspection of the records (sometimes at item level). Following our experience with this accession, we wrote procedures and adjusted policies to tie appraisal much more closely to records management and functional analysis. Ideally, of course, policies come before the processing work, but they have helped our decision making for future accessions. If I could do it again, I would still ultimately "learn by doing" (and suggest the same to all e-records novices), but perhaps a bit more deliberation would have accelerated the learning process or at least have prevented some of the more time-consuming processes.

One lesson that I wish I had learned earlier was that relationships with creators and key stakeholders are much more important than technical skills for an electronic records program. As my experience shows, all of the policies, procedures, and technical knowledge in the world are worthless if you can't convince the records creators that their electronic records are worth preserving. Support from top leadership and institutional IT set good examples for others to follow. At the same time, talking to the creators directly about e-records—and demonstrating our ability to handle them—proved vital for starting the flow of transfers.

The primacy of relationships aside, I do not wish to discount the importance of also having the technical skills to work with the records once transferred. When our early electronic accessions arrived, our lack of knowledge of digital preservation best practices meant that we made a number of bad decisions in handling files. As a result, file metadata was altered, file formats were converted without reversibility, and—significantly—a huge amount of time was spent on low-level analysis of files. Once I acquired some knowledge of tools and practices, we were able to greatly increase the efficiency of our acquisition, ingest, and appraisal procedures and simultaneously were able to minimize the alteration of the digital objects being transferred. By creating and documenting these processes, we have been able to standardize our treatment of electronic records from all sources.

Another insight that did not come until well into the electronic records process was the need to examine existing tools in new ways to facilitate the program. Using Archive-It as a records management tool was at least part of our justification for purchasing the service (because it allowed campus units to remove captured documents, etc.), but using records captured by the service as an extension of existing archival series did not initially occur to us. In capturing and keeping the webpages as a separate collection, the individual documents would still have been captured and searchable. By shifting how we thought about the captured static records, however, we were able to make them more discoverable by researchers and administrators by linking them to existing collections and finding aids.

Last, we discovered that the key to buy-in was making the process as painless as possible for the records creators. The early training materials I developed on electronic records were very prescriptive, in part because I was hoping that people would create records in a way that made the archivist's job easier. I lost sight of the fact that people don't want to do extra work if their records workflow is already working for them; small wonder this advice was sparsely followed! Later iterations of training focused on ways to improve active workflows in ways that coincidentally helped with documentation of electronic records, such as creating well-organized index pages for documents stored on web servers. By influencing the way records are created in the first place, and making transferring those records to archives as easy as uploading to the web or an online drop box, we receive more electronic records with better contextual information.

CONCLUSION

Moving to an active electronic records acquisition program is not easy by any stretch of the imagination, but nor is it that much more difficult than active acquisition of institutional records in any format. For both electronic and physical materials, records management is vital both for delineating the functions of your institution and for communicating which series of records are important for permanent preservation. Both traditional and electronic records management require constant building of trust and goodwill with records creators. I happen to have a strong public records law behind my efforts, but the rhetoric of persuasion has, for me, always been more effective than naked appeals to statutes and administrative codes. Even in this era of "paperless offices," records creators can be resistant to the idea that their born-digital materials are archival—or records at all. Resistant, however, does not mean unpersuadable.

As with the therapist in the old light bulb joke, it is our job as archivists practicing active acquisition to make the bulb (or records creator, as the case may be) *want* to change. Ultimately, my ability to successfully appraise and accession electronic records has come down to my ability to persuade campus units of the importance of electronic records and the benefit to them in working with the University of Wisconsin–Milwaukee Archives. In my own case, a "seed" collection from my institution's highest office gave me the impetus to build my electronic records competencies and the example to use to display those competencies to skeptical IT professionals and records creators. In other contexts, other collections from lower levels of organizational hierarchy—even documents manually harvested from a division's web presence or intranet—may serve as the example needed. Even without an exemplar, though, laying the groundwork through training and especially through direct contacts can leave an impression of the archives' role and send that first accession your way sooner than you expect.

***Brad Houston** is the university records archivist at the University of Wisconsin–Milwaukee.*

NOTES

1. "Records of State Offices and Other Public Records," 2009, Wis. Stat. 16.61 (2) (b), accessed May 27, 2014, http://docs.legis.wisconsin.gov/statutes/statutes/16/III/61/2/b (emphasis added).

2. "Electronic Records Management—Standards and Requirements," Wisconsin Administrative Code (2001), chapter Adm 12, accessed May 27, 2014, http://docs.legis.wi.gov/code/admin_code/adm/12.

3. InterPARES Authenticity Task Force, "Requirements for Assessing and Maintaining the Authenticity of Electronic Records," in *International Research on Permanent Authentic Records in Electronic Systems (InterPARES) 2: Experiential, Interactive and Dynamic Records*, ed. Luciana Duranti and Randy Preston (Padova, Italy: Associazione Nazionale Archivistica Italiana, 2008), accessed May 27, 2014, http://www.interpares.org/book/interpares_book_k_app02.pdf.

4. Key to my understanding of OAIS was the Information Package construction, each "variety" of which includes not just the object to be preserved but also the preservation description information necessary to render the object and place it in context with other objects in the collection. This construction provided needed justification for the metadata generated and extracted during ingest of digital records. For more on OAIS, see the Consultative Committee for Space Data System Practices, *Reference Model for an Open Archival Access System*, Magenta Book (Washington DC: CCSDS Secretariat, 2012), accessed May 27, 2014, http://public.ccsds.org/publications/archive/650x0m2.pdf.

5. Lisa Christie worked with me on this project in fall 2012 and provided much of the initial testing of tools and possible preservation and access solutions. Jia He, my fieldworker during spring 2013, provided use testing, refinement, and scalability testing of Lisa's workflow and was primarily responsible for creating an inventory of electronic records hidden in existing accessions and collections. I am deeply indebted to both Lisa and Jia for their hard work during these first few months of the active electronic records program.

6. Since electronic records tools are constantly being updated or made obsolete, I will not go into great detail on the particular tools we used here, instead describing them in terms of their function. A reasonably current list of tools archivists have found useful is available through the POWRR tool grid, http://digitalpowrr.niu.edu/tool-grid/.

7. Digital Preservation Coalition, "Decision Tree for Selection of Digital Materials for Long-Term Retention," 2006, accessed June 9, 2014, http://www.dpconline.org/advice/preservationhandbook/decision-tree. The DPC's digital preservation handbook (cited below) provides additional reasoning and justification for appraisal decisions based on content, rights, technical issues, cost, and robustness of documentation.

8. Neil Beagrie and Maggie Jones, *Preservation Management of Digital Materials: The Handbook* (Digital Preservation Coalition, November 2008), 93, accessed June 10, 2014,

http://www.dpconline.org/component/docman/doc_download/299-digital-preservation-handbook.

9. Capstone is an approach to email appraisal in institutional settings that seeks to schedule and classify email according to the account owner, rather than strictly according to content. For more information on this project, see NARA Bulletin 2013-02, "Guidance on a New Approach to Managing Email Records," August 29, 2013, accessed June 10, 2014, http://www.archives.gov/records-mgmt/bulletins/2013/2013-02.html.

TEN

Weaving the Web of Influence

Maximizing Archival Appraisal and Acquisition through the Use of "Spider Advocates"

Shelley Sweeney, University of Manitoba

When I first came to Winnipeg, Manitoba, in 1998 to become the head of Archives & Special Collections, I was faced with a completely new and unfamiliar donor community. I did not grow up in Manitoba, but I quickly understood something about the culture of this place that made one thing glaringly apparent to me. The people of this province, and particularly this city, value connections of every sort—with family, coworkers, neighbors, and friends. If there is a relationship to be discovered, people in this community are eager to identify it. I realized that if I were to conduct a broad and vigorous acquisitions program for our institution, I could not go it alone as I had been accustomed to doing in my previous place of employment. I would have to rely heavily on the assistance of others.

Over time I gradually created what I now recognize and call "the web of influence." The web of influence plays on the notion of the archivist as spider (dare I say "big fat spider"?) at the center of a web who relies on a combination of enthusiastic amateurs, advocates, and experts at the end of each strand as needed to assist in specialized appraisals or acquisitions. These "spider advocates" work on behalf of the organization in specific ways using their own specialized or community knowledge and relying on their own webs of influence, each advocate individually coordinated by the archivist to realize a richer, more substantial, and better-grounded archive.

This chapter will discuss a number of examples of how the web of influence works and how the lessons learned in my particular place can be employed by other archivists wherever they may be. Archives with a broad collecting mandate, whether they target private papers or the official records of a large parent institution, can never have experts in every area of acquisition. Yet archivists often rely on only their own research and abilities to determine what is going to be collected and to make the necessary time-consuming contacts with donors. This, combined with serendipity, the desires of donors, and organizational preferences, can lead to quite chaotic acquisitions, even for those archives with well-articulated acquisition policies. To combat this, we archivists need to consider going beyond our desire to meet the needs of others, to ask: what can other individuals do for us?

PLANNING

When I became head of the University of Manitoba Archives & Special Collections, I joined a very small permanent staff with one other assistant archivist, one librarian, and a support staff member; the assistant archivist and I were responsible for all acquisition activities for both university records and private papers. Granted, by the time I arrived, the acquisition program was well established, being in its twentieth year, and my predecessor, Dr. Richard Bennett, was a master of acquiring outstanding archives. But how was I, a newcomer to the community, to continue this tradition? I had acquired archival material in my previous position as head of the University of Regina Archives for eleven years, but the emphasis there had been on university records and far less on private papers.

So after arriving in Winnipeg, I mulled over several options for assistance with my acquisition activities. Archival manuals often tell you to form an advisory committee to assist you, and so I briefly pondered that possibility. However, I felt it was difficult to accomplish anything by committee. The few committees I worked with when I was assigned responsibility for applying freedom of information and privacy legislation to the University of Manitoba were very clumsy and a heck of a lot of work for very low returns. And who would sit on this acquisitions committee? And would the members get along with each other? How would I manage the dynamics of a disparate group of people when I would not know any of them? These are some of the questions I had when I first thought about forming an advisory committee for acquisitions.

I also considered trying to inject some life into the somewhat moribund friends group for the library. The group was supposed to help raise awareness of the library, but in fact they did not have the opportunity to provide much advice or practical support. A friends group seemed very similar to an advisory committee, just with a more informal group of people, including both staff members and those external to the university. Furthermore, members of this group would have differing motivations to be involved in such a committee, in some cases with agendas of their own, and would not be particularly oriented to the archives as opposed to the library. Therefore I thought it would be simpler and more straightforward to proceed without working through the formal structure of either an advisory committee or a friends group.

It is not that I had never depended on relationships to acquire materials before I got to the University of Manitoba, but as a young archivist, I had not reflected very much on how I could employ those relationships to improve my acquisition activities. Looking back, I realize now that I really did not take advantage of my connections. I became sensitized to the issue of relationships in Winnipeg, however, while listening to my assistant archivist talk to donors and potential donors. Then I began to discern the underlying connections that linked all of those involved in the archives' acquisitions, from scouts for collections to donors to researchers to individuals with ideas of what they would like us to do. Once I became aware of the importance of this web of relationships, I concentrated on discovering them for myself and over time began to develop my own personal relationships with specific individuals who showed particular interest in the archives. I soon realized that because of their interest I could harness their energy and enthusiasm to assist me with my acquisitions so that I didn't have to start from zero. They would be our eyes and ears in the donor community. They were well placed to note potential acquisitions, and they had the relationships and connections to persuade individuals to donate to us. I now refer to these individuals "spider advocates."

The development of these spider advocates was gradual over time and always an informal arrangement. I only needed the approval of management when we were making a significant, controversial, or large acquisition. The finer details of acquisition, however, have never been of particular interest to our administration. They trust me to display good judgement in adding to the collections. And in turn for me, the primary importance of the spider advocates is that they are people I can trust and rely on, and they feel similarly—that they can trust and rely on me.

IMPLEMENTATION

There are three examples I can offer that exemplify the different ways in which these spider advocates have been able to assist the University of Manitoba in acquiring private records. The examples cover spider advocates who have close familial and community ties, those with collegial connections, and a lone spider advocate with knowledge of a specialized field of acquisition.

My first example is a group of experts and prominent members of the local Ukrainian Canadian community. Many are associated in some way with the University of Manitoba, and each acts as a scout for likely collections of interest or importance, employing his or her own contacts and connections. Because they are important experts or are well known in their community, they are looked up to and relied upon for their advice, particularly when individuals are interested in placing their archives. But what makes this example stand out for me is how these advocates are connected to each other (see figure 10.1). This example shows the importance of having individuals who are valued experts with their own sphere of influence and of appreciating the sometimes invisible web of relationships between the advocates that can exist within a specific community.

Like many of the ethnic groups that settled in Winnipeg around the turn of the last century, the Ukrainian Canadian community is undergoing significant changes. Organizations that were established to assist immigrants in adjusting to their new home are dying out for lack of younger

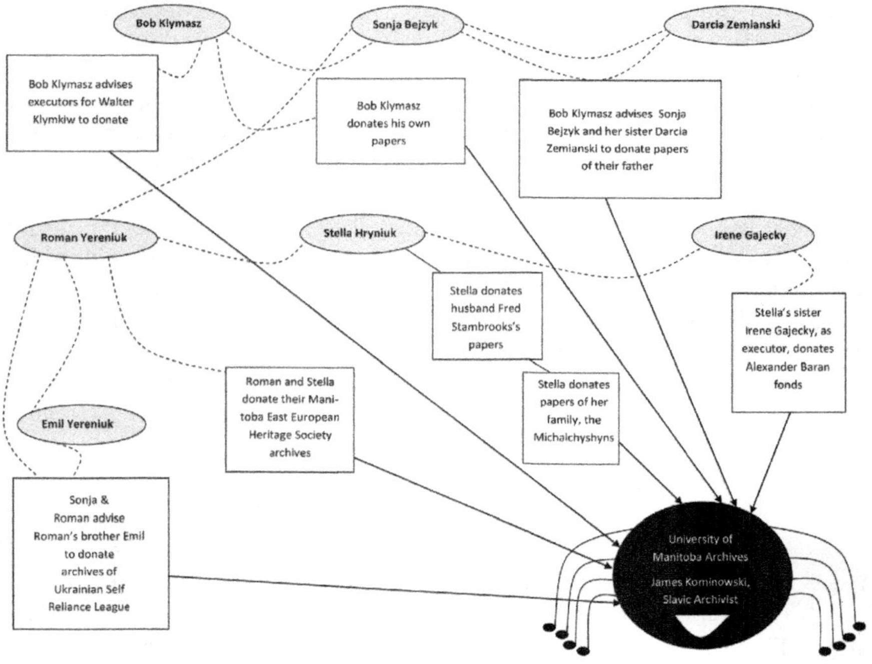

Figure 10.1. The relationships of some of the Ukrainian Canadian spider advocates who assist the archives.

members and leaving behind large collections of papers with no homes. In 2001, Natalia Aponiuk, a professor in the Centre for Ukrainian Canadian Studies, came to the university librarian to ask her to support the establishment of a Ukrainian Canadian archives at the university. There were already a number of organizations within the city who were collecting such archives but none that could absorb any large new collections. The university librarian was convinced, and thus a new direction for Archives & Special Collections was initiated.

One might be tempted to think of each ethnic community as an organized whole, where individuals all get along and think the same way. The reality of course is nothing like this. Relationships are messy. In this particular ethnic community, there are significant historic divisions. There are also strong bonds between many individuals as well. Each of these relationships builds on a myriad of connections—familial, collegial, and others.

For example, our first collection came as a result of the efforts of Bob Klymasz, a graduate and a former staff member of the University of Manitoba who had returned to Winnipeg to retire. Bob contacted us because he was advising the executors of the estate of history teacher and conductor Walter Klymkiw on what to do with his papers. Bob had retired from a long career at the then Canadian Museum of Civilization in Ottawa as its first program director for Slavic and East European studies. Because of his perceived expertise and his long-standing relationship with the Klymkiw family, on his advice the family donated Walter's collection of materials relating to Ukrainian Canadian music and the award-winning O. Koshetz Choir to the university.

The donations did not stop there however. Bob then donated his own papers, including a significant study he had done of life in Gimli, Manitoba, a nearby Icelandic community. Bob knew Sonja Bejzyk through Walter Klymkiw, as both Walter and Sonja had attended Holy Trinity Ukrainian Orthodox Church together. Bob then advised Sonja and her sister Darcia Zemianski to donate their father's papers to the University of Manitoba. Their father, J. Nicholas Mandziuk, had been a member of Parliament for Marquette, a small rural community outside of Winnipeg. Sonja then turned around and, with Roman Yereniuk, the head of the Centre for Ukrainian Canadian Studies on campus, advised the Ukrainian Self-Reliance League (USRL) to donate their papers here. Sonja knew Roman as she was the external representative at the Centre's departmental meetings. Sonja's father had been president of the men's section of USRL. Roman's brother, Emil Yereniuk, was the current president, and Roman himself had been part of the Union of Ukrainian Youth, a division of USRL. Roman in turn donated his material relating to the Manitoba East European Heritage Society, which had been documenting Ukrainian Catholic and Orthodox churches throughout Manitoba. Roman did this study with Stella Hryniuk, a colleague.

Stella, meanwhile, another graduate and retired professor of history at the University of Manitoba, first deposited her own papers in 2008. She followed that donation by depositing the papers of her late husband, Fred Stambrook, a fellow professor of history at the University of Manitoba, soon after. Later she donated papers from her family, the Michalchyshyns, pioneers who were involved in Ukrainian Catholic churches. She then persuaded her sister Irene Gajecky, who was acting as executor, to deposit the Alexander Baran fonds. Reverend Baran was the chaplain of "Obnova," the Ukrainian Catholic students organization at the University of Manitoba beginning in 1964, who became a full-time professor of history in 1966.

As diagrammed in figure 10.1, we see that there is an almost Byzantine web of relationships between individuals within the community and how one donation leads to another. The organizations and families can feel safe in placing their records with the university because they trust the advocates who give them advice based on the stature these advocates have among them. In turn, these advocates have ties of loyalty to the University of Manitoba as graduates and employees.

My second example—the Lone Dog Winter Count—is intriguingly different but also employs the advice of a combination of experts. There is what might be considered an archive of Sioux communities on the Plains in the form of a so-called winter count. The winter count was a pictorial history of the community. A symbolic event was chosen by elders each year to represent the history of the time between snowfalls—or "winter." A keeper, in this case the last being a man named Lone Dog, then inscribed a pictograph representing that event onto a buffalo hide to preserve the community's history and underpin the tribe's oral histories. This particular winter count covered the period 1800 to 1870 and exhibited many identifiable events, such as the flood of the Missouri River when a number of tribe members drowned in 1825–1826 and the Leonid meteor storm of 1833.[1] The pictographic symbols begin in the center of the hide and spiral outward in a counterclockwise direction (see figure 10.2).

At various times since 1870, other aboriginal people have copied this count onto a variety of hides. Some were copied specifically at the request of people who were studying aboriginal culture.[2] Most surviving winter counts were copied for sale.[3] Colonel Garrick Mallery published information about the Lone Dog count in the *Fourth Annual Report of the Bureau of American Ethnology* published in 1886, complete with an illustration of a copy that had been drawn on muslin.[4]

An antiques dealer in town offered to sell me what he described as a 1930s copy of the Lone Dog Winter Count inscribed on a buffalo hide. He offered it to the university for $75,000, after having already tried to sell it unsuccessfully to an American institution. I had never heard of winter counts, but the photos he sent me were very interesting, and a quick look

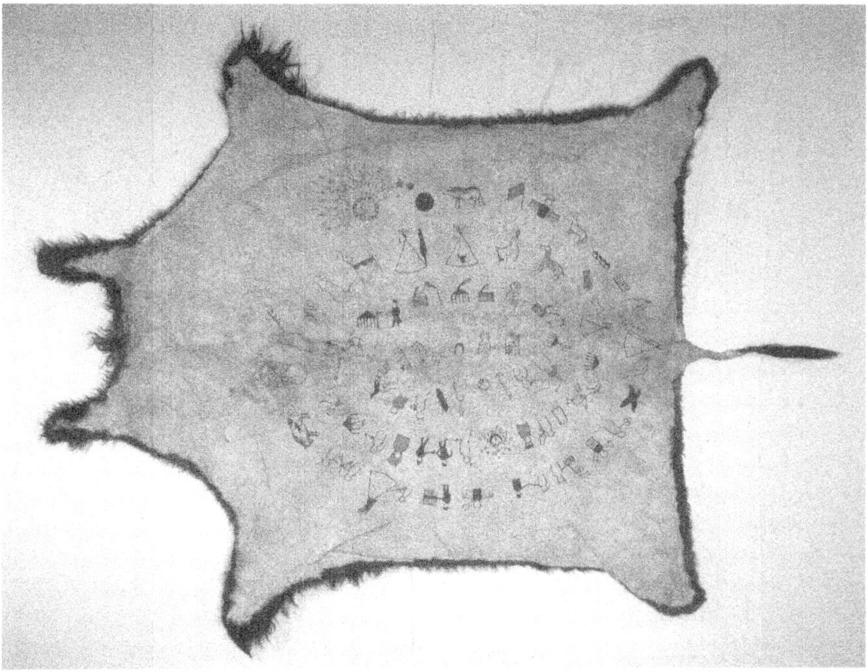

Figure 10.2. Lone Dog (Shunka Ishnala), Nakota (Yankton Sioux). Winter count recording events from 1800 to 1870. A Lone Dog Winter Count similar to this one was offered to the University of Manitoba Archives for purchase. *National Museum of the American Indian, Smithsonian Institution (1/617). Photo by Janine Sarna Jones.*

online turned up plenty of information from reputable sources, such as the Smithsonian's National Museum of the American Indian.

If the count on offer was a relatively early copy, created by an Aboriginal person, it would indeed be extremely valuable and useful for teaching purposes, and with consultation and approval from the appropriate tribe from which it came, it could be an exciting acquisition. It would also help support our university's strategic plan of promoting Aboriginal achievement. If, however, the count turned out to be a fake, it would be disastrous for our institution's reputation to have acquired it. Likewise, if it turned out to be an early cultural appropriation by a nonindigenous person, for purposes of decoration for example, that fact could be equally damaging. No one would want to study a faux winter count that was made by a nonindigenous person even if it was created with no intentions to deceive. What might have been acceptable almost one hundred years ago is no longer acceptable by today's standards.

Unfortunately, right from the start, the offer had all the makings of a fraud. The antique dealer was selling the hide on behalf of another dealer. That man had acquired it from his partner who was dead with no remaining family. The partner had bought it from a woman (name unknown) who supposedly had a summer cottage (location unknown) next to a former minister of Mines and Northern Resources who gave her the count, which he himself had received as a gift during an unknown event sometime in the 1930s. Thus not only was the provenance unknown, but also it was virtually impossible to establish. I knew I was badly out of my depth on this acquisition. Fortunately for me, Katherine Pettipas, a graduate of the University of Manitoba and recently retired from the provincial museum where she had been responsible for curating aboriginal artifacts, had turned to her alma mater to look for volunteer opportunities. I enlisted her assistance, and we headed over to the antique store to view the hide.

What we saw in the store made both of us wonder—and not in a good way. To me, the filthy condition of the hide and the wear marks from what looked like furniture made me think it had spent most of its life on a floor serving as a rug. Furthermore, it didn't have the right feel to me; the yellow color was very bright, not consistent with an original application in the 1930s, although it was possible that somebody had re-laid the color sometime later. Katherine was concerned by the fact the horseshoe symbols were pointed and not round, as if the painter had not understood their significance, and by the fact that there were no holes where the hide would have been stretched. She noted that the black coloration normally should have faded to a brown in the intervening time. But she was not willing to dismiss this item without further research.

We needed more information to make a firm decision. I ran into Anne Lindsay, one of our former archival studies students who I knew had deep connections in the Aboriginal community because of a former position. She is also a crackerjack researcher. I mentioned our quest because I knew she would find it of interest. She immediately leapt into action, delving deep into various databases and extracting a vast amount of information. She contacted an Aboriginal scholar she knew who could review the potential acquisition. Meanwhile, Katherine contacted the former Canadian Museum of Civilization, the Royal Ontario Museum, the Smithsonian's National Museum of the American Indian, and a number of retired curators. She did further research herself on the history of Lone Dog Winter Counts.

Katherine's main conclusion was that there were more robes than you could shake a stick at, some stolen, some without provenance sitting in quiet obscurity in museums, and a few made specifically for display. And, of course, at least some fakes. Anne discovered, among other things, that one Lone Dog Winter Count had disappeared from a museum in the western part of the province. Her colleague at the University of Winnipeg spoke with a Swiss Aboriginal couple who run a bison ranch, and they pointed out a number of inconsistencies, including the fact that the hide had not been brain tanned as it should have been had it been authentic, leaving an uneven, instead of smooth, surface.

When all was said and done, and all the various people were consulted, the evidence was certainly not conclusive but leaned toward the likely possibility that the item had either been created for an exhibit or deliberately faked to sell. If we were wrong and the count was authentic, then there was the strong likelihood that it was stolen somewhere along the line. None of these scenarios was palatable, and even the slim possibility that the item was authentic did not outweigh the risk. In this instance, the spider advocates pulled in their own experts to assist us in coming to a final judgment that I felt comfortable with. I did not know enough about the subject to come to the right decision for the university on my own. In the end, I sent a long explanation providing all the reasons for our decision to the antique dealer and of course kept a copy for our files. I truly felt I had done my due diligence.

My final example is an individual who is a blend of enthusiastic amateur and knowledgeable expert. Walter Meyer zu Erpen is a practicing archivist whose daytime consulting has nothing to do with his personal interest in life after death.[5] His connection to the University of Manitoba, since he lives full-time in another province far from Winnipeg, lies in his interest in our Hamilton family fonds of séance archives. He began doing research on the collection in 1990, long before I appeared at the university, and he quickly realized the importance of this unique collection. In the course of his visits, it became clear that the archives was very supportive of his personal interest. As a result, over the years Walter has been responsible for the archives acquiring no less than sixteen parapsychological collections. Two collections in particular stand out. The H. A. V. Green collection, passed on to Walter by the Vancouver Psychic Society, and donated by him to our collection, contains an album with a selection of photographs of the Hamilton family séances. A similar album sold for close to $100,000 (US) at auction in New York in 2013. The real value in these albums however is in seeing how the Hamiltons distributed their photos to others with similar interests; in addition, the Green album was annotated by a participant in the séances who was a lawyer for the Canadian Pacific Railway, so it contains valuable first-person information by an identifiable individual as well.

The second of Walter's notable acquisitions for us are the papers of New Yorker Alexander Imich, who before his death in 2014 at age 111 was briefly declared the oldest man in the world. He left behind a wide variety of materials relating to parapsychology gathered over a significant length of time from the 1930s to 2012. Imich's archives hold extensive correspondence he maintained with many organizations and well-known figures in the field, including the Academy of Religion and

Psychical Research, the Exceptional Human Experience Network, the Lady of Light Association , the Amazing Kreskin, Stephen Hawking, and Uri Geller, among many others.

In addition to Walter's assistance in acquiring parapsychological archives, as time has passed, he has come to Winnipeg to give lectures. He has also established an endowment to support our paranormal archives and future possible research in this area at the university and has been actively raising money for this fund. But for us his most important contribution has been his increasing work as our representative in collecting psychical archives.

Because Walter has been intensely studying this topic and the history of its activities for a long time, and because he has been able to write on the topic and travel extensively, he himself has become part of an enormous web of enthusiasts throughout the world. His knowledge of the history of psychical investigation has allowed him to track down descendants of people directly involved in psychical research and Spiritualism, including the children and grandchildren of mediums and those hosting séances, individuals with significant private libraries of ephemeral and hard-to-find publications, as well as other researchers and institutions and organizations also having a common interest in life after death or related subjects. His ability to negotiate the acquisition of these parapsychological archives on our behalf is critical to building our collection. His dedication and willingness to travel to scout out collections, to meet with potential donors, to keep up an extensive and thorough correspondence and documentation of his contacts and the donations make his value to our institution immeasurable. Simply put, we could not have built a parapsychological archives without him. With his help, we have been able to build a substantive archive of materials that normally would require a very careful vetting. However, we can feel secure that Walter's knowledge and expertise ensures the authenticity of these materials has been established before they are offered to us.

These three examples then show how complex relationships between the spider advocates and the university as well as between the advocates and other external experts create a web of influence. Of course, it is much easier to start building such a web when you are not starting from scratch. In all of these examples, I was building on established relationships. Right at the creation of the Ukrainian Canadian archives, we hired a half-time Slavic archivist (who is also the Slavic librarian), James Kominowski. James is a University of Manitoba graduate in Slavic studies who had taken courses with many of the individuals who have deposited their records with us. He is a well-known and highly thought of member of the Ukrainian Canadian community. Through James, I have come to know many of these spider advocates, and he has vouched for me within the community.

In the case of our two experts on the Lone Dog Winter Count, I have developed individual relationships with each of them based on Katherine's volunteering at the archives and Anne's working for the archives of the Truth and Reconciliation Commission. The commission's archives will be coming to the University of Manitoba, and I am cochairing the implementation committee for the center that is being developed to house the archives; thus we have had opportunities to work together in another sphere.

And, in the famous Winnipeg way, I went to school with Walter the psychical researcher in the archival studies program at the University of British Columbia—he was one year behind me—and furthermore he was best friends with a good friend and fellow student from my year. So we were not starting our relationship cold.

RESULTS

The acquisitions have been a spectacular success. Archives staff are happy to have the expert input, management is pleased with the high profile that the institution has achieved with these acquisitions, and visitors are busy making use of the collections.

In each case, it was important that the archives validated the worth of each of the collections before their acquisition. However, where we did not have the expertise to make that validation on our own, we were relying on community knowledge or subject expertise to assist us in making a final decision. Based on this input, we felt on solid ground in pursuing extra funds where needed to process these archives—as we did with the Ukrainian Self-Reliance League—or in turning down an acquisition, as with the Lone Dog Winter Count. Refusals that have turned out to be wrong can cause heat for institutions. There is nothing worse than hearing about some amazing acquisition that you missed because you did not realize its significance, and there is nothing universities hate more than missing an opportunity to shine. But if you do your due diligence and come to a reasoned decision, then at least you can defend that decision however wrong it may turn out to be. In our case, the experts provided solid backup to our decision making.

Although missing out on a great acquisition is painful, it can sometimes be even worse to acquire something. In two of my examples, the aboriginal and psychical archives, the acquisition of fraudulent or, at the very least, inauthentic archives could be very damaging to our reputation. We want to have the provenance of each collection clearly established and not rely on the word of the seller or donor. It's not good enough to simply say, "This looks like an interesting collection; I think we should get it." The fallout if you accepted a collection on university history, for example, that turned out not to be what the donor represented it to be would be considerably less than if you were paying an enormous amount of money or you were acquiring materials in a high-risk subject area like parapsychological investigation. For low-risk collections, where you are not concerned about fraud, once you have established the provenance, you expect researchers to determine the papers' authenticity through their own internal investigation.

Clearly our experience having outside expertise to guide us in making our decisions to acquire, or not acquire, materials has helped us avoid such mistakes. What makes this web work is the confidence or close relationships spider advocates have with donors, other members of the community, and experts. Appreciating these relationships and the knowledge and expertise of our spider advocates, we are happy to rely on them. But what makes these spider advocates, well, advocate? Why work on our behalf? I posed that question to some of them, and their answers may give some insight into what motivates this kind of advocate.

Irene Gajecky, who was responsible for donating the papers of Father Baran, sought out the University of Manitoba because Father Baran himself had mentioned his wish to leave his papers to the university. But it was Irene's sister Stella Hryniuk that pointed Irene in our specific direction and helped walk her through the donation process. I asked Irene what her own motivation was for donating, and she said that she was personally interested in history and iconography in particular. She also said that she felt strongly that the archives of ethnic peoples other than Anglo-Saxons should be included in a public, secular university and made available for research.

Katherine Pettipas has retired but says she still enjoys conducting research and employing her expertise. She has a passion and the personal interest to be involved in the archives. She wants to discover the truth behind an object or an item. And she's particularly interested in how you find a story of an object when you do not have the provenance. She describes her interest in history and particularly in objects as "an obsession." She loves to keep digging. She feels the biggest motivator for her, however, is to be of service to the public.

Anne Lindsay feels herself to be an avocational historian. In fact she described herself as a "research addict." She said that she derived a great deal of satisfaction from engaging and finding a solution to an interesting problem as she did with the winter count. She also enjoys working with her contacts and experts, and she said that she felt these relationships were a bit like muscles; if you didn't use them, they would waste away.

Walter said that psychical research is his passion and that he feels the research gets to the very nature of human existence. Because the area is an understudied area of human endeavor, the archives of these studies become even more important. Individuals spend their lives studying psychical phenomena, and then when they die, Walter said, their archives are destroyed or dispersed or stuck into dumpsters, making his efforts to preserve these records all the more urgent.

What connects almost all of these advocates are strong ties to the university or, in the case of Walter, the psychical researcher, a strong attraction to something the university holds. That loyalty motivates them to support the university's archives. They also have deep personal interests in and an overall concern for the advancement of education and the preservation of culture. They have a sense of their role in that public good.

LESSONS LEARNED

The most important lesson we have learned from using spider advocates is not to do all appraisal and acquisition by ourselves. We have come to recognize that not only do we not have to be the soul arbiters of acquisition decisions, but also by calling on our spider advocates and citizen archivists, together we make better decisions about what to acquire and, equally important, what not to acquire. By relying on the input of people such as Katherine Pettipas, a giant of specialist knowledge and herself at the center of a significant international web of expertise, and Anne Lindsay, a remarkable researcher who also can tap into a web of local experts, we do not have to wonder whether we just passed up the opportunity of the lifetime and that our decision to not acquire the Lone Dog Winter Count is going to haunt us later on in the future.

We have also learned that the basis of any good acquisition program is a solid mandate supported at the highest level of our organization, as demonstrated in the decision to begin acquiring archives of the Ukrainian Canadian experience. We needed to have a very clear acquisition mandate with strict parameters, and we needed to stick to these very carefully as we provided guidelines to our spider advocates. By having support at the highest level, we acquired a half-time dedicated staff member, James Kominowski, who has himself been able to develop a web of enthusiastic supporters over time. Any criticism that we encountered when we first began to acquire in this area about whether we were in effect competing with other organizations who had been acquiring these types of archives in the past could be countered with the information that the University of Manitoba Libraries had chosen to become involved in this area at the behest of the community and we were carrying out the members' wishes. Community concern quickly melted away when it became apparent that with the best will in the world, the other organizations collecting records of the Ukrainian Canadian experience had few resources in terms of space and staff to deal with any more significant acquisitions, which is why the community had approached the libraries in the first place. By having that mandate, however, we felt comfortable in our acquisitions.

Now if an opportunity comes up to acquire archives outside of our mandate, we return to our library administration to ensure that the acquisition we are contemplating is appropriate and that we have a defensible position for making that decision to acquire.

We have learned when and how to communicate with our spider advocates; we do not necessarily interact regularly with them. We communicate with them when we have something to tell them that meets their interests, or they communicate with us when they have something specific to tell us. But as Anne Lindsay said, it is important to keep up the relationship. In practical terms, that means determining the spider advocates' level of interest; for example, some advocates only want to come to events that are squarely in their area of interest, while others are more broadly interested in what the archives is doing. We have established email lists with very narrow subject areas, such as Slavic or parapsychological topics, and I augment these lists with personal emails of people I think might be particularly interested in a piece of news or an event we are hosting. When any of us involved in acquisition leave or retire from the university, it will be important for us to communicate to our replacements the names and interests of our spider advocates, and to that end, we need to begin recording salient details about their individual interests and expertise.

It is important for us to keep in mind that not everyone is appropriate to become a spider advocate. We always need to recognize and assess the strengths and abilities of each individual before we "recruit" them. Even though this is an informal network, we still have had to spend time in choosing whom we could trust to become an advocate. People may be knowledgeable without having a sympathetic or even instinctual understanding of archives. This can cause them to provide advice that can actually be misleading. We have to judge each spider advocate's abilities both by what they do as much as what they say. This means that we have to spend time with them and listen for subtexts hovering below their conversation. And at the same time, we need to recognize their limitations because sometimes people's enthusiasm takes them beyond their expertise.

While it is difficult at times, we have to be careful not to get too wrapped up in an advocate's enthusiasm, as with some of our spider advocates in the Ukrainian Canadian community. They feel their community has immense importance, and they feel a strong need to ensure thorough documentation of pretty well all of the organizations that have contributed to their history. Not every organization and individual is equally prominent or even worthy of documenting, and we have had to walk a delicate balance between our spider advocates' interests and our institution's interests. Ultimately we cannot allow an advocate's enthusiasm to dictate what we are going to acquire. And we still need to go through all of the usual processes we would normally go through when determining whether we will acquire a collection. Does this collection fit our collecting mandate? Does it support our institution's goals and objectives? How does it fit in with our other collections? Has the spider advocate's authentication been done to our satisfaction? Do we feel comfortable with the final decision?

With Walter Meyer zu Erpen, we have needed to work out between us how far he can go on our behalf. Fortunately because Walter is himself an archivist, he is very cognizant of this requirement and has been careful to consult and seek prior approval in writing before making any approaches. He is an ideal external advocate because he is so fully aware of exactly how much work, time, and money such acquisitions can absorb, but this is not true with other spider advocates. Luckily we have not had to deal with any advocate who has made any promises on our behalf, although they have sometimes brought potential donors to us that we have not ultimately pursued. We have tried to encourage interest but not allow that interest to push us into doing something we ultimately cannot support. Although we have made our administration aware of how we work, we have not had any formal approval mechanism for each acquisition. It has not posed a problem in our own organization, but that would not be true for all archives.

Our spider advocates have been both internal and external to our parent organization. If, however, archivists are solely collecting records within an organization, they can still develop these advocates in other departments who keep an eye on institutional records and provide information and assistance that will aid the archivists in acquiring materials—a type of mole in the organization. Even with robust records management programs, there is still room for advocates.

CONCLUSION

By creating the web of influence, I have enlisted spider advocates who work, in very defined and limited ways, on our behalf. These experts, professionals, knowledgeable amateurs, and interested members of the public become surrogates for the archives. This requires work on our side to communicate openly with these advocates at all times. We need to respect them, their abilities, and their knowledge and listen with a careful ear to what they have to tell us. We also have to ensure we provide proper guidelines and parameters as to what they can and cannot do on our behalf.

The web of influence of course does not only apply to appraisal and acquisition, but these two areas in particular benefit the most from expert and knowledgeable input. We have recognized one of our advocates by naming her an ambassador of our archives at her retirement party that we hosted. This was simply presenting her with a certificate and naming her as an honorary ambassador before all the staff. It was informal, and fun, but I know she was very pleased by the recognition. I think there needs to be more substantial recognition of these advocates, however. Their roles also need to be documented in finding aids for transparency purposes, something that we have not done in any systematic way to date but plan to do in the future. Thus, we would note their participation in the acquisition of a collection under the custodial history. This would help explain to future researchers why and how particular collections were chosen and acquired. Further, because advocates play such an important role in authenticating and evaluating collections for acquisition, their own bona fides need to be recorded so that future archivists and researchers will know what our decisions were based upon.

What you are doing when you establish spider advocates is creating a giant web where many people, not just your own staff, are all working toward an established goal. This suggests that archives have a much larger purpose and mission than the one that is written in their internal institutional policies. Universities are much more prone to consider themselves stewards for a larger public, but private or public, if your archives allows external users to access your collections, then you are working ultimately for these users, for society as a whole, for history and community memory. We simply cannot do everything ourselves, nor should we. The more we integrate members of our community into our appraisal and acquisition plans, the more solid the results of that acquisition will be. In turn, our reliance on these spider advocates binds them to the archives; they have a stake in the results and want to see the archives flourish. The web of archival acquisitions can only get stronger with all of us spinning together.

***Shelley Sweeney**, PhD, is the head of the University of Manitoba Archives & Special Collections, the Libraries.*

NOTES

1. National Museum of the American Indian, *Lone Dog's Winter Count: Keeping History Alive*, accessed May 17, 2014, http://nmai.si.edu/sites/1/files/pdf/education/poster_lone_dog_final.pdf.
2. Anh-Thu Cunnion, *Lakota Winter Counts: An Online Exhibit*, March 3, 2005, accessed September 1, 2014, http://wintercounts.si.edu/html_version/html/index.html.
3. Candace Greene, "Art until 1900," in *Handbook of North American Indian*, vol. 13, *Plains, Pt.1 and Pt. 2*, ed. Raymond DeMallie and William Sturtevant (Washington, DC: Smithsonian Institution, 2001), 1043.
4. "The Smithsonian Collection," accessed May 17, 2014, http://wintercounts.si.edu/html_version/pdfs/overview3.pdf.
5. Walter Meyer zu Erpen is president of the Survival Research Institute of Canada whose members investigate life after death and other related phenomena.

ELEVEN

Reappraisal and Deaccessioning

Building for the Future by Removing Some of the Past

James Gerencser, Dickinson College

Before I became the head of the Archives and Special Collections Department of Dickinson College, I worked there as a graduate intern. During my internship, I ran across many items that seemed curious and out of place, such as salt and pepper shakers featuring John and Jackie Kennedy, scrapbooks containing letters and engravings of relatively obscure eighteenth-century English writers and nobles, business records for a gun shop in Philadelphia dating from the late 1800s, a brief letter from Bram Stoker to an unknown recipient, and the logbook of the voyages of a mid-nineteenth-century merchant ship, showing stops at Madrid, New York, and San Francisco. There were also shelves upon shelves of uncataloged books on all variety of subjects, with some being recently published and others hundreds of years old. I wondered, how did such materials end up on these shelves, and how likely was it that they would ever be used? What were the chances that a professor would incorporate this content into classes being taught or that a student would stumble across these items and use them to answer some research question?

In 1998, I was named acting college archivist and special collections librarian, the sole professional in a department of two. In my new role, I began supervising undergraduate student workers in the processing of manuscript collections. I spent quite some time reviewing the collections, trying to match each person's level of experience to the amount of complexity presented by the materials. In examining the various collections, it became more and more clear that while many of these personal papers were useful as instructional tools for undergraduates learning how to process, they were often far less useful as content that might be mined by our faculty and students for teaching and research. The mission of Dickinson College, a small liberal arts institution chartered in 1783, is focused on undergraduate learning. But yet the kinds of material I was finding among our holdings seemed ill-suited to the curriculum being taught by our faculty and to the kinds of research being pursued by our students.

With all that in mind, I began to consider the possibility of deaccessioning materials that seemed a poor fit for Dickinson College. Why have today's students spend their time processing collections that will likely never be used by subsequent generations of students or faculty? Why catalog a random letter by a famous person if it has no research potential? Why devote scarce shelf space to duplicate books or books not particularly rare or books on topics that probably will never be taught at Dickinson? And why keep manuscript collections here that would better serve researchers in other repositories?

Having looked at the scarce literature on the topic of reappraisal and deaccessioning available at the time, I turned to the Archives and Archivists listserv for some feedback from fellow archivists. I posted a message asking what others thought about our obligations to maintain special collections materials that had, presumably, been donated in the past on the understanding that they would stay there, whether or not any formal agreements had ever been signed. I wondered, too, if materials should only be donated elsewhere if deaccessioned or if sale was a viable alternative. From a management perspective, I was curious about the amount of time one should reasonably spend on reappraisal activity. Finally, I was curious to hear what my colleagues might say regarding ethical considerations.[1]

On this particular occasion, the denizens of the listserv had very little to say. My post garnered only one response, which contained practical guidance but which was presented more as a lecture than as a position up for discussion. The most notable sentence of that message was, "Quit dithering, James."[2] While I hadn't really thought that seeking the opinions of fellow professionals constituted dithering, I nonetheless heeded this advice and determined to move forward with plans to rid the repository of materials that seemed out of keeping with the needs of our primary audience, the students and faculty of Dickinson College.

PLANNING

Recognizing that there were materials among the special collections that did not support the current curriculum—and that likely had not supported the teaching and learning that took place at Dickinson in the past—was the first step. Ensuring that no additional gifts would be made or donations accepted that were not a particularly good fit for the college was a high priority. In order to provide for coherent collecting going forward, I had already begun working with a campus-wide Committee on Archives and Special Collections to develop a mission statement and to review and refine an outdated collection development policy. The committee included the director of the library, the dean of the college, the treasurer, the assistant to the president, the director of alumni relations, and seven faculty members from across the disciplines (including the director of the college's art gallery). This broad campus representation ensured that the concerns of stakeholders throughout the institution were taken into account as we began debating the future directions for the special collections.

The earlier collection development policy had been written in such a way that almost any potential gift could be considered appropriate to accept, with breadth of subjects generally being seen as more important than depth in any particular collecting area. The newly revised policy, which is still in force, provides much more focus, with a stated aim to collect materials directly related to the college and the many individuals associated with the college through the centuries. The revised policy also supports continued acquisitions in already-established collecting areas, most of which are of local or regional importance. Finally, the revised policy provides for acquiring materials in subjects not yet represented among the collections. However, the opening of any new area of collecting, which should support the curriculum and the research needs of the faculty and students, is to be pursued only with the input of faculty members and other colleagues.

Added to the revised collection development policy was an appendix, which addressed the deaccessioning of existing holdings. Criteria for evaluating materials include the relevance of the item to the college mission, appropriateness according to the collection development policy, necessity of the item to support the educational needs of the college community, authenticity or uniqueness, the manner of acquisition of the item, and the ability of the college to maintain and provide access to the item. Guidelines for the proper manner of removing materials from the existing holdings include due consideration for the intent of the donor, disclosure of all relevant information to any potential new owner of the material, sharing any information regarding the deaccession of materials upon request, and not allowing the direct acquisition of deaccessioned items by a college employee. Finally, a record of all deaccessions shall be retained permanently.[3]

With the committee members in agreement that the reappraisal and potential removal of materials from the special collections was a natural part of more carefully refining and shaping the content of our holdings, the next issue to discuss was how best to dispose of items that have been deaccessioned. Donation to other appropriate repositories was recognized as the best option in some cases, when it was clear that the items bear directly on that institution or complement existing holdings. For example, if we have two cubic feet of Arthur Prinz papers that were donated to us by his widow thirty years ago but another repository has ten cubic feet of his personal papers that were deposited there by Prinz himself at an earlier time, then offering our two cubic feet to that repository would seem to make the most sense.

In other cases, such as individual letters, documents, and pieces of ephemera that hold little significance beyond the signature of the author, sale seemed to offer an alternative. Just as the college had purchased most of these items from manuscript and autograph dealers in past decades, we could in turn offer them up for sale to interested parties. In the case of duplicate books or titles not considered appropriate for our collecting needs, sale again seemed to be a reasonable means of disposal. Proceeds from such sales could then be used to better preserve existing collections as well as to acquire new materials deemed more desirable for our needs.

One or two members of the committee were initially concerned about selling deaccessioned materials, feeling that reappraisal decisions might be made solely based on the funds that could be realized from such sales, which would then leave the special collections with a lot of relatively worthless content while all the valuable things would have been sold off. Other members successfully argued, however, that the review process, which required the approval of the committee before any item was deaccessioned, would guard against such occurrences. In addition, a fear was expressed that money received through the sale of materials would simply be used to offset annual budgetary needs, meaning the special collections would not realize any meaningful benefit from such sales, other than freeing up space. The committee agreed this was a legitimate concern that needed to be addressed.

Having established that implementing our deaccession policy could include the selling of materials, the committee needed to develop a policy specifying what would be done with the funds realized through such sales. The proceeds were to be placed in a restricted account, the Archives Deaccession Fund. The account would operate like an invested endowment, with the principal not being expended but with annual returns available for spending by the department for new acquisitions, conservation of existing holdings, purchase of supplementary supplies, or hiring of consultants or interns to perform short-term work for the department. Perhaps most importantly, the policy included language explicitly stating that money from the account could not be used to replace any part of the annual operating budget.[4]

With the policies in place, we next considered options for how to handle the potential sale of materials. Many years earlier, a process had been followed that involved placing books removed from special collections on a cart near the library circulation desk. Books could be purchased for $2.00 the first week, $1.50 the second week, $1.00 the third week, $.50 the fourth week, and thereafter were free. On a few other occasions, books and other materials had also been sold through silent auctions, which typically lasted for a week or two in order to allow interested buyers ample opportunity to visit and inspect items available for bid. Several faculty members told me that they had always been uncomfortable with such auctions, and committee members agreed that neither of these activities were appropriate or desirable going forward.

These earlier approaches revealed several shortcomings we wanted to avoid. One problem was the assumption that those working in the archives knew enough to judge the monetary value of holdings, even though such monetary appraisals were not the focus of the job or the particular area of expertise of any employees. In addition, by selling locally with very little advertising, the potential audience for such purchases was quite small, and the likelihood that the best return on a sale could be achieved was unlikely. These kinds of activities also required a certain amount of time and effort to manage, and given our limited staff resources, we preferred to minimize such demands on our time. While the committee briefly considered using online means such as eBay to sell unwanted books, which would address some of our concerns, we quickly decided that such an approach would also consume too much staff time and resources.

Weighing our various options, we ultimately decided to make arrangements with a dealer we trusted who was experienced in appraising and selling rare books and manuscripts. The dealer had secured rare books for the special collections on more than one occasion in response to faculty requests to support their teaching. A few years earlier, this dealer had also done a large appraisal job for the college, examining and evaluating nearly 2,000 books donated by John and Mary Dickinson in 1784. The care that went into the physical inspection of the volumes and the detail provided in the appraisal report convinced the committee members that this dealer's expertise would prove invaluable in assessing any material that might be deaccessioned and set aside for sale. Through our agreement, the dealer is authorized to sell deaccessioned materials on behalf of the college, and he then takes a fair commission for those sales. The dealer has the advantage of using his particular knowledge, research skills, experience, and connections to properly evaluate materials and then identify appropriate means of sale, whether through auction, consignment, or working directly with an interested buyer.

For more than a year, the committee members had debated issues regarding how to redefine and reshape the special collections of the college going forward. The various concerns of the committee had also been shared with legal counsel, who in turn provided information, advice, and some recommended language for the policies that were being drafted.

Our deliberative process resulted in a shared understanding among all the stakeholders for a working plan moving forward. The collection development policy and its appendix on deaccessions, as well as the policy on funds generated through deaccessions, were both approved by the Committee on Archives and Special Collections in April 2001.

IMPLEMENTATION

With a policy in place, approved by a committee with representatives from all parts of the college that explicitly supported deaccessioning and the sale of such items, we were able to begin implementing our plans for unneeded materials. We started, naturally enough, by clearing out the most obvious things on the shelves. In our special collections' periodicals section, there were several hundred titles for which our holdings were limited to one or two loose issues or just a single bound volume. Working with the cataloging librarian, we spent several months reviewing each title against the holdings information recorded in the library OPAC. As we confirmed the accuracy of the information to ensure that our single volume was not part of a longer run of the journal housed elsewhere, we assessed whether or not it made sense to retain each title.

During our evaluation process, we considered how valuable each journal might be for our primary audience, with particular consideration for the content of the issues or volumes we held. We also tried to assess how rare or unique the title was by checking the holdings of other libraries. In the case of individual issues, we examined the contents to see if the item had been kept because of articles that mentioned the college or else were related to alumni or other people with a college relationship. We also looked at the item to see if there was any indication how or why the journal was among our collections in the first place. Was there a bookplate showing previous ownership, a note written directly on the issue, or some variety of college ownership mark—such as ink stamps or embossing—that might indicate when the item originally entered our library? Taking all this into consideration, we selected more than 350 titles for deaccession.

We also evaluated a few hundred books that were shelved in an area of uncataloged volumes. With the books, we again checked the titles against existing holdings, looking for duplication or the possibility that these uncataloged items would fill gaps in incomplete multivolume sets. When there was duplication, the uncataloged book was compared with the one already on the shelves to see if conditions would warrant swapping out copies or potentially even keeping both if there was a compelling reason to do so, such as interesting marginalia in both or some other unique quality. And once again, we checked the holdings of other institutions through OCLC in order to determine relative rarity of individual titles and editions. Just over one hundred books from among those reviewed were deemed appropriate for deaccession.

Finally, we selected a few manuscript items for review, all of which had come from the same donor in the 1960s. This donor had made several large gifts of manuscript material, much of which had still not been sorted and was simply piled in dozens of disorganized boxes. The items that we selected for review were all single bound volumes of various origins, including scrapbooks, business or account ledgers, photo albums, and notebooks. Of those evaluated, fifteen items were set aside for deaccession.

The periodicals, books, and manuscript materials were all inventoried and shelved in order by subject and content type. According to the procedures outlined in our deaccession policy, once these inventories of the items slated for deaccession were created, they were shared with the Committee on Archives and Special Collections for review and comment. We chose to post the inventories on our internal website and sent committee members a detailed email message describing our selection process, along with a link to the inventories. Faculty members on the committee in particular were invited to visit the archives and inspect the materials personally to ensure that we would not be removing items of potential use to their departments' teaching or research. They were given six weeks to reply. The email ended by saying that we hoped every committee member would respond with his or her thoughts and concerns but that silence would denote consent.

Questions were raised about a few books, the subject matter of which was deemed of interest to individual faculty, but in those instances, the items to be deaccessioned were duplicates, and the faculty members were satisfied that the copies being kept in the collection were adequate. Faculty were also encouraged to share the inventories with their colleagues if they felt any materials might be useful to others, but no one outside the committee inquired about the periodicals, books, and manuscripts listed. After the six weeks had passed with no items being deemed worthy of retention, we proceeded to the next stage of the deaccession process.

We contacted the rare book and manuscript dealer who agreed to act on the college's behalf to sell or otherwise distribute the deaccessioned material appropriately. We arranged a time when he could travel to the college to collect the deaccessioned materials, and he informed us that he wanted to examine the items on the shelves before packing them. When the dealer arrived on-site, we signed a formal agreement with the deaccession inventories attached. The agreement provided the dealer with written authorization, in case anyone should question how he had obtained the materials and whether he had the right to sell them. He instructed us how he wanted the materials packed, and then they were loaded into his van and taken away.

Nine months later, a check for $7,281 arrived from the dealer, being the first returns for deaccessioned items that he had sold on behalf of the college. The check did not represent the total return for sale of all of the materials deaccessioned since some books and periodicals had been placed with different auction houses and had not yet gone under the hammer, while other books were still being shown at various rare book fairs. With this first check, the restricted account was established for the proceeds of all future sales of deaccessioned collections. At the time of deposit, the treasurer for the college remarked, "It's a good start."

The first deaccession established a process that has been repeated fifteen times over the past twelve years. As each group of materials is taken away for sale, we consider the next books and manuscript items to review. We continued to try to identify first those materials that most obviously did not fit the collecting and research needs of the college, as well as those books that were not yet formally cataloged. For example, over the years, we have been working our way through roughly 5,500 books that were moved to an off-site facility prior to the archives and special collections moving to new quarters in 1998. Most of these books had been loosely organized into subject groupings before being boxed up and sent off to storage. Categories included "philosophy and religion," "poetry and prose," "science," "history," "periodicals," and "foreign languages." As one group was unboxed, the books were all inventoried by work/study student employees and checked against the library catalog to look for duplication or to see if the book might fill a gap for an incomplete set.

For collections of personal papers and other miscellaneous manuscript material, the process has been somewhat similar. A survey of all unprocessed collections led to several dozen of them being set aside for further review and possible deaccession, and these collections were physically relocated to a different area of shelving. For these collections, we next sought information about the original source of the gifts or purchases to inform our decision making. In some cases, a brief correspondence between the librarian and the donor were all that remained to tell the story of how the materials came to the college. In other cases, detailed inventories—and sometimes even estimates of the value of the items—were found.

Many of these unprocessed collections, comprising more than a hundred cubic feet, represented the donation of a single individual in the mid-1960s. This donor, from Philadelphia, had been both a lawyer and a manuscript collector. From what I have been able to gather, he had been somewhat opportunistic in his collecting, presumably using his connections with colleagues to clear out nineteenth-century papers from other law offices around Philadelphia. Toward the end of his life, he sought a home for these hundreds of cartons of papers. Dickinson College accepted much of this material despite the fact that the contents did not reflect either the college or the local region, nor did they relate to the curriculum or the activities of the faculty and students. While some of these papers had been inventoried through the years, some fifty cubic feet remained completely unsorted four decades later.

Besides the collections of papers from that donor, there were also about 2,000 individual letters, documents, and pieces of ephemera. Most of these materials had been single-item purchases, acquired solely because of the autograph of some notable politician, military figure, religious leader, or artist. There had clearly been an attempt to acquire the signature of every U.S. president, though not necessarily during his term of presidency. A concentration of signatures of authors, poets, and essayists also revealed an interest in literary figures. These letters and documents seldom had any content of note, often being invitations to dinner, pro forma appointments or legal filings, and simple acknowledgements of a previous exchange. The pages from sale catalogs, which were often found in the folders alongside the purchased item, were a testament to the bargain-basement approach to collecting that had been pursued in the mid-twentieth century.

Due in part to the marginal quality of most of the material that has been set aside for deaccession, the process for review of such materials has changed over time. For one thing, faculty members became less interested in examining each group of material, particularly since I routinely contact people directly to seek their input on their areas of expertise. Faculty who had been on the Archives and Special Collections Committee expressed a preference for being consulted only regarding items related to their discipline. As an example, we recently reappraised a collection of material regarding a little-known early twentieth-century British author and playwright. As part of the reappraisal, we sent an inventory and description of the collection along to all of the faculty members in the English and theatre departments. No one voiced any misgivings about deaccessioning the materials, though several individuals expressed appreciation for having been invited to take part in the process.

Modifications to our administrative structure since the deaccession policy was first approved necessitated other changes in the review process. For one thing, the move to a more hierarchical arrangement of responsibilities within the library suggested that approval should more appropriately follow the chain of command. For another, a second professional position—a special collections librarian—was added to the department, offering another perspective to the reappraisal decisions. Finally, the Archives and Special Collections Committee itself ceased to meet as a body, with issues of concern regarding the college's unique holdings being handled through other college governance structures. Our policies have been updated accordingly, and the result is a review process that is more targeted and streamlined, with faculty being consulted directly based on their interests and expertise and the library director being the only administrator to review and approve the recommendations of the professional staff of the Archives and Special Collections Department.

RESULTS

Since 2002, there have been sixteen separate deaccession shipments, roughly one every ten months. More than 115 cubic feet of manuscript material and 4,500 books have been removed from the special collections in that time. The space that has been freed up among the manuscript collections has been taken by new donations and purchases that adhere to the collection development policy and reflect the current research and teaching needs of students and faculty members at the college. Space freed up among the bookshelves has allowed room for newly acquired books and has also provided a place for books awaiting cataloging and manuscript material being processed.

Several manuscript collections have been donated to other archival repositories, particularly when that institution has a substantial collection on the same person or topic. In a few cases, it was clear that the material among our holdings should have been added to the collections already held elsewhere but that instead they were given to Dickinson College out of convenience following the death of an individual who had resided nearby. Over the past ten years, recipients of personal papers from our special collections have included the Pennsylvania State Archives, Bryn Mawr College, the University of Pennsylvania, Depauw University, the Leo Baeck Institute, Beloit College, Princeton University, the American Philosophical Society, the University of Southern California, and Bethune-Cookman College.

In numerous other cases, single documents or a small file of materials have been donated elsewhere. Recipients over the years have included more than half a dozen different county historical societies throughout central and eastern Pennsylvania, nine different colleges and universities, one preparatory school, and five different public libraries, museums, and archives. One item was also recently identified that should most appropriately be housed with the U.S. National Archives and Records Administration.

Of the manuscript material deaccessioned and set aside for sale, the overwhelming majority was drawn from the 1960s donation of the lawyer-collector from Philadelphia. Again, many of those papers reflected the work of nineteenth-century lawyers from that city. Other material deaccessioned has included hundreds of individual letters that had been purchased in the mid-twentieth century solely for the author's signatures. Finally, a few collections of personal papers purchased and donated by a friend of a former college trustee that reflected his interests, but which have not been used in the past and do not support teaching and research interests of our faculty and students, have been removed from our holdings and sold.

Since the first deposit to the Archives Deaccession Fund twelve years ago, the account has grown steadily. Through the sale of materials, the fund currently has a principal balance in excess of $180,000. The annual returns have provided nearly $30,000 for dedicated special collections spending over the past decade, which has provided some flexibility and relief when opportunities arise that exceed available budget in any given year. This money has been used to pay for new acquisitions, conservation work on existing holdings, consultancies, and internships: acquisitions have included letters written by prominent college alumni as well as a diary kept by a mid-nineteenth-century student, conservation work has included the rebinding of several eighteenth-century books, consultancies have provided assistance for review of historic film footage and for a digitization project, and paid internships have been provided for undergraduates and graduate students alike.

Besides the obvious benefits of removing unneeded materials from our shelves to free up space for more desirable items and generating revenue from the sale of some of these materials, other benefits of this process have become apparent. Perhaps the most important of these is the fact that so many collections are now housed at other more appropriate repositories. By donating to other institutions various collections that fulfill their collecting policies and complement their existing holdings, we provide a greater opportunity for the research community at large to discover and make use of these materials.

A particular benefit to us is the visibility and awareness among the faculty about the holdings of special collections. Each time that members of a department are contacted regarding a possible deaccession, they always express appreciation for being included in the decision-making process. Transparency is important for maintaining trust as well as for building understanding with one of our primary audiences. Faculty are also reminded of our interest in shaping the collections to suit the needs of them and their students, which often leads to conversations about what types of material they would like to see added to our holdings in the future.

For our students and interns, the reappraisal process provides educational opportunities. As one example, a graduate intern who was interested in gaining experience with cataloging was tasked with reviewing books, checking both our OPAC and OCLC to learn more about each item and whether it might be needed and complementary to our holdings. The intern made initial recommendations about the disposition for each title, and then for those books ultimately retained, she received training to perform the work of adding those items to the OPAC. In other instances, our undergraduate work/study employees are asked to inventory and describe manuscript material that is undergoing reappraisal.

They sometimes need to perform additional research to better understand the content of the collections in order to help assess its potential use or relevance. This is just one of many activities performed by our student workers that provides opportunities for enhancing analytical and evaluative skills.

Finally, the Archives and Special Collections has benefited from the positive reactions to our reappraisal and deaccessioning process from colleagues across the college. The development of a source of revenue to supplement our annual budget is especially appreciated by the director of the library. At the time the deaccession policies were being developed, the treasurer of the college was impressed by the potential for building long-term financial reserves by removing unnecessary content, essentially reinvesting past resources to support future growth. From her perspective, this was an effective way to steward scarce college resources, in terms of physical space, material assets, and money, in a thoughtful and responsible manner. And as mentioned, faculty members have appreciated the transparency of the process, being given the opportunity to be involved in shaping the collections in ways that will support them and their students.

LESSONS LEARNED

When we first began to implement our deaccessioning process, the holdings we selected for evaluation were obvious candidates for removal. Duplicate copies of nineteenth-century novels and numerous other publications that had been donated in previous decades, though never formally cataloged, were easily reviewed and judged for either deaccession or retention. Likewise, manuscript collections that included strong documentation of provenance, but which bore no relationship to the college or the local community and reflected none of the criteria within the collection development policy, were easily moved along.

As the deaccession process continued, we began to run across more materials where the chain of ownership was more difficult to determine. While many of these materials have been deemed inappropriate for permanent retention, without more information about how they came to be housed at Dickinson College, I am hesitant to deaccession them. One outcome of this process is that we've learned quite a bit about the acquisition and donation practices employed in the mid- to late-twentieth century and how they relate to the relationships among many donors and the librarians responsible for special materials, as well as the relative informality in documenting the acquisition process.

We have also learned that some materials, which had not been well documented in our own catalog, had nonetheless been recorded in larger union catalogs. On one occasion, a university digitizing nineteenth-century newspapers contacted us for issues of a somewhat obscure and short-lived news magazine for young people. The library staff members at the university had seen Dickinson College listed among institutions with holdings for this title according to the Library of Congress's Chronicling America site. It had never occurred to us that Dickinson librarians in the past would have taken the time to share holdings information with a national service for two loose issues of a news magazine, particularly since our own library OPAC did not even include a record for that title.

On one other occasion, a researcher contacted us regarding a manuscript item—an office notebook for a nineteenth-century private school—which we had deaccessioned a few years earlier. The notebook had apparently been mentioned in an article from the 1970s. The researcher wished to examine the notebook for himself, and he was naturally disappointed to learn that the item was no longer among our collections. We were quite surprised that anyone had ever been aware of the existence of the item, let alone that someone had referred to it in a scholarly article. We did contact our dealer to see if we could track the item down for the researcher, but unfortunately we discovered that in this case the notebook had been sold to another dealer and that its further whereabouts were unknown.

Through our process of reappraising and deaccessioning, we have discovered more about how holdings information was shared many decades ago, how scholars and other researchers discovered our materials, and how such information spread among peers. Knowing more about those past communication networks has led to changes in our review process, encouraging us to check other sources to see if our holdings were more widely shared than we had suspected. Our manuscripts and published materials seemed at first glance to only have ever been used, if at all, by local audiences, but we have since learned that was not always the case.

As our reappraisal process has continued through the years, the time needed to perform the research to properly evaluate the materials has increased. As mentioned, we began with some of the more obvious candidates for deaccession, where the documentation regarding transfer of ownership was readily available and the content was clearly out of scope for our repository. We also targeted whole collections of material since it took less time to review coherent collections of personal papers compared to loose, individual documents. With much of the material that remains to be reappraised, documentation is scarcer and individual documents are far more prevalent than collections. In short, the reappraisal process is becoming a more time-consuming one. Weighing that time against other priorities has been leading quite naturally to a decreased amount of deaccessioning activity.

CONCLUSION

A large exhibit in our reading room currently celebrates some of the more unusual and eclectic items from our holdings. The student who curated the exhibit had worked in the archives for several years, and she had seen various things that piqued her interest. Planning to pursue graduate study in the museum field, she spent several months digging into our collections to develop an exhibit inspired by the "cabinet of curiosities." Images of the royal family of Nepal in the 1950s, an autograph book with the signatures of numerous Confederate officers, a piece of scientific equipment from the lab of Joseph Priestley, signed photographs of Bette Davis and Albert Einstein, five Christmas cards featuring Robert Frost's poetry and his signature, and one of the first models of Edison's phonograph to be manufactured are all among the items featured.

In looking through the displays, it strikes me that for all of the books and manuscripts that have been deaccessioned in past years that did not meet our collection development criteria, we still have thousands of unique items that at first glance would not seem to belong but that in fact reveal interesting connections with Dickinson College and its personalities. Why keep an item purchased in 1952 simply because it bears the signature of a U.S. president when we have many other presidential signatures among our collections that reflect direct interaction with the college and its personalities, such as our letter from John Quincy Adams written to the Dickinson students' two literary societies? Why keep among our collections a letter from Grover Cleveland in which he thanks a fellow politician for the birthday flowers he received?

As a result of reappraisal and deaccessioning activity over the past twelve years, the special collections are now more properly aligned with the teaching and learning that takes place at the college, and the holdings better reflect the history of Dickinson College and the many people associated with the institution. Richness and depth in a few key collecting areas have been enhanced, and new areas of collecting have been explored. Space that had been briefly freed up is now occupied by materials that reflect the collecting interests of our faculty and students. As one would expect, there is less material to be reappraised and considered for possible deaccession as the process continues. Perhaps within a few years, all of the material deemed of dubious value to Dickinson College will have been donated elsewhere to interested repositories or sold through book fairs, auctions, and dealer catalogs. When that time comes, we will be satisfied that we honed and shaped our collections in a way that appropriately supports our institutional teaching and research mission and that we developed a valuable funding source that will continue to provide for growth and maintenance of the Archives and Special Collections for the foreseeable future.

James Gerencser *is the college archivist at Dickinson College.*

NOTES

1. James Gerencser to Archives and Archivists listserv, "De-accessioning stuff," October 23, 2000.

2. Judith Robins to Archives and Archivists listserv, "Re: De-accessioning stuff," October 23, 2000.

3. "Collection Development Policy," Archives and Special Collections Department, Dickinson College, 2001 (revised 2010), http://archives.dickinson.edu/sites/all/files/Collection_Development_Policy.PDF.

4. "Policy on Funds Generated through Deaccession for the Dickinson College Special Collections Department," Archives and Special Collections Department, Dickinson College, 2001 (revised 2010), http://archives.dickinson.edu/sites/all/files/Collection_Development_Policy.PDF.

TWELVE

Tap into History

The Birth of the Oregon Hops and Brewing Archives

Tiah Edmunson-Morton, Oregon State University

Oregon is a special place, known for stunning natural beauty, a good amount of rain, and a predilection for pushing the boundaries of cultural norms. Its cities are surrounded by rural landscapes of agricultural farmland and forests; much of our history and heritage is intertwined with the politics of environmental protection and land use, the economics and sustainability of farming, and social considerations related to labor and employment. Oregonians are generally interested in knowing who grows their food—and who brews their beer.

Brewing and imbibing aren't new to Oregon's economy and culture, and it's fair to say that our state has a complicated relationship to its vices. Our history includes a healthy pre-Prohibition brewing scene, early local and statewide prohibition tied to state suffrage and temperance movements, counterculture hippies with an interest in mind-altering substances, and home brewing that certainly predates its legalization in 1978.[1] When Chuck Coury opened Oregon's first microbrewery in 1980, he stepped into this legacy and paved the way for an artisanal, commercial craft brewing industry. It wasn't long before the state took its place at the epicenter of a renaissance, one with brewers that were both curious and dedicated to their craft.

The modern community of consumers, farmers, and brewers continues to connect with their predecessors. Today, brewers recreate historic styles and pride themselves in using traditional ingredients, many sourced from the hop farms that have been a staple on the landscape since the first commercial hop yard was established in Buena Vista, Oregon, in 1867.[2] As the state's land grant school, research at Oregon State University (OSU) on these communities and industries has its own historical roots. Scientists at Oregon Agricultural College planted the first experimental hops on campus grounds in 1895, and seventy-six years later, Dr. Alfred Haunold made an indelible mark on the industry with the release of Cascade and other superstar hop varieties. University scholarship and research grows with the work of OSU's Aroma Hops Breeding Program at the Plant Breeding and Genetics Program and the U.S. Department of Agriculture's Agricultural Research Service programs. Food science and studies on fermentation have long been a part of research at OSU, but since the establishment of a Fermentation Science Program in 1995, OSU has been a leader in training brewers.

While scholars and laypeople alike are interested in digging into the topic, there was no single repository dedicated to gathering the history of hops farmers, scientists, and craft brewing communities. A project to collect and provide access to these primary materials would be invaluable for informed scholarship and accuracy of the historical record. Inspired by an involved community, a growing body of scientific research, and a need for documentation and aggregation, in 2013 the OSU Libraries and Press's Special Collections and Archives Research Center (SCARC) established the Oregon Hops and Brewing Archives (OHBA). OHBA's mission is to preserve the story of hop production and the craft brewing movement in Oregon through a range of diverse activities. OHBA is the first archive in the United States dedicated to saving and telling these intertwined stories, capturing all facets of the industries, and uniting social and cultural aspects with the scientific research work at OSU. We have the opportunity to document a vibrant living culture and the rich historic past of industries that have made a significant impact on the culture, science, agriculture, law, and economy of our state. Beer is also part of our regional identity, and its study allows exploration of topics like prohibition and government regulation, ecology and environmentalism, gender and representation, marketing, and business practices.

While in retrospect, starting OHBA seems like a natural for SCARC, the original spark was a personal one. I am a native Oregonian who came of age in the first decade of the craft beer explosion, and I still remember my dad's excitement when we went to our first brewpub, illegal in Oregon until 1985, because he could have a meal and a beer brewed on-site. The Edmunson family also had a hop farm in Goshen through the 1920s, until it was replaced by sour cherries when downy mildew wiped out many of the hop crops throughout the valley.

In addition to my family heritage, the birth of OHBA also includes a wedding, a trip, and a fortuitous meeting. In June 2013, two friends of mine were married at the Rogue Farms Hopyard, and since one was an archivist, the daylong fete included a history lesson on Oregon hops. I was among many guests who were captivated by the legacy of the crop in our region and how craft beer was affecting agricultural practices. A week later, I attended the Archives Leadership Institute in Iowa, where two important things happened. The first was meeting Rachael Woody (Oregon Wine History Archive) and Doug Boyd (Kentucky Bourbon Tales) and hearing them talk about the crossover between academic research and popular history collections. The second was a tour of Seed Savers, where we learned about their work to conserve and promote America's food crop heritage. They collect and share heirloom seeds, but to do so they have to grow them—like the stories that live in archives live because they are used, the plants persevere because they are grown.

I returned from Iowa with the kernel of an idea to create an archive that would celebrate science, business, and culture. The idea grew after I heard historian Peter Kopp lecture on "The Origins of Hoptopia." After his talk on place, culture, and the international nature of the hop trade, I introduced myself, and we had the first of many conversations. Fortunately for me, he was turning his dissertation on hops in the Willamette Valley into a book; he'd used our university history collections for that dissertation and was an excellent person to talk to about what he'd found there, but his work also spoke to a larger need to preserve heritage and culture by saving the story of science and agriculture.

My vision for what would eventually become OHBA included more than just collecting items and putting them in boxes. I imagined a destination for researchers and a portal for historical documentation housed not only in OSU collections but also in outside repositories and in the communities. I wanted to work with a variety of donors to collect traditional and nontraditional materials produced by the community, digitize collections we don't own, collect secondary literature to support scholarship in the form of rare books and historic industry journals, and conduct oral histories. I'm fascinated by the principles and practical applications of community archiving and post-custodialism,[3] and I wanted to find ways to allow for community involvement and curation and explore how current technologies offer alternatives to physical possession of items in order to provide access to informational content.

I had identified a new collecting area with outreach potential and scholarly interest and in which I had a strong personal connection. I was bursting with ideas about how to make this into a collaborative, community-oriented resource, but it took more than just ideas and my enthusiasm to make OBHA a reality. Although it has been only slightly more than a year since we debuted the effort, we have completed the essential steps of planning and launching the new archive, as well as conducting essential outreach to our donors and collaborators. In many ways, we are still finding our way and defining OHBA, but there have been some lessons and successes that I hope can help others interested in starting similar community documentation efforts.

PLANNING

Our organizational culture was ideal for nurturing an idea like mine. I am fortunate to work at a library that prides itself in being innovative, and we are encouraged to experiment. From the earliest conceptual stage, both my boss and others in library administration completely supported establishing the new archive, and they helped guide me through the crucial elements of planning and getting the new effort off the ground.

SCARC has several signature collecting areas that are managed by curators who serve as the main contact for donors, media, researchers, and people generally interested in the subject. I wanted this to be another established collecting area, highlighting existing collections with materials pertaining to hops and brewing research at OSU and also adding new materials and serving as a portal to collections in other repositories. In line with our Oregon Multicultural Archives, the hops and brewing archives would be comprised of many different individual collections and materials in existing SCARC collections. When I approached Larry Landis, my supervisor and the director of SCARC, in July 2013, I knew OHBA could follow the same model as our other collecting areas.

With Larry's support after pitching the initial idea, I needed to prepare a project proposal that detailed mission and scope, as well as staffing and plans for outreach. Though I wrote the majority of the narrative, I worked closely with Larry to discuss and sketch out project details. SCARC staff and our administration reviewed the proposal iteratively; most suggestions were editorial, but others were more substantive, such as including ideas for student engagement and not forming an official advisory board.[4] I revised it five times before settling on the final document that my library administration approved in August 2013.

In developing the proposal, defining the scope was the most difficult piece. I'd identified forty-five promising physical collections, so I knew that we had ample material in our holdings on which we could build; however, during the planning phase, I did outside research to make sure OHBA's scope complemented rather than competed with other collecting initiatives. Once I confirmed no one else was collecting in this area, I worked with Larry to determine categories for OHBA's scope, including location, time period, topic, and type of material. Should we collect for the entire Pacific Northwest? Should we collect from the post-Prohibition and pre-craft-brewing period to show change over time? Should we include home brewing? Would we collect artifacts? Were we in the business of collection development (acquiring collections) or content creation (oral histories)—or both? In the end we decided that OHBA was a place for materials pertaining to Oregon hops since the 1800s and commercial craft brewing since the late 1970s. To accommodate our desire to collect from a wide range of sources, we also established the Oregon Hops and

Brewing Collection, a "catchall" for donated materials that aren't appropriate for separate manuscript collections.[5]

Creating the project proposal was necessary for many reasons, but it also required me to have conversations with a variety of people to articulate what we all wanted the archive to become and so strengthened everyone's vision of our goal. It also forced me to explain the rationale for the archive in a coherent narrative! The finished proposal included a description of need; mission statement and scope; collection development and arrangement ideas; project phases and course of action for year one; potential advisers, stakeholders, and partners; project promotion; areas of student engagement; staffing; budget; and future steps.[6]

With the plan approved and many connections made through my outreach activities, I needed to learn about growing hops, brewing beer, and all the people involved.

IMPLEMENTATION

As in many projects, there was overlap between the early stages of implementation and the development of the proposal. And like other collecting initiatives geared at reaching people in a diverse and active community, in the first year, I prioritized donor relations and outreach activities over acquiring new collections.

In developing the proposal, I had explored collections at other repositories from afar and identified some key contacts, but once the proposal was approved, I actively sought out opportunities to connect with people in person, talking with them not only about the importance of history and the impact of saving records and stories but also about my mission and goals. I also spent time thinking generally about the members of the communities I wanted to reach, what kinds of questions I should ask about the types of records they create, where to connect with them, and what more I needed to learn. In many of my early outreach efforts, I was reminded of just how much I needed to adjust my own expectations for this new collecting area. For example, when I presented at an Oregon Brewers Guild meeting in December 2013 about OHBA and the types of records archivists typically collect, I offered meeting minutes as an example. One brewer very kindly told me, "We don't have many meetings, and if we do, we don't keep notes—plus our hands are wet."

Throughout the year, I gave formal presentations and hosted promotional events, had one-on-one meetings and informal conversations at festivals, went on public tours, conducted oral histories, coproduced a short OHBA documentary, worked with researchers and journalists, submitted press releases and articles, and was on the radio several times.[7] Meeting with people in heritage and history communities, state agencies, hop farms, craft breweries, university departments, and allied communities helped me make connections I could build on in the future for donations, collaborations, and outreach. For instance, during the summer of 2013, I visited local university and historical society archives to look at materials, talk to them about OHBA, glean ideas for leads for further research, and discuss potential digitization collaborations. In that same period, I talked individually with my informal advisors about how this project could best serve a variety of researchers and how to raise the profile of the initiative as a whole. In summer 2014, with support from a library fund for faculty development, I made multi- and single-day trips to make connections and pick up materials at breweries and hop farms that were further afield.

As my sense of the community and their records keeping practices solidified throughout the summer and fall of 2013, I had a series of meetings with SCARC and library IT staff to talk about a digital portal for scanned materials, as well as ideas I had for OHBA's online presence and spaces for community contribution. We have in-house resources for digitization and web design, as well as multiple ways to provide access to digitized photos, textual items, and audio content. I haven't made as much progress as I'd have liked in uniting our access points for digital content, but I'd like to offer three examples of how I have provided access to different formats. I should note that while I'll briefly address born-digital records in the results section, my examples here are of my work with digitized physical items. Further, our procedures and policies for both born-digital and digitized materials are still being solidified, and this has had some impact on options I had for preservation and access. For instance, because my library was transitioning from CONTENTdm to Hydra for image management, our workflow for digitizing and providing access to images was in flux, so I didn't have a good option for presenting digitized images. Fortunately, because SCARC has a Flickr account, I was able to upload the images and companion metadata I'd identified in CONTENTdm to Flickr. While our department goal is to have all digital images together in one system for both preservation and access purposes, creating Flickr sets provided a temporary access point for those interested in visual material, as well as a space for contemporary public programming pictures and place for me to deposit the nearly 348 images of hops, brewing, and barley I've located in our collections.[8]

Our department is discussing whether separating images from textual items makes sense for researchers, but our current policy for textual items is to deposit them in our institutional repository, ScholarsArchive. I had identified existing OHBA-related items in ScholarsArchive, mainly university theses and dissertations and also college and research reports from our archival collections. In May 2014, I added a few other sets of interesting items to the repository, such as the hop investigation reports from 1930 to 1969—crucial years in USDA/OSU hops research—and issues of *The Hop Press*, an Extension Services serial publication written by hop specialist Godfrey Hoerner for farmers published between 1948 and 1955.[9]

I identified analog audio content as well, both in our collections and in neighboring repositories. The latter offered opportunities for collaboration for preservation and access. For instance, the Benton County Historical Society has a collection of oral histories of hop-pickers, farmers, and researchers from 1980 on cassettes; we borrowed the tapes and transcripts, digitized both, returned the originals and digital access copies to the museum, and uploaded the files to OSU's Media Space, which is where we provide access to other OHBA and SCARC media files.[10] So, while our current infrastructure doesn't allow us to provide a unified space for storing or accessing these different kinds of materials, I have been working to assemble a diverse range of formats "into" OBHA.

To support broader outreach for the new archive, I prepared a variety of promotional materials. Included in my arsenal were copies of the full proposal, a single-page document with the project mission and background about the history of the industries and research at OSU, and an informational brochure suitable for a general audience. I worked with a graphic design student to develop a style to convey the message that OHBA was a repository for both "historic" and "current" materials. Working within the brand guidelines defined by our university relations and marketing office, we picked colors and graphics that represented hops, barley, and brewing. These colors and icons were used on all of our promotional material, including buttons, brochures, and handouts, as well as the website, blog, and social media. The assortment of promotional items evolved over time, but the message was consistent and publicity constant.

I wanted a place to write about my research findings and almost immediately (July 2013) set up a Tumblr blog called "The Brewstorian"; it has become an important place to share updates and reflect on the work I've done. A barebones OHBA webpage was created in November 2013, and over the next months, I deepened the content on this page with more information about OHBA and the history of the region.[11] I still plan to create a more robust site that unites digitized materials, oral histories, historical background, user contributions, related resources, and information about events, and feel optimistic that we will be able to do more in this area next year.

I use social media and networking sites personally and professionally and know that there are many tools for connecting with audiences and sharing information. I've already mentioned using Tumblr and Flickr to promote OHBA, but I had additional audiences available through SCARC's established Facebook and Twitter accounts. For the first six months, I used both to share information about our new archive, but in the long run, I felt the audiences who would be most interested in OHBA were rather dissimilar from the general SCARC audience. However, because I was concerned about fracturing the existing audience for SCARC's social media accounts, I discussed adding OHBA accounts on Facebook and Twitter with the head of our Emerging Technologies Services Department, and she approved the plan. I created the Facebook account in January 2014 but concluded that the brewing community was much more involved with Twitter, and the audience was different enough that I felt good about adding Twitter in March 2014.[12] I have both accounts linked to the other, which mean that all posts and tweets appear on both channels.

RESULTS

Our first year brought new acquisitions for OHBA and six new collections have been established. The first was the "catchall" Oregon Hops and Brewing Collection (OHBC), which offers a home for materials not destined for an individual archival collection. Included are items I collect and those donated by others; the bulk of the materials added in the first year were ephemeral in nature (e.g., coasters and posters). In many ways, this collection is the most useful of our acquisitions because if we want an archive that reflects a community, we need to have a way for people to donate individual items that are meaningful to them. Additionally, I have received numerous requests from people who "want to come look at the archive," and these visually appealing items are great to show. However, also found in the OHBC are a collection of notes from a judge who presided over a court case related to Oregon's brewpub law, a nearly complete run of the 1990s publication *Brewing Techniques* from a local brewer, and a folder of stockholder files from Portland Brewing, so it is more than just ephemera. I've established a relationship with the publishers of the *Oregon Beer Growler* and have added all their issues.

This first year also saw the start of the OHBA Oral History Collection. So far I have conducted eight interviews with people from both the hops and brewing industries in Oregon, and I have commitments from several other interviewees. Documenting the story of a community through oral histories is an excellent way of recording, preserving, and making connections in advance of the donation of more "tangible" archival collections.

My relationships with the farming community is growing, and though our OSU research collections are strong in hops research, apart from the digitized oral histories from the Benton County Historical Society and two oral histories I've conducted with farmers, I haven't added anything new for hops. However, two collections have been established for thriving breweries. The first, the Ninkasi Brewing Company Collection, is comprised mainly of art department materials, which are particularly important since this company is known for its outstanding growth and engaging marketing strategy. To date, I have accessioned physical and electronic marketing and art materials, design files, and an eclectic array of company files. As previously noted, because we are refining our department procedures for accessioning, describing, and providing access to electronic records, much of what I have accessioned from this collection is stored on our servers but isn't available to researchers. However, as we develop our policies, this will no doubt change, and I expect that the bulk of future accessions will contain even more electronic material. The second important acquisition in this area is the McMenamins Brewery Collection; McMenamins is Portland-based and is known both for its beer and its work preserving and restoring historic properties. The collection contains brewing and art records, as well as ephemeral items such as a wooden cask and rare 1995 six-pack of one of their first beers. We have plans for adding company records (e.g., brewing sheets) and conducting oral histories with the founders, artists, and employees.

Another category of new acquisitions in OHBA is publications. Several have been "acquired" by OHBA by transferring them from other parts of the library. We created a new collection for the previously mentioned *Hop Press*, which was pulled from our circulating library and I had digitized and added to our institutional repository. Our rare books librarian has also identified and transferred other items from the circulating collection to SCARC, including the *Oregon Hop Grower* (first published in 1933). For this publication we didn't create a new collection since it was a widely circulated publication without a direct connection to OSU; however, we thought it was important to have it protected in closed stacks. The final "publications" collection, the Robert Daly Beer Publication Collection, came when a gentleman involved with the Portland home brew club donated a modest book collection, news clippings, and issues of the club's publication.[13]

While we hadn't established any formal assessment measures, I am pleased with the progress at the end of the first year for OHBA.[14] In addition to the collection additions detailed above, I have worked with thirteen researchers on projects related to brewing and hops history in Oregon and given fourteen interviews in which I talked about OHBA. Our measurable results for social media are encouraging given the relatively short time they've been active. Library faculty and student interns share information about OHBA with their friends on Twitter and Facebook, and public interactions are steady; we have 292 fans on Facebook and 253 on Twitter. I have added sixteen sets to the OHBA collection in Flickr, and the total views for all is 1,991, with 812 views of those being of the historic photographs set. The support provided for gathering statistics for views on Tumblr are disappointing and are limited to followers, likes, and notes rather than visits or duration, so to gather more meaningful information, I embedded a Google analytics code in August 2014. Results for the first two months of monitoring show a good number of views (425 sessions, 682 page views) but a disappointing page visit duration (1:38 minutes) given the length of my posts. There have been sixteen downloads of the thirty-six publications in ScholarsArchive and one hundred views of the thirty-seven audio and video files in Media Space.

LESSONS LEARNED

Looking back, the time I spent this year planning and laying the groundwork for acquisitions has had more benefits that I realized at the time. For example, I spent significant time getting to know the OSU collections and collections at other repositories related to OHBA's focus. Talking with other curators was important since I wanted to respect the collecting scope and mission of other repositories, but having a familiarity with collections was also helpful when contacting potential donors. It meant I could offer concrete examples of related materials and be specific about how their donations would complement our holdings when I was making my initial contacts.

In addition, the time I spent observing and talking with the community before bringing up donations gave me a better idea of the types of materials they had, gave us time to learn about each other, and checked my own tendency for a full-scale assault of enthusiasm. As a curator of a new archive in a state with 173 brewing companies and 22 commercial hop farms, it was easy to become overzealous and overwhelmed. I consider personal outreach to be one of the biggest keys to the success of OHBA, but I also didn't want to be the scary archivist who was suddenly at every event ready to pounce. Each conversation and interview offered me a chance to refine my message and the way I engaged with people; the more times I explained what OHBA was and why it was important, the better I got at tailoring the message. So while my networking and promotional activities were all designed to get the word out about OBHA, they were also helping me learn in ways I hadn't necessarily expected.

As I spent more time in the community, I learned that OHBA is a great archive for "translating" science and archival work for lay people or beginning researchers, and I have learned to adjust to working with a wide a variety of audiences. Further, various aspects of the project appeal to different people, so I've developed an arsenal of videos for public events, fun facts and compelling stories for our library administration, and pithy quotes and pictures for journalists. Scholarly researchers are also an important audience, and their work shapes mine. I don't plan with one researcher in mind or let them dictate collection development, but I do talk with them about collection development efforts.

This project has also taught me important lessons about the need for balance. I have opinions and preferences, but my job is to collect and chronicle. An important part of my role is to be engaged and enthusiastic, and at times it can be difficult to do that and remain impartial. I've worked to maintain a balance between collection development (acquiring donations) and content creation (conducting oral histories and my collecting of ephemera), keeping in mind that I'm not creating an archive of things that catch my fancy. In addition, as I've gained experience documenting multiple voices in the same community, I've learned the importance of not alienating one contributor to connect with another. These are competitive businesses with zealous fans that can be both laudatory and ruthless!

Since the start of OHBA, there have been a wealth of options for promoting the new archive, and during this first year, I've learned to be more selective about my engagement. Being involved means being flexible and aware of community issues and events and considering where and when you participate. I learned to take advantage of opportunities to network in person or engage on social media but also to balance that participation. For example, in a state where there is an event within driving distance every weekend, it can get overwhelming, and I had to remind myself that, while OHBA could take up all of my time, I need to balance that with the other facets of my job (and life) that also need my attention.

And finally, since a lot of my promotion of OHBA has been simply talking face-to-face with new people who are curious about the project—and me—I've learned to be ready for unexpected and different questions. The three things people interested in OHBA most commonly want to know are:

- What's your favorite beer?
- Is this really your whole job?
- Who pays for this?

Personal interest, time management, and funding are all predictable questions, but I was still caught off guard by these at first. I'm not a huge beer drinker, so the first question was always awkward until I developed a standard answer. Early on, I had a relatively banal response that referenced something about ingredients and appreciation, but now I have decided to be more decisive and say "Cartwright Brewing" to honor the short-lived yet unsuccessful first craft brewery in Oregon. For the second question, I am honest ("No, but it feels like it"), and for the third, I am transparent ("The library, but we're exploring other options").

CONCLUSION

Getting OHBA off the ground has offered me opportunities to talk with potential donors about research value, records retention, corporate privacy and trade secrets, and the types of materials they produce, as well as how the traditional definition of an "archive" comprised of records that are no longer actively useful fits into the discussion. It has challenged me to think about my own definitions of an "archive" and how the theories of community archiving and post-custodialism might be liberating or calamitous in situations like ours. While both are appealing from a theoretical perspective, I continue to struggle with practical application. How do you work with creators to save their history in a community archiving and post-custodial environment, encouraging them to save and share valuable records of their work? How do you document a living history? How often do you make additions?

Oregon's early craft brewers were (and are) a gregarious bunch, which is great for an archivist; they were (and are) both living in the moment and thinking about the future, which can be a challenge for an archivist. Yet they love to talk about their beer and its impact, as well as their craft and uniqueness, and that gives me great opportunities to think about what is appropriate and necessary to document this part of our culture. Hop farmers don't seem to be as overtly gregarious, but they are certainly creative and engaged in their craft. Gayle Goschie and Blake Crosby, both part of multigenerational hop farming families, talk about walking the soil that their grandparents walked, farming in a place that's been in their families for over a century, and adapting to changing tastes or values. They know it's important for people to know where food products come from and important to connect with the history of farming. I have to agree.

It's an understatement to say that OHBA has fundamentally changed my job, shifting me into a world of collection development and donor relations, but as different as the details are, my core duties still revolve around teaching people about archives. The principles of post-custodialism and community archiving may challenge many of our professional philosophies, but they also offer unique opportunities to think about the work we do. Working with living communities and corporations can be messy and complicated, but it is also exciting to be close to creators and facilitate connections between them and researchers. Each day, I learn something new, make a new connection, and add my bit to the history of hops and brewing in Oregon. It's not a bad job to have, and the fringe benefits are great.

Tiah Edmunson-Morton *is archivist for instruction and outreach and curator of the Oregon Hops and Brewing Archives at the Special Collections and Archives Research Center, Oregon State University.*

NOTES

1. "Homebrewing Rights Statutes," American Homebrewers Association, last modified 2013, http://www.homebrewersassociation.org/homebrewing-rights/statutes/.
2. Peter A. Kopp, "Hop Industry," *The Oregon Encyclopedia*, accessed April 26, 2014, http://oregonencyclopedia.org/articles/hop_industry/.
3. "Post-Custodial Approach," Paradigm, last modified January 2, 2008, http://www.paradigm.ac.uk/workbook/collection-development/post-custodial.html.
4. My library has an advisory council and has decided that other advisory boards are not necessary. I have a group of people that I consult with about the project but who do not serve in an official capacity.
5. "Oregon Hops and Brewing Collection, 1993–2014," accessed May 15, 2014, http://scarc.library.oregonstate.edu/coll/ohbc/index.html.
6. Proposals for years one and two and first-year report are not available online but will be provided upon request.
7. National Council on Public History, Northwest Archivists, Oregon Brewers Guild, and Corvallis Beer Week. Articles in the *Oregon Beer Growler*, the OSU Libraries, and Northwest Archivists newsletters. OHBA Stories short documentary promotional piece, https://media.oregonstate.edu/media/t/0_ddr6tr59. Interviewed for pieces in *Library Journal*, *Modern Farmer*, and the *Register Guard*. On Oregon Public Broadcasting's *Think Out Loud*, *Beer Radio*, *Beer O'Clock*, Jefferson Public Radio, and KQEN's *Morning Conversation*.
8. All OHBA Flickr collections, http://bit.ly/OHBAFLICKR; photo tally for archival images in this set, http://bit.ly/OHBAimages.
9. Oregon Hops and Brewing Archives community, https://ir.library.oregonstate.edu/xmlui/handle/1957/49145.
10. Special Collections and Archives Research Center in Media Space, http://bit.ly/SCARCmedia.
11. OHBA Tumblr, http://thebrewstorian.tumblr.com/; OHBA website, http://scarc.library.oregonstate.edu/ohba.html.
12. OHBA Facebook, https://www.facebook.com/brewingarchives; and Twitter, https://twitter.com/brewingarchives.
13. "MSS Robert Daly, 1978–2004," accessed November 5, 2014, http://scarc.library.oregonstate.edu/coll/daly/index.html.
14. All statistics gathered October 7, 2014.

Index

About the Editor

Kate Theimer is the author of the popular blog *ArchivesNext* and a frequent writer, speaker, and commentator on issues related to the future of archives. She is the editor of the Rowman & Littlefield series, Innovative Practices for Archives & Special Collections, in which volumes on management, description, outreach, and reference and access were published in 2014. She is also the author of *Web 2.0 Tools and Strategies for Archives and Local History Collections* and the editor of *A Different Kind of Web: New Connections between Archives and Our Users*, as well having contributed chapters to *Many Happy Returns: Advocacy for Archives and Archivists, The Future of Archives and Recordkeeping*, and the forthcoming *Encyclopedia of Archival Concepts, Principles, and Practices.* She has published articles in the *American Archivist* and the *Journal of Digital Humanities.*

Kate served on the Council of the Society of American Archivists from 2010 to 2013. Before starting her career as an independent writer and editor, she worked in the policy division of the National Archives and Records Administration in College Park, Maryland. She holds an MSI with a specialization in archives and records management from the University of Michigan and an MA in art history from the University of Maryland.